Second Edition

FUNDAMENTALS OF MUSIC THEORY

A Program

BERTRAND HOWARD
University of Arkansas

HARCOURT BRACE JOVANOVICH, INC.
New York Chicago San Francisco Atlanta

ISBN: 0-15-529461-X

Library of Congress Catalog Card Number: 75-3530

Printed in the United States of America

Cover Illustration by Pat Avallone.

PREFACE

The Second Edition of *Fundamentals of Music Theory* may be used successfully in a variety of situations: with the beginning music student who has no prior theoretical training, the more advanced student in need of remedial instruction in basic theory, the education student who requires knowledge of fundamentals, and any music student seeking a source for review. The programed format is suitable for both individual and classroom use; in either case, instructor supervision is recommended but not essential.

The book has been reorganized to reflect recent developments in programing techniques and has been enlarged to include C clefs and modes as well as much additional material in all areas covered in the First Edition. Each chapter of the Second Edition has been divided into several short units to facilitate learning by minimizing fatigue and encouraging frequent evaluation of the student's progress.

An important new feature of this edition is the inclusion of "Listening Frames" and corresponding recordings. Together they provide aural reinforcement of theoretical concepts through illustrations from the standard music literature. They are not intended to provide a basis for ear training but rather to establish a rewarding bridge from concept to musical application.

The "Self-Quizzes" concluding each chapter are also new. These are primarily intended to assist students in evaluating their own progress (answers are provided at the back of the book), but they may also be used for testing in the classroom.

Many of these changes were prompted by suggestions made by users of the First Edition, who represent widely varied teaching and learning situations. The result is a more efficient, thorough, and flexible presentation that allows students to progress at their own speed with less chance of error and more rapid assimilation of the material.

To achieve maximum effectiveness from the text, it is important that all students understand and carefully observe the procedures outlined in "To the Student" on page ix. The programed sequence requires that chapters be taken up in order unless a student already has a solid knowledge of the material in earlier chapters. Frequent use of the piano or other instrument is extremely important and should be encouraged at every opportunity. Additional aural and performance activities relating to the material being studied are also strongly recommended. The examples used in the Listening Frames can easily be supplemented, since scores and recordings of these works are readily available in most music libraries.

The author wishes to thank Professors John R. Fitch, Carolyn R. Hickson, and Madelene Zachary, all of the University of Arkansas at Fayetteville, and Mr. Charles Ward for their valuable assistance in the preparation of the Second Edition. The book also reflects the continuing important contributions of Professors Janet McLoud McGaughey and Nelson G. Patrick, both of the University of Texas at Austin, and Guy Alan Bockmon of the University of Tennessee at Nashville, who assisted with the First Edition. Special gratitude is due the many students in each of these universities for their cooperation in testing this program, and the numerous persons throughout the country who offered substantive suggestions.

Bertrand Howard

CONTENTS

RECORDED EXAMPLES

All examples are excerpts unless otherwise noted.

Record 1, Side 1

Band 1. ★ Bach, Fugue No. 1 in C, from *The Well Tempered Clavier*, Vol. I, BWV 846 (Anthony Newman, harpsichord)
2. * Purcell, "Thy Hand, Belinda!" from *Dido and Aeneas*
3. ★ Beethoven, Symphony No. 1, fourth movement (The Cleveland Orchestra, George Szell, Cond.)
★ Brahms, Symphony No. 4, fourth movement (Columbia Symphony Orchestra, Bruno Walter, Cond.)
4. ★ Beethoven, "Archduke" Trio, Op. 97, in B flat Major, first movement (Eugene Istomin, piano; Isaac Stern, violin; Leonard Rose, cello)
★ Mozart, Symphony No. 41, third movement (The Cleveland Orchestra, George Szell, Cond.)
▲ Brahms, Symphony No. 1, second movement (Columbia Symphony Orchestra, Bruno Walter, Cond.)
★ Desmond, "Take Five" (Dave Brubeck)
5. ★ Mozart, Piano Concerto No. 27 in B flat Major, K. 595, last movement (Columbia Symphony Orchestra, George Szell, Cond.)
* Sousa, "El Capitan March"

Record 1, Side 2

Band 1. ★ Handel, "Joy to the World" (The New York Philharmonic, Leonard Bernstein, Cond.; The Mormon Tabernacle Choir, Richard P. Condie, Dir.)
▲ Handel, Flute Sonata No. 3 in B minor, second movement (Jean-Pierre Rampal, flute; Robert Veyron-Lacroix, harpsichord)
2. ★ Bach, Partita No. 4 in D Major, BWV 828, first movement (Glenn Gould, piano)
★ Mendelssohn, Symphony No. 4 ("Italian") in A Major, Op. 90, second movement (The New York Philharmonic, Leonard Bernstein, Cond.)
3. ✠■ Mozart, *Don Giovanni*, Overture (Glyndebourne Festival Orchestra, Fritz Busch, Cond.)
★ Mozart, Piano Concerto No. 24 in C minor, K. 491, first movement (Members of the Cleveland Orchestra, George Szell, Cond.; Robert Casadesus, piano)
4. ✠★ Bartók, Mikrokosmos No. 40 (complete) (Gyorgy Sandor, piano)
5. ★ Stravinsky, *Petrouchka*, Tableau I, Russian Dance (Columbia Symphony Orchestra, Igor Stravinsky, Cond.)
★ Tchaikovsky, Serenade for Strings, third movement (opening) (The Strings of the Philadelphia Orchestra, Eugene Ormandy, Cond.)

Record 2, Side 1

Band 1. ★ Tchaikovsky, Serenade for Strings, third movement (end) (The Strings of the Philadelphia Orchestra, Eugene Ormandy, Cond.)

2. ∗ Haydn, Symphony No. 104 ("London"), first movement

▲ Corelli, Trio Sonata, Op. 4, No. 8, Prelude (Max Goberman and Michael Tree, violins; Eugenia Earle and Jean Schneider, continuo)

3. ★ Bach, Fugue No. 16 in G minor, from *The Well Tempered Clavier,* Vol. I, BWV 816

4. ★ Saint-Saëns, *Danse macabre,* Op. 40 (The Philadelphia Orchestra, Eugene Ormandy, Cond.)

★ Copland, Sonata for Violin and Piano, first movement (Isaac Stern, violin; Aaron Copland, piano)

★ Bartók, *Concerto for Orchestra,* second movement (The New York Philharmonic, Pierre Boulez, Cond.)

5. ● Purcell, Sonata for Trumpet and Strings, Z. 850, third movement (complete) (Rhenish Church Orchestra, Cologne, Kehr, Cond.)

6. ★ Haydn, Symphony No. 94, second movement (two excerpts) (The New York Philharmonic, Leonard Bernstein, Cond.)

★ Bach, *Brandenburg Concerto* No. 2 in F Major, third movement (two excerpts) (Marlboro Festival Orchestra, Pablo Casals, Cond.)

Record 2, Side 2

Band 1. ★ Brahms, Symphony No. 3, Op. 90, first movement (The Cleveland Orchestra, George Szell, Cond.)

★ Chopin, Prelude No. 20 in C minor (complete) (Nelson Freire, piano)

2. ∗ Bach, Mass in B minor, "Crucifixus" (complete)

★ Courtesy of Columbia Records.
∗ Courtesy of Vanguard Recording Society, Inc.
▲ Courtesy of Odyssey Records.
■ Courtesy of Vox Productions, Inc.
● Courtesy of Nonesuch Records.
✢ Electronically re-recorded to simulate stereo.

TO THE STUDENT

The programed design of this book allows you to reason your way through the material at your own pace. Information is presented step by step in small portions called *frames*. Your understanding of each frame is immediately tested, so that you will be constantly aware of your progress.

The basic procedure for working through this program is described below. Follow it consistently throughout the book in order to absorb fully the material presented.

1. Before beginning your work, make a "mask" by folding a piece of typing paper lengthwise to the width of the left-hand column of the programed pages.

2. Place the mask over the left-hand column of frames on page 1 and read the information in the chapter introduction and in frame 1. Then fill in the blank in frame 1; the information called for is found within the frame itself.

3. Slide the paper mask down just far enough to uncover the answer in the left-hand column. If that answer matches yours, proceed to frame 2. If your answer is incorrect, reread the frame until you understand the reason for your error *before* you go on to the next frame. In most cases your answer will be correct and you can proceed directly to the next frame. Continue in this way through each frame in the book.

4. Be sure you actually write your answers in the spaces provided. The process of *writing* rather than merely thinking each answer will reinforce your learning and will become increasingly important as you go through the book.

5. If you miss three or four answers in a row, retrace your steps until you understand the reasons for your incorrect responses. If any confusion remains after you have done this, consult your instructor for clarification.

6. Refer to the keyboard, or another instrument, as often as possible. This will greatly increase your understanding of the material and will accelerate your progress through the text.

7. *Listening Frames:* These form an important part of the material in each chapter, so be sure you work through them as they appear, before moving on to the next section. The recordings found in the book contain all the music needed for these frames. Listen to each example several times before responding to the questions. To facilitate replaying, "locked grooves" stop the needle at the end of each band.

8. *Self-Quizzes:* Each chapter ends with a Self-Quiz, the answers to which are found at the end of the text. Use these to evaluate your progress, or as directed by your instructor.

If you apply sufficient concentration and carefully follow the directions provided here, you should make very few errors and will acquire a solid basis for later musical studies.

KEYBOARD DIAGRAM

For those with little or no keyboard orientation, the keyboard diagram below will be helpful. It depicts a section of the piano keyboard; the keys in the diagram are lettered according to their corresponding pitch names. The symbol [C] locates Middle C, which is the C nearest the center of the piano keyboard. The meaning of these pitch names is explained in Chapter I.

Students unacquainted with the keyboard should compare this diagram with an actual piano keyboard. Further comparison is to be encouraged where similar keyboard diagrams occur within the text. The value of these diagrams will be enhanced when the student produces on the piano the concepts they illustrate.

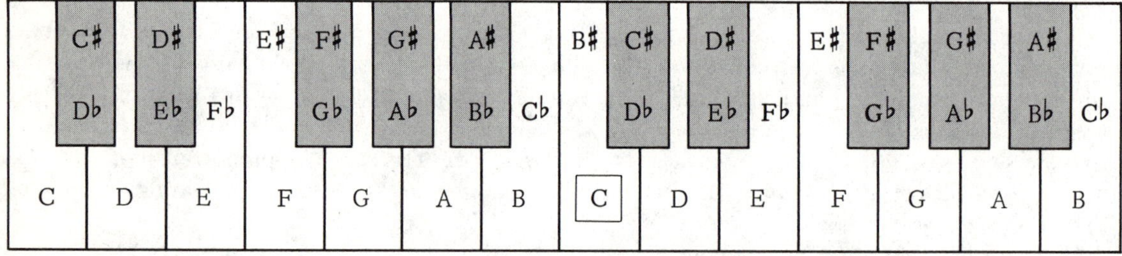

CHAPTER ▪ I ▪ PITCH NOTATION

One of the major accomplishments of music in Western civilization is the development of a system of written symbols that makes it possible to communicate on paper the intentions of the composer, editor, or arranger in considerable detail. Our system of written music, called *notation*, has evolved to its present form through centuries of trial and error and invention, and is continuing to evolve as new musical styles and ideas call for new kinds of notated information.

The notation that is still used for most music today is largely based on practices that became relatively uniform in the seventeenth century. This book deals with the basic principles underlying those notational practices, and will serve as a foundation from which to explore additional aspects of notation.

Some differences exist between printed music and manuscript music, music written by hand. Several of these differences are indicated where appropriate in this chapter.

While working through this program, always bear in mind that although the symbols of notation serve to *represent* music visually, they are not the music itself. While a thorough knowledge of notation is a necessity for the serious musician and a useful tool for the layman, this knowledge is meaningful only in relation to the actual experience of music through living performance.

THE STAFF; PITCH NAMES; THE G AND F CLEFS; THE GRAND STAFF

notation	**1.** Musical *notation* consists of symbols that represent sounds, silences, and their duration. The symbols used in musical ____________ represent sounds, silences, and their duration.
Tones Pitch	**2.** Musical sounds are called *tones*, some of which sound higher or lower than others. This relative highness or lowness of tones is called *pitch*. __________ are musical sounds. __________ is the relative highness or lowness of tones.

notation Pitch	**3.** Tones are represented by symbols in musical ________. ________ refers to a tone's highness or lowness.
Duration	**4.** Some tones sound for a longer or shorter time than others. This relative longness or shortness of tones is called *duration.* ________ refers to the length in time of a musical tone.
Pitch Duration	**5.** Two of the qualities of musical tones are duration and pitch. ________ refers to a tone's highness or lowness. ________ refers to the length in time of a musical tone.
Notes whole note	**6.** The symbol commonly used to express the pitch and duration of a musical tone is the *note.* One form of note is the *whole note,* shown below. o ________ are symbols commonly used to express pitch and duration of musical tones. This form of note (o) is a ________ ________. (Observe that "tone" refers to sound and "note" refers to symbol.) Different note forms are used to express duration, which is covered in Chapter II. For convenience, this chapter, which deals with pitch notation, will use only whole notes.
o o o o o	**7.** Draw five whole notes below, following the given example.* o ____ ____ ____ ____ ____ * Whole notes in printed music usually have varying thickness of line, as shown. In manuscript, however, you may more easily draw them as simple oval shapes; either way is acceptable.

8. To indicate pitch, a note is placed on a *staff* consisting of five horizontal parallel lines and the four intervening spaces. The relative highness or lowness of its tone corresponds to its position on the staff.

On this staff, note 1 is visibly higher than note 2, indicating that note 1 *sounds* higher than note 2.

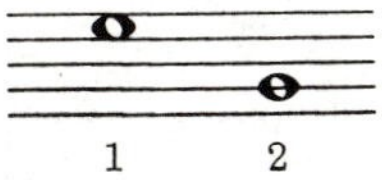

1 2

higher

On this staff, note 2 sounds __________ (higher/lower) than note 1.

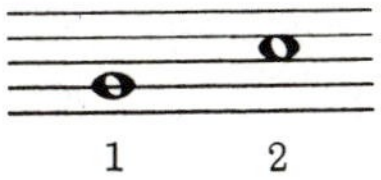

1 2

---

lower

9. On this staff, note 1 sounds __________ (higher/lower) than note 2.

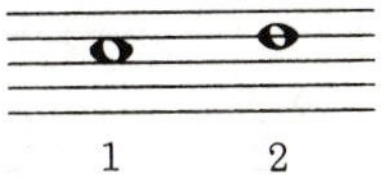

1 2

---

whole

10. In this example, a __________ note appears on each line and in each space of the staff. Copy the example on the staff below it.

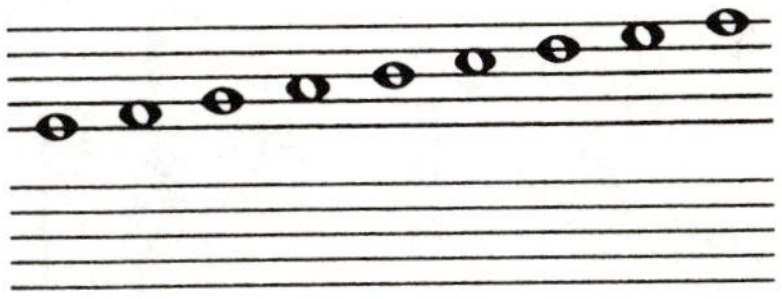

---

symbols (If your answer was "notes," remember that notes represent sounds, while silences are represented by other symbols to be dealt with later.)

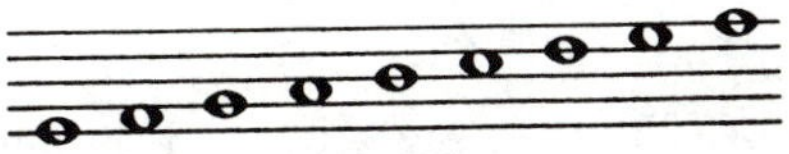

11. Musical notation consists of __________ representing sounds and silences.

---

12. The lines of the staff are numbered from bottom to top, as are the spaces.

Lines Spaces

5 4 3 2 1 — 4 3 2 1

four

The staff has five lines and __________ spaces.

G five	**13.** Pitch names on the staff are derived from the first seven letters of the alphabet—A, B, C, D, E, F, and G (low to high). After G, continuing to move upward in pitch, the same letters are repeated as often as necessary, A through G. Names of notes on the staff correspond to the alphabetical letters A through ____. The staff has four spaces and ________ lines.
	14. To identify the pitch name of each line and each space in the staff, a symbol called a *clef* is placed at the beginning of the staff. Several clefs are commonly used in notation. The clef in this example is the G *clef*, or *treble clef*. It locates the pitch G on the staff where the clef curls around the second line, which is the only line crossed four times by the clef. identifies G
clef treble	**15.** A ________ is used at the beginning of the staff to identify pitch names of notes. The G clef, or ________ clef, identifies the pitch G on the second staff line.
	16. An easy way to draw the G clef is to proceed in three steps: 1. 2. 3. Draw a G clef (treble clef) on each staff below. Observe carefully the discussion above and the example provided.* G * As was pointed out with reference to whole notes, manuscript forms of these symbols may differ slightly from the printed forms. Remember that the G clef must clearly identify the second staff line as G. Refer to frame 14 if necessary.
G treble (either order) B C D E F G	**17.** The clef that locates the pitch G on the second line of the staff is called the ________ clef, or ________ clef. The consecutive pitch names of notes are A ____ ____ ____ ____ ____ ____.

18. The G located by the G clef is the G above Middle C* on the piano keyboard, as shown below.

C G

Draw a staff below and place a treble (G) clef at the beginning. Then draw a whole note G on the staff where indicated by the clef.

* "Middle C" is the C nearest the center of the piano keyboard. In the remainder of this book it will be represented by the symbol [C]. Refer to the keyboard diagram, p. x, as often as needed.

---

treble

19. Once you have located G, it is possible to identify the other notes on the staff. Study the example below. Notice that some pitch names appear twice on the staff, and that the spaces above and below the staff also contain pitches.

G A B C D E F G

Another name for the G clef is __________ clef.

(E) G

B D F

20. The spaces of the G clef, starting with the lowest, are F A C E.

The names of the lines, starting with the lowest, are E ____ ____ ____ ____.

4 3 2 1 F A C E

E 5 4 3 2 1

---

* Notes in parentheses have two possible staff locations. Either is correct for our present purposes.

21. Draw a G clef at the beginning of the staff. Then draw, in whole notes, the pitches indicated.

G A F C

G B D A	**22.** Write below the staff the pitch names of these notes. ___ ___ ___ ___
B E F E	**23.** Continue as in frame 22. ___ ___ ___ ___
C F D E	**24.** Continue as in frame 23. ___ ___ ___ ___ It will be helpful at this point to find and play at the piano keyboard all the notes appearing in frames 18–24.
lower	**25.** For pitches lower than those which the G clef accommodates, the *F clef,* or *bass clef,* is commonly used. The F clef accommodates pitches which are ________ (higher/lower) than those of the treble clef.
bass	**26.** The two dots of the F clef (𝄢) surround the fourth line of the staff, identifying it as F. The fourth line is also where the upper curve of the F clef sign begins. Draw an F clef sign on each of the adjacent staves, observing carefully the example provided. F Another name for the F clef is ________ clef.

27. The F located by the F clef is the F below Middle C on the piano, as shown below.

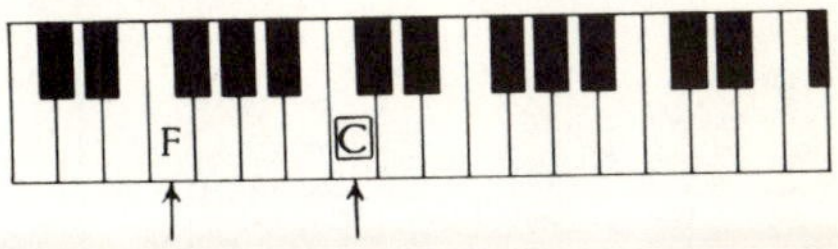

F C

Draw an F clef on the staff and place a whole note F where indicated by the clef.

---

28. Once again, locating one pitch makes it possible to find the remaining notes on the staff.

Study carefully the example below.

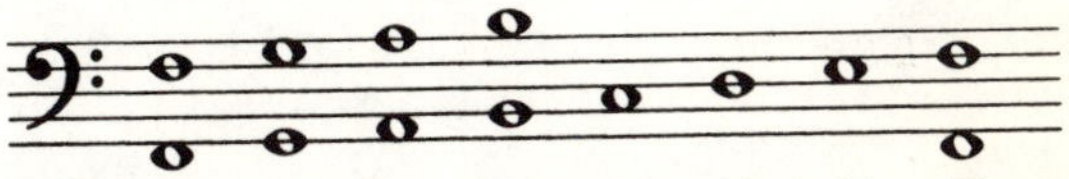

F G A B C D E F

Another name for the bass clef is _____ clef.

F

---

29. The spaces of the F clef from bottom to top are A C E G.

The names of the lines, starting with the lowest, are _____ _____ _____ _____ _____.

4 3 2 1

A C E G

5 4 3 2 1

G B

D F A

---

30. Write beneath the staff the pitch names of these notes.

— — — — —

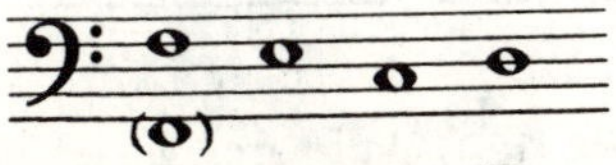

G D A B F

---

31. Draw the indicated pitches in whole notes.

F E C D

Now sound at the keyboard all the notes appearing in frames 27–31.

F E C D

Leger lines

32. To indicate pitches lying beyond the range of the staff, short additional lines called *leger*° *lines* are used. For example, Middle C is shown below as it appears on the G clef and on the F clef.

__________ __________ are used to indicate pitches above and below the staff.

° Also spelled "ledger." This book will use the more traditional spelling, "leger." It is pronounced "lej-er."

treble

bass

33. Leger lines are a convenient means of extending the pitch range of the staff. As many leger lines may be used as are necessary.

A B A C F B

Another name for the G clef is __________ clef.

Another name for the F clef is __________ clef.

A C B A C E D C

34. Write beneath the staves° the pitch names of these notes. Then copy the examples on the blank staves below.

° The plural form of "staff" is either "staffs" or "staves." "Staves" will be used in this book.

higher

35. Pitches notated on the treble (𝄞) staff are generally __________ (higher/lower) than those on the bass (𝄢) staff.

36. Draw an arrow to the single specific notes on the keyboard located by the G and F clefs. Write the pitch names of the two notes on the corresponding keys.

Now sound at the keyboard all the notes appearing in frames 32–36.

grand staff

37. By placing the treble staff above the bass staff, a greater range of pitches can be more conveniently expressed than with either staff alone. This two-staff arrangement, with the treble above the bass staff, is called the *grand staff.*° Notice in the example below that Middle C occurs on a leger line midway between the two staves.

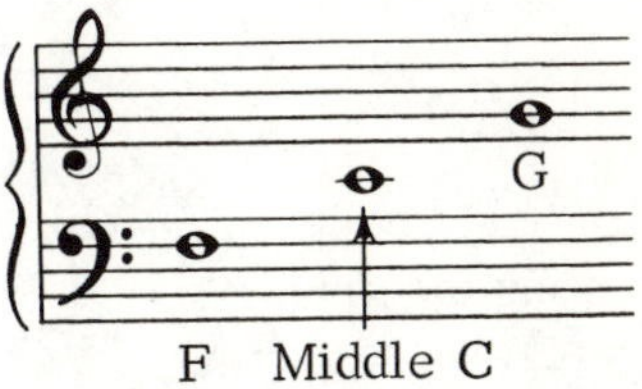

The two-staff arrangement shown above is called a __________ __________.

° Also called "great staff," but in the remainder of this book "grand staff" will be used.

A F D B C E F

38. The grand staff is often used in keyboard music, condensed scores (for example, a piano score of an opera), and elsewhere. Notice that the two staves are connected on the left with a line and a brace.

Write the pitch names below the grand staff.

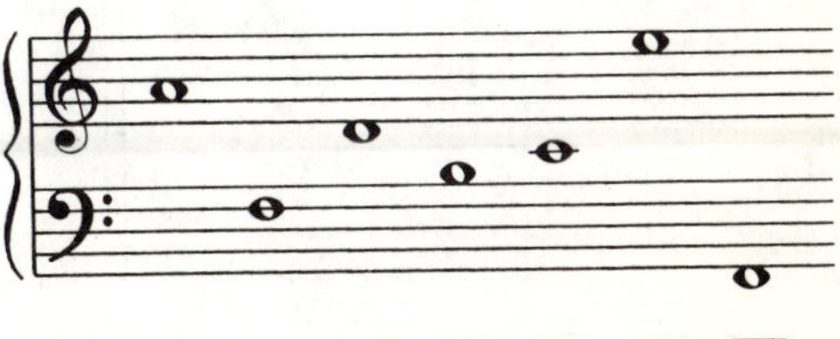

— — — — — — —

39. Notice that Middle C on the treble staff alone 

and Middle C on the bass staff alone occupy the *same* leger line when written on the grand staff.

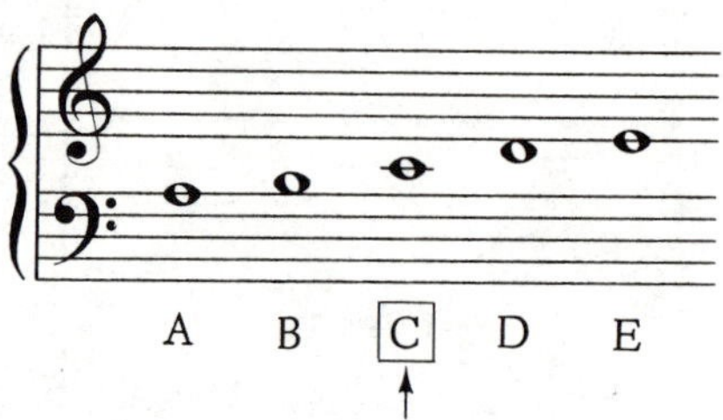

On the grand staff, therefore, pitches may continue in consecutive order from one staff to the other.

(Check the following:
1. a brace connecting the staves
2. a line connecting the staves
3. leger line)

40. Complete the grand staff below. Then notate Middle C as a whole note.

(Check the following:
1. a brace connecting the staves
2. a line connecting the staves
3. both clefs added)

41. Complete the grand staff below. Place whole notes on the staff corresponding to the pitches indicated on the keyboard, and write the pitch names below the staff.

42. On the grand staff, Middle C is usually placed closer to one staff than to the other when it is part of the music notated on that staff. Unequal spacing between staves does not affect the names of the pitches between them (B–[C]–D).

Thus, Middle C can be written on the grand staff in three ways.

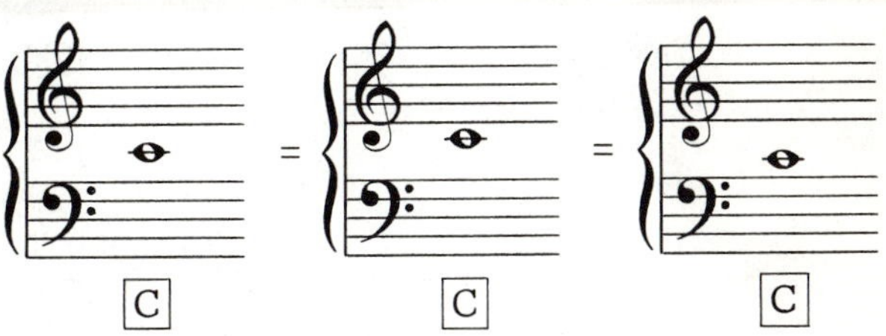

Name the pitches written on the treble staff in this example.

G G A B C D E

43. Name the pitches written on the bass staff.

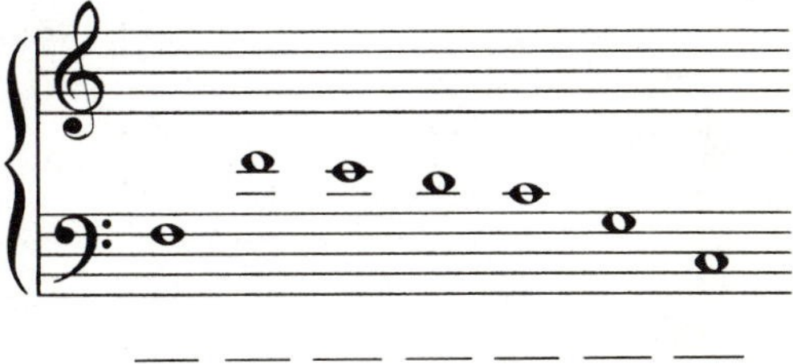

F F E D C G C

44. Both staves of the grand staff are used in this passage. Write the pitch names below the example.

C	G	F	F	A	G
C	E	F	D	F	E

LISTENING FRAMES

3	**45.** Listen to Example 1-1, the beginning of J. S. Bach's Fugue No. 1 in C from *The Well-Tempered Clavier,* Vol. I. Which of the following staves would be most appropriate for notating this music? (Listen to the entire excerpt before you answer.) _____ 1. 2. 3.
higher	**46.** Listen again to the first four tones of the excerpt. After the first tone, each subsequent pitch is __________ (higher/lower) than the one preceding it.
2	**47.** The notation (in whole notes) that most nearly corresponds to the opening of the excerpt is __________. 1. 2. 3.
higher 4	**48.** Listen again to all of Example 1-1. Further into the passage the same melodic line enters at another pitch level, while the first continues. The second melodic entrance is __________ (higher/lower) than the first. As the passage continues you will hear more entrances of this same melody. How many are there in the entire passage? __________

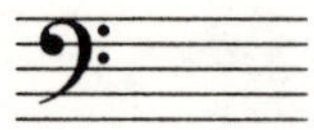

CHROMATIC SIGNS

Any pitch may be raised or lowered without changing its basic letter name. Notation of these pitches uses symbols called *chromatic signs.* Working through this portion of the chapter near a piano keyboard will prove especially helpful.

49. The lines and spaces of the staff all correspond to the white keys of the piano keyboard.

Write the names of these notes on the corresponding keys of the keyboard.

C

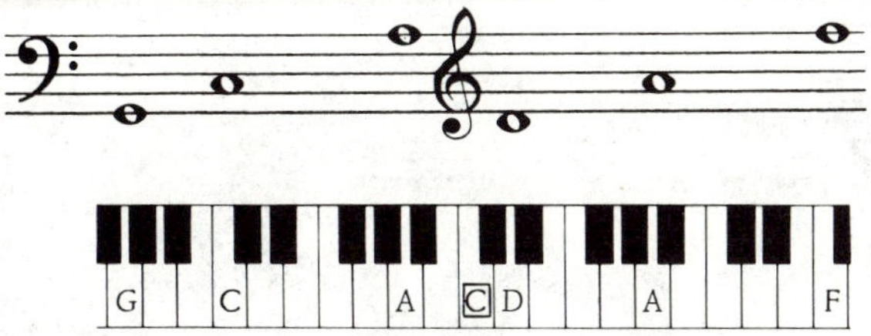

G C A C D A F

50. A *sharp* (♯) placed before a note means that the pitch is *raised* to that of the next key to the right on the keyboard.

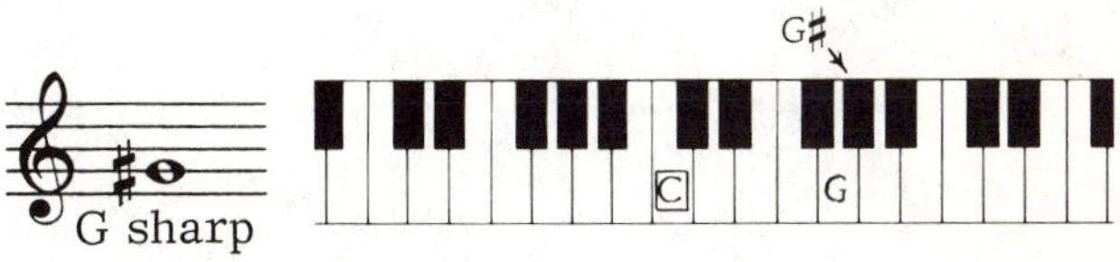

G♯

G sharp

C G

The symbol ♯ is called a ____________.

sharp

51. In notation, the sharp is placed *before* the note to which it applies.

When naming the sharped note, however, the word "sharp" *follows* the letter name: for example, F sharp, C sharp. These may also be written F♯, C♯.

52. Study these notes carefully. Then write the pitch names of the last three, observing the clefs. Refer to frame 51 if necessary.

G♯ C♯ A♯ __ __ __

F♯ G♯ C♯

raises

53. Notice that the sharp (♯) is centered on the same line or space as the note to which it applies.

Thus 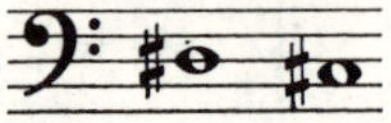, not 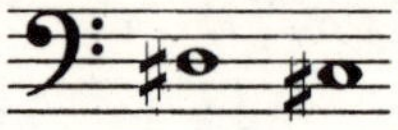 or 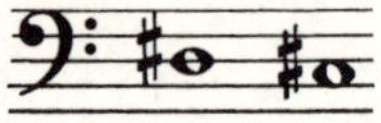.

Place a sharp before each of the following notes.

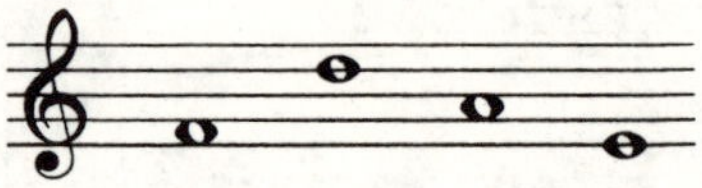

The sharp (♯) __________ (raises/lowers) the note that follows it.

---

2 3

54. Which of the following are correct? __________

1. ♯F 2. G sharp 3. 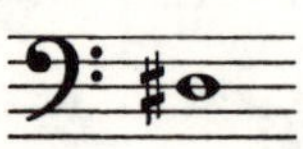 4. 

---

3 4

55. Which of the following are correct? __________

1.  2. ♯D 3. 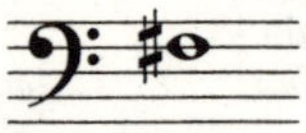 4. E sharp

---

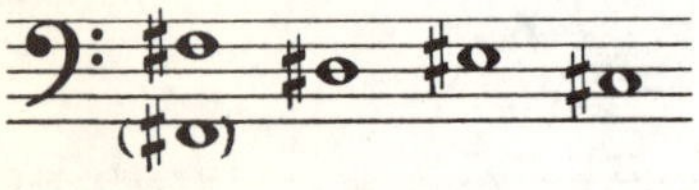

2

56. Notate these pitches in whole notes on the bass staff. (Do not use leger lines.)

F♯ D♯ E♯ C♯ 

Which of the two below is the higher pitch? _____

1.  2. 

57. Draw an arrow to the location of these pitches on the keyboard, following the given example.

58. A *flat* (♭) placed before a note means that the pitch is *lowered* to that of the next key to the left on the keyboard.

E♭

E

C

E flat

What is the symbol ♭ called? ____________

flat

59. Name these symbols.

1. ♯ ____________

2. ♭ ____________

3. ____________

4. ____________

5. ____________

1. sharp
2. flat
3. staff
4. grand staff
5. leger line

60. The flat (♭) ____________ (raises/lowers) the following note.

Which of these is the lower pitch? _____

1. 2.

lowers

1

61. The loop of the flat sign (♭) encircles the same line or space as the note to which it applies.

Thus , not or .

Draw a bass clef at the beginning of the staff; then place a flat before each of those notes. Write the name of each pitch below the staff.

_____ _____ _____ _____

$E^{\flat}$ $A^{\flat}$ $D^{\flat}$ $B^{\flat}$

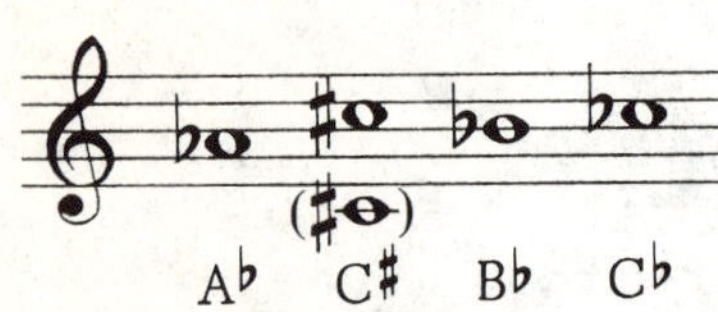

1

62. Using whole notes, notate these pitches on the treble staff.

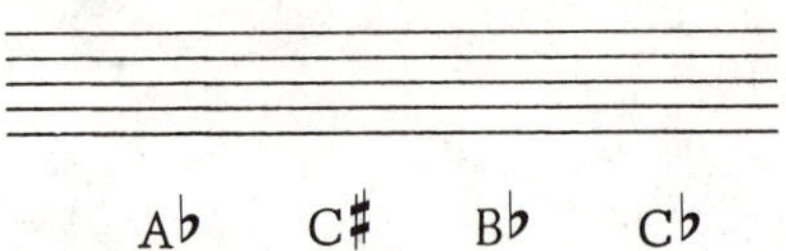

Which is the lower pitch? ____

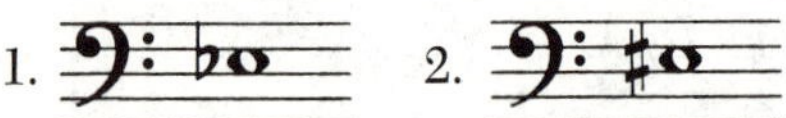

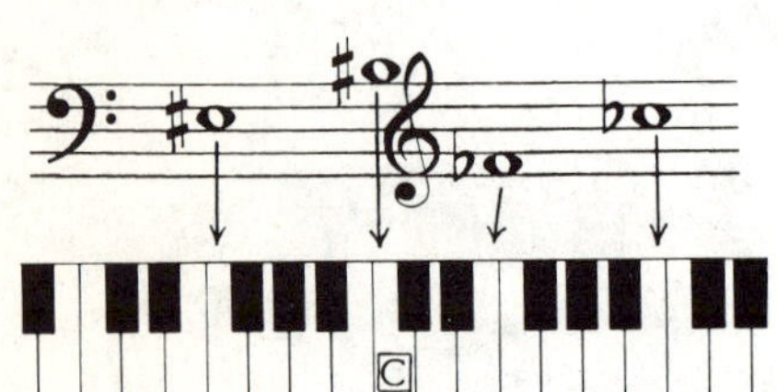

63. Notice that E♯, B♯, F♭, and C♭ are found on *white* keys of the piano keyboard. All other pitches with "sharp" or "flat" in their names fall on *black* keys. The musical applications of this principle will be discussed later.

Supply arrows to complete the example below.

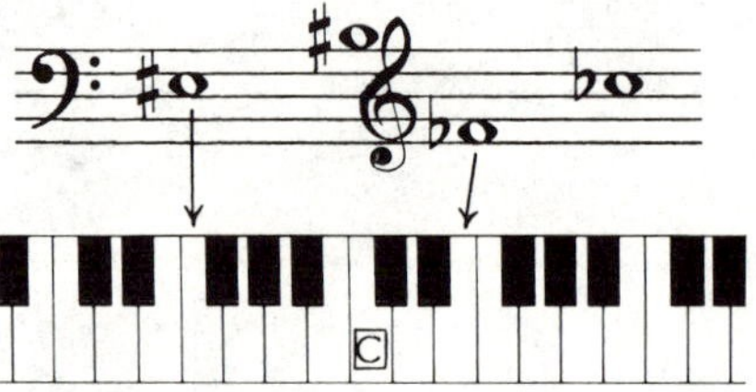

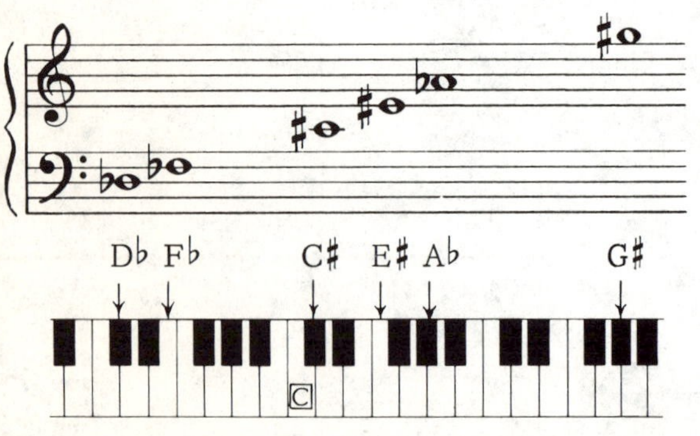

64. Complete the notation of these pitches; then draw an arrow to their locations on the keyboard.

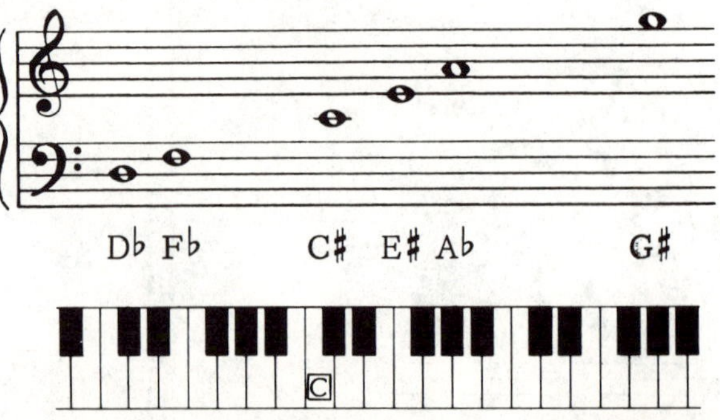

65. Name these pitches below the staff. Then draw an arrow to their locations on the keyboard.

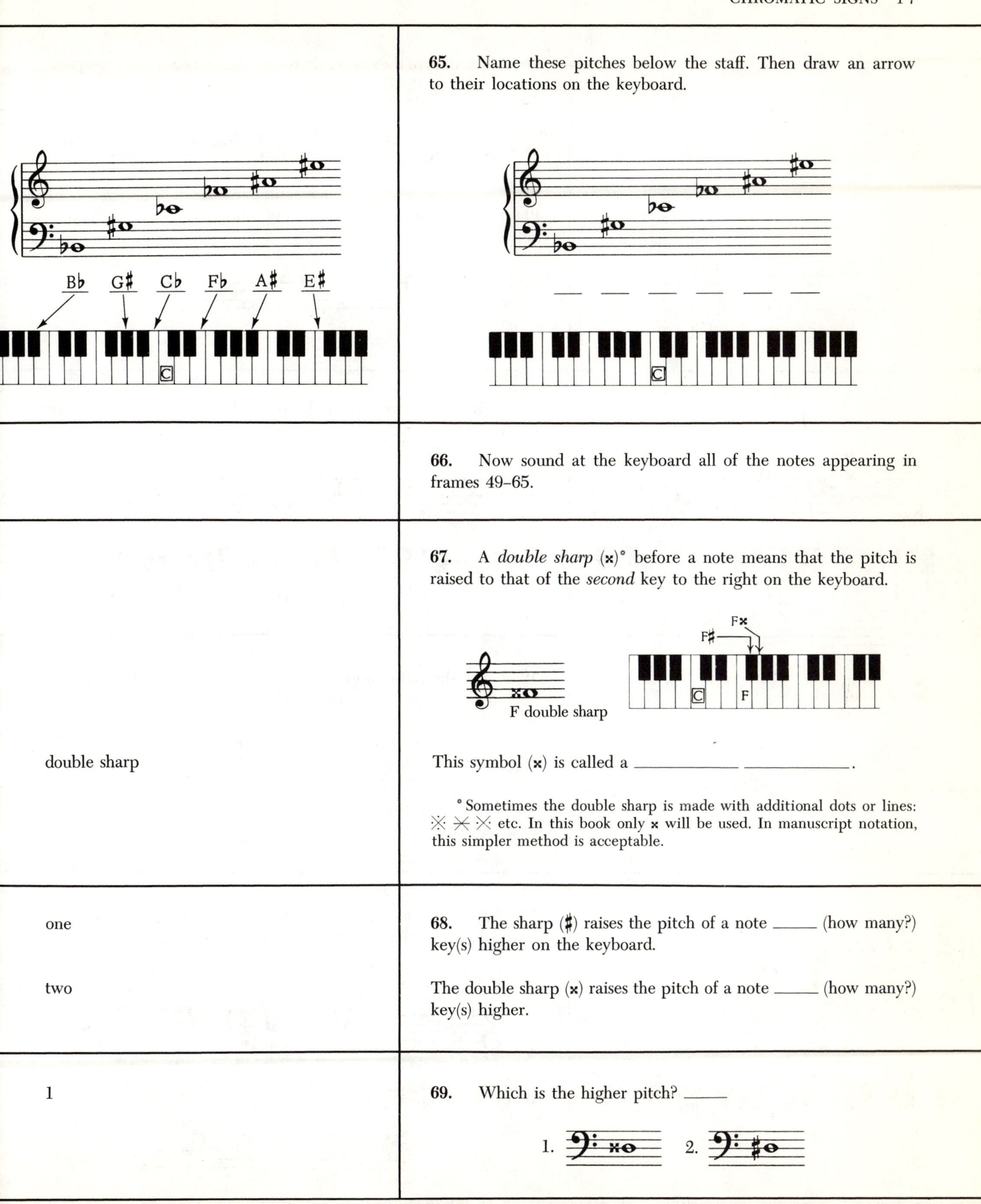

66. Now sound at the keyboard all of the notes appearing in frames 49–65.

67. A *double sharp* (𝄪)* before a note means that the pitch is raised to that of the *second* key to the right on the keyboard.

F double sharp

This symbol (𝄪) is called a ________ ________.

double sharp

*Sometimes the double sharp is made with additional dots or lines: etc. In this book only 𝄪 will be used. In manuscript notation, this simpler method is acceptable.

68. The sharp (♯) raises the pitch of a note ____ (how many?) key(s) higher on the keyboard.

one

The double sharp (𝄪) raises the pitch of a note ____ (how many?) key(s) higher.

two

69. Which is the higher pitch? ____

1

1. 2.

70. The lines of the double sharp (×) intersect on the line or space of the note to which it applies.

Thus [staff], not [staff] or [staff].

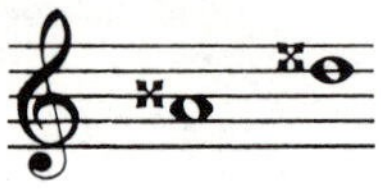

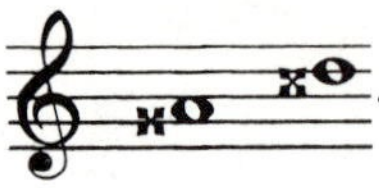

Place a double sharp before each note below. Then name each pitch below the staff.

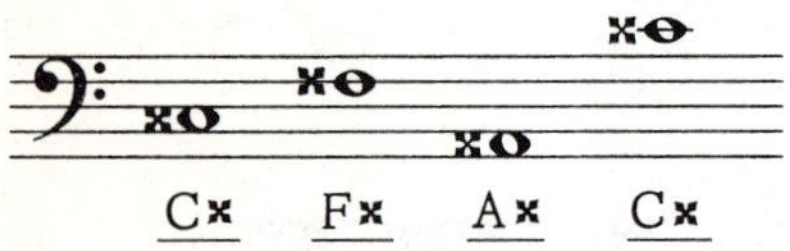

___ ___ ___ ___

Cx Fx Ax Cx

71. Draw an arrow to the keyboard location of each of these pitches, following the given example.

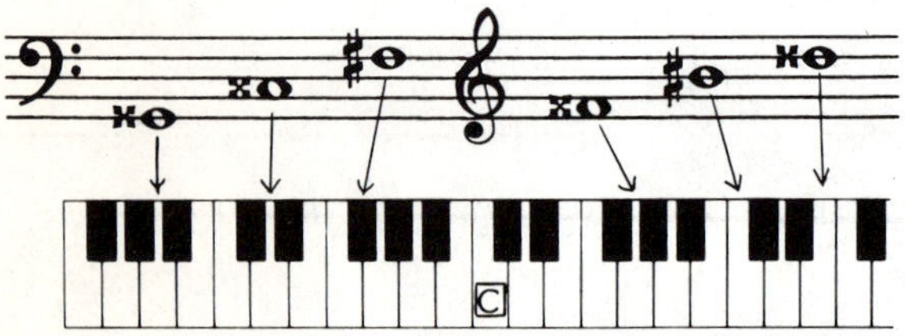

C

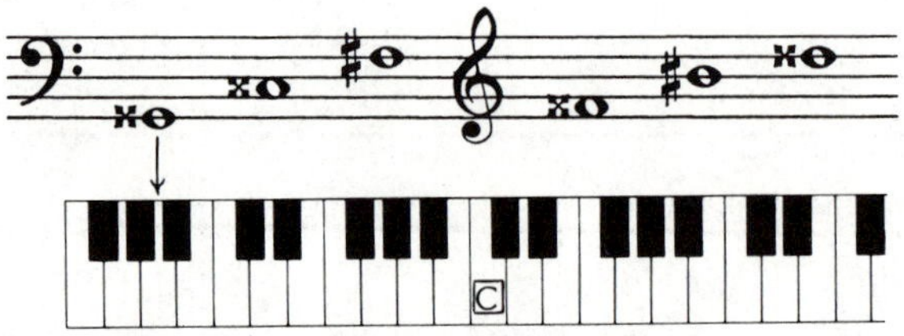

C

1

72. The sharp (♯) raises the pitch of a note ____ (how many?) key(s) to the right on the keyboard.

2

The double sharp (×) raises the pitch of a note ____ (how many?) key(s) to the right.

1

The flat (♭) lowers the pitch of a note ____ (how many?) key(s) to the left on the keyboard.

73. A *double flat* (♭♭) before a note means that the pitch is lowered to that of the *second* key to the left on the keyboard.

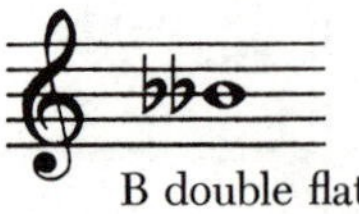

B double flat

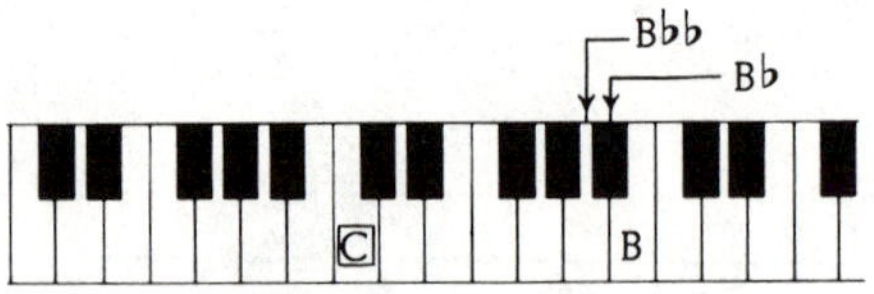

B♭♭

B♭

C

B

2

Which is the lower pitch? ____

1. 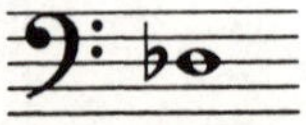 2.

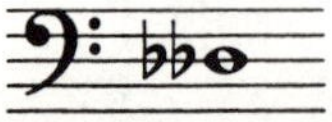

two two	**74.** The double flat (♭♭) and the double sharp (𝄪) affect the pitch of a note by the same amount but in opposite directions. The double flat (♭♭) lowers the pitch of a note _____ (how many?) key(s) to the left. The double sharp (𝄪) raises the pitch of a note _____ (how many?) key(s) to the right.
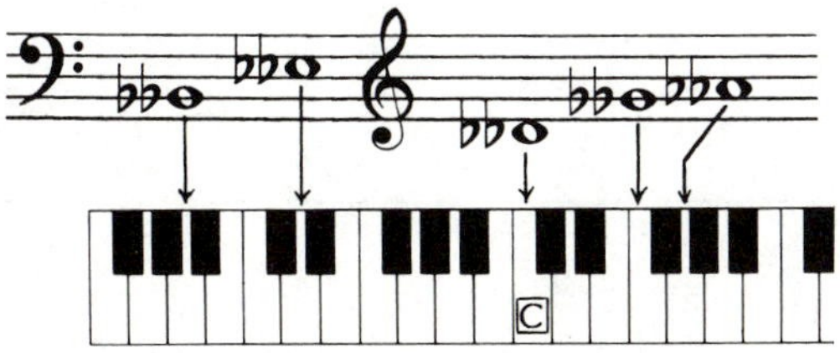 C	**75.** Place a double flat before each note below. Then draw an arrow to the keyboard location of each. C
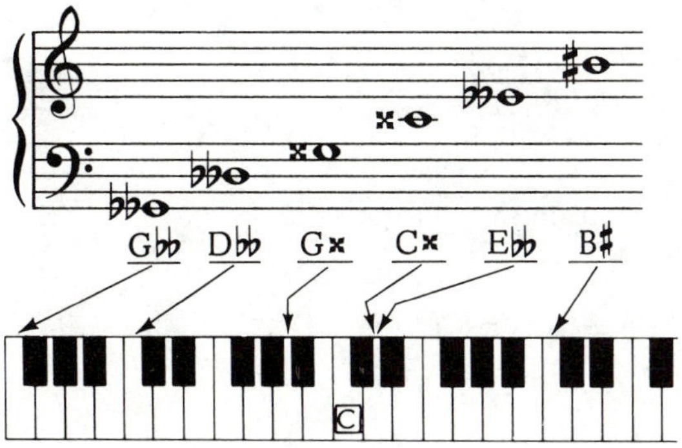 G♭♭ D♭♭ G𝄪 C𝄪 E♭♭ B♯ C	**76.** Name these pitches below the staff. Then draw an arrow to their locations on the keyboard. ___ ___ ___ ___ ___ ___ C
	77. Now, at the keyboard, sound all the notes appearing in frames 67–76.
1. flat 3. double flat 2. double sharp 4. sharp	**78.** Name these symbols. 1. ♭ __________ 3. ♭♭ __________ __________ 2. 𝄪 __________ __________ 4. ♯ __________
1. G♭♭ 2. G♭ 3. G 4. G♯ 5. G𝄪	**79.** Arrange these pitch names from lowest to highest. G♯ G G♭♭ G𝄪 G♭ 1. _____ 2. _____ 3. _____ 4. _____ 5. _____

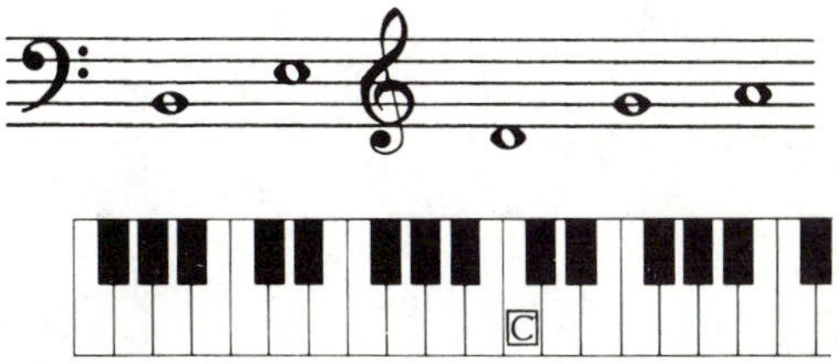

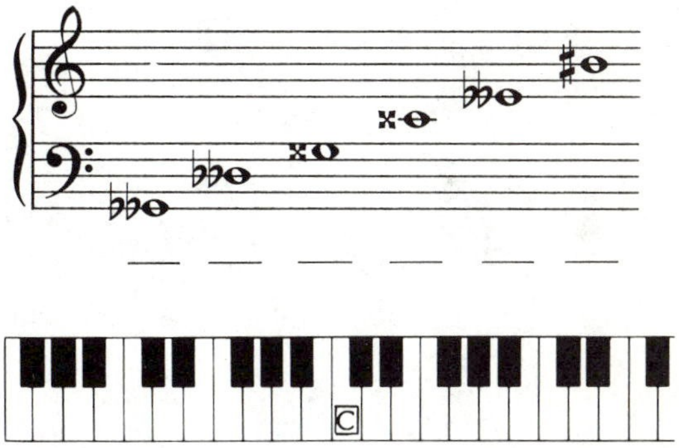

80. To *cancel* a sharp, double sharp, flat, or double flat, a *natural* sign (♮) is used. When placed before a note, it restores the original pitch of the note.

G natural

What is this symbol (♮) called? ______________

natural

81. A *single* natural sign is sufficient to cancel a double sharp or double flat.

Name the pitch that results from this natural sign.

____ ________

G natural

82. Draw on the blank staves the pitches that are restored by these naturals.

1. 2. 3. 4.

1. 3.

2. 4.

83. Note that the natural (♮) is centered on the same line or space as the note to which it applies.

Thus [staff], not [staff] or [staff].

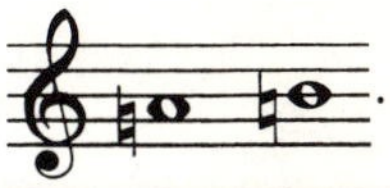

Draw an F clef at the beginning of the staff. Then place naturals before these pitches.

---

84. Name these symbols.

1. ♭ ____________
2. ♮ ____________
3. ♭♭ ____________ ____________
4. × ____________ ____________

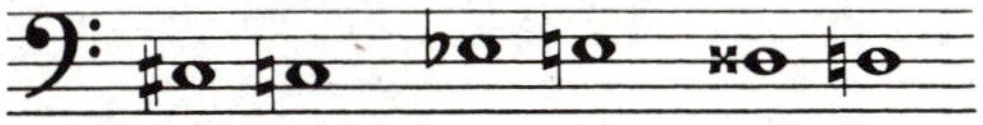

Answers:

1. flat
2. natural
3. double flat
4. double sharp

---

85. Using whole notes, notate these pitches on the bass staff.

C♯ C♮ E♭ E♮ D× D♮

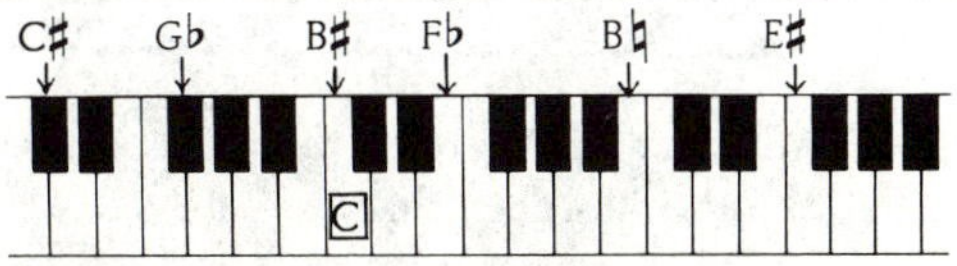

---

86. Write the pitch names of these notes below the staff; then draw arrows to their locations on the keyboard.

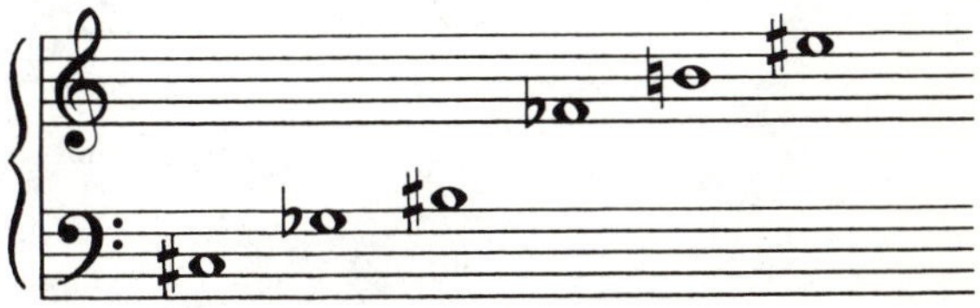

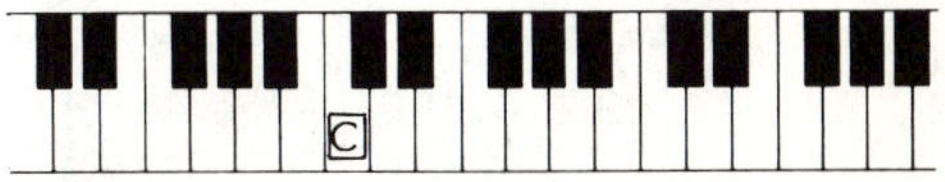

Answer: C♯ G♭ B♯ F♭ B♮ E♯

C

1	**87.** The sharp, double sharp, flat, double flat, and natural are called *chromatic signs,* or *accidentals.* Which of these is the higher pitch? _____ 1. ♯ 2. ♮
2	Which of these is the lower pitch? _____ 1. 𝄪 2. ♮
1. natural 2. double flat 3. sharp accidentals	**88.** Write the names of these chromatic signs. 1. ♮ ______________ 2. ♭♭ ______________ ______________ 3. ♯ ______________ Chromatic signs are also called ______________.
2	**89.** Which of these is the higher pitch? _____ 1. ♭♭ 2. ♮
1	Which of these is the lower pitch? _____ 1. ♭ 2. ♮
chromatic signs	Accidentals are also called ______________ ______________.

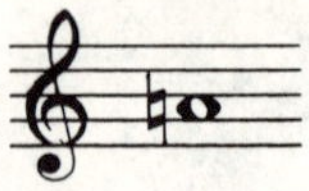

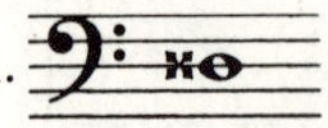

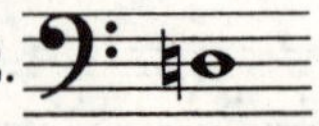

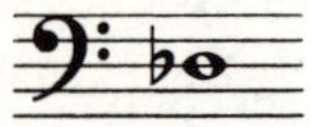

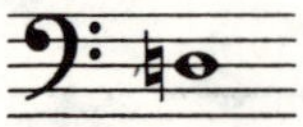

LISTENING FRAMES

lower	**90.** Listen to Example 1-2, a portion of Henry Purcell's song "Thy Hand, Belinda!" from his opera *Dido and Aeneas.* In the first seven tones, each pitch is ______________ (higher/lower) than the preceding one.
3	**91.** The first ten pitches form a melodic pattern that is repeated after the singer enters. How many times does this melodic pattern occur in the passage? _____

2

92. The notation (in whole notes) that most closely corresponds to the opening of this excerpt is ____.

1. 

2. 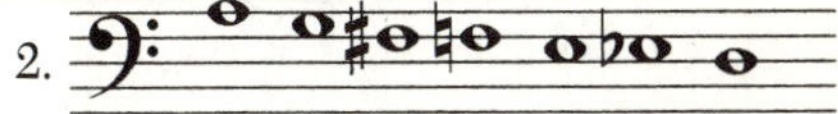

3. 

---

higher

the same

93. Listen to Example 1-2 again. When the singer enters later in the passage, each of the first three tones is ________ (higher/lower) than the preceding ones.

The third and fourth pitches are ________ (the same/different).

THE C CLEF

In addition to the G and F clefs, the *C clef* is often used in notation. The C clef was once widely used in vocal music and may be encountered in early editions of older music. Today it is used primarily to notate music for certain instruments whose ranges would necessitate an awkward number of leger lines if the G or F clef were used. Because the C clef is an essential tool in notation for those instruments, the student who plans to continue music-theory study beyond this book should work through this section, frames 94–107. Other students may omit this section.

The C clef has the distinction of being movable; that is, it may be used in various positions on the staff. The line or space marked by the inner part of the clef is always Middle C (see below).

While the C clef may be used on any line or space of the staff, it is used most frequently on one of the first four lines; each position gives it a different clef name.

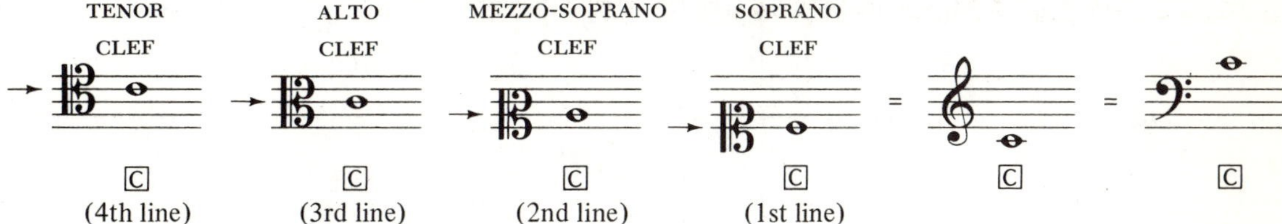

Of these four, the first two—tenor and alto clefs—are by far the most widely used today. The alto clef is commonly used in notating music for the viola, while the tenor clef is sometimes used for the higher notes of the trombone, bassoon, and cello. In addition, the movable nature of the C clef makes it useful in transposition and score reading. In manuscript notation it is sometimes simplified to 𝄡.

Since the alto and tenor clefs currently enjoy the most frequent application, the frames that follow will focus on these.

Answers	Frames
Middle C	**94.** The C clef always identifies the location of ______ ______. Draw four alto clefs, following the given example.
Third	**95.** The alto clef locates Middle C on which line of the staff? ______ (number) Draw an alto clef at the beginning of the staff. Then write beneath the staff the pitch name of each given note. ___ ___ ___ ___ ___
C B A D E	
1. F 2. E 3. G 4. D tenor	**96.** Write beneath the staff the pitch name of each note. 1. ___ 2. ___ 3. ___ 4. ___ The C clef used in 4 above is known as the ______ clef.
C A D E E	**97.** Draw a tenor clef at the beginning of the staff. Then write beneath the staff the pitch name of each given note. ___ ___ ___ ___ ___
tenor B G C B♭ F♯	**98.** Draw the indicated pitches in whole notes. (Do not use leger lines.) The C clef used in this example is the ______ clef. B G C B♭ F♯

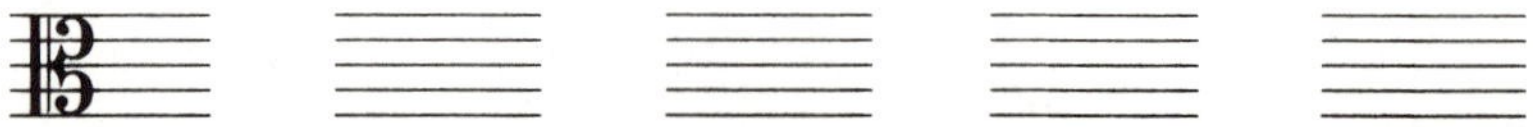

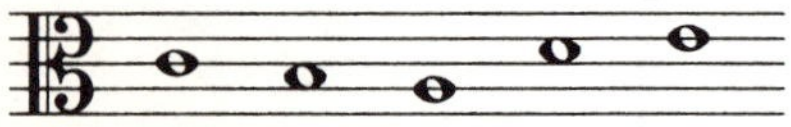

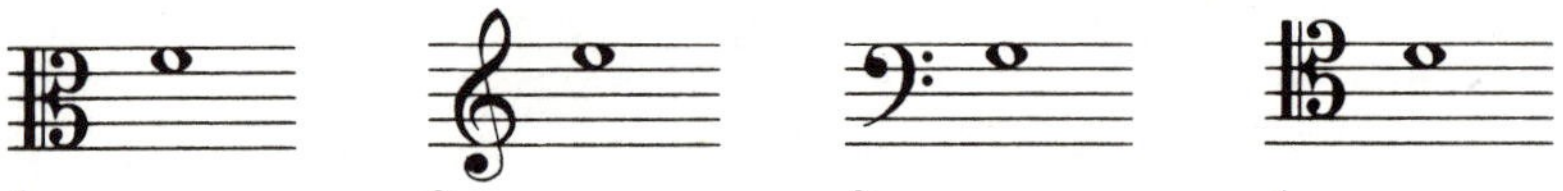

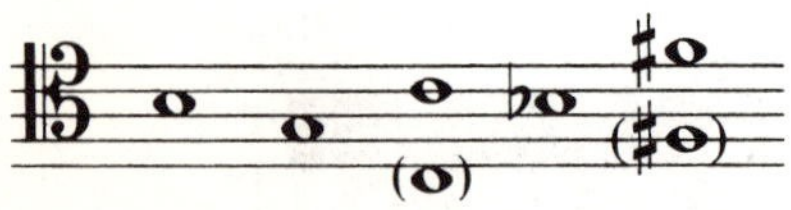

alto

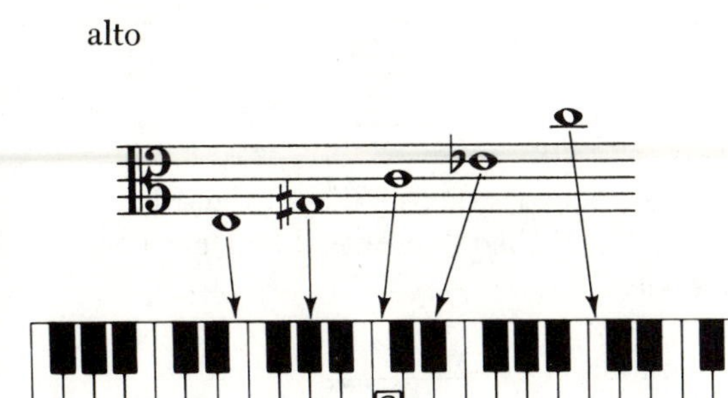

99. Draw an arrow to the keyboard location of these pitches, following the given example. The C clef in this example is the ____________ clef.

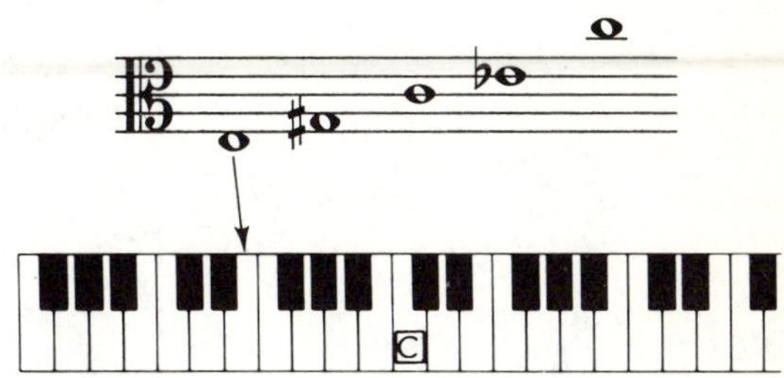

tenor

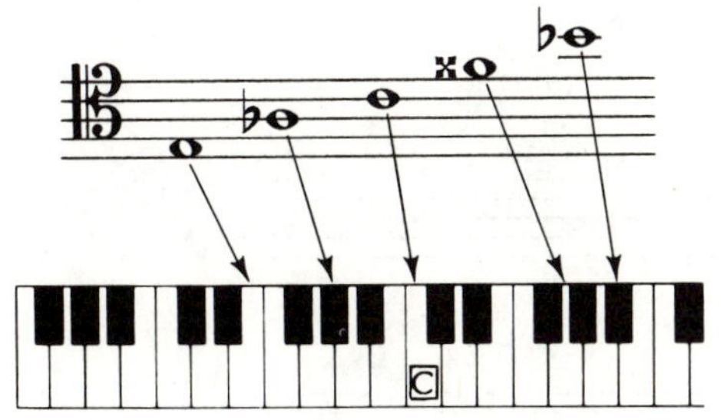

100. Continue as in frame 99. The C clef used is the ____________ clef.

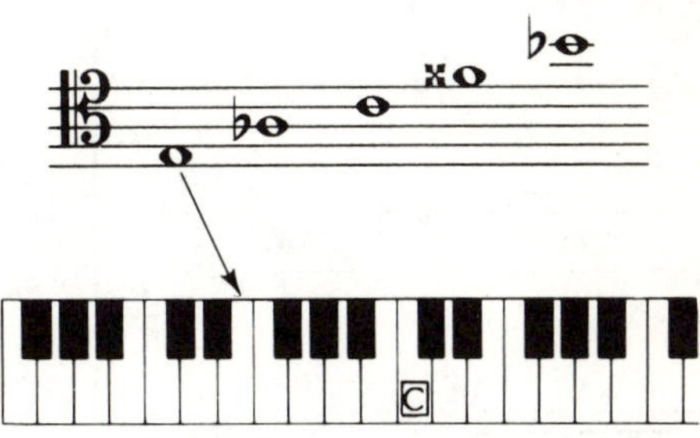

C

101. Alto and tenor clefs are both _____ clefs.

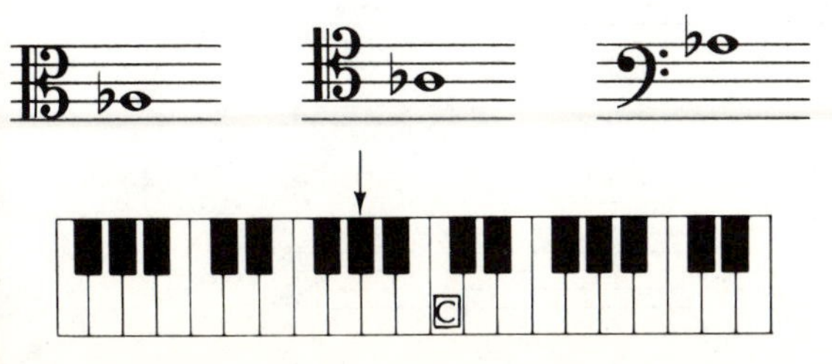

102. Observing each clef carefully, notate this pitch on each staff below. Then draw a single arrow to its keyboard location.

Middle C

103.

This diagram illustrates the pitch position of the alto and tenor clefs within the grand staff. The dashed lines would be leger lines when using the indicated clefs.

All C clefs identify the location of ________ ____.

F♯ F♯ B G E♭♭

104. Name the given pitches. Then, observing the clefs, rewrite each note on the blank staves. Use leger lines as necessary.

___ ___ ___ ___ ___

G♭ C♯ B♭ D♮ D𝄪

105. Continue as in frame 104.

___ ___ ___ ___ ___

A♭ C♭ F♯ C♭ E♭ A♯

106. Continue as in frame 105.

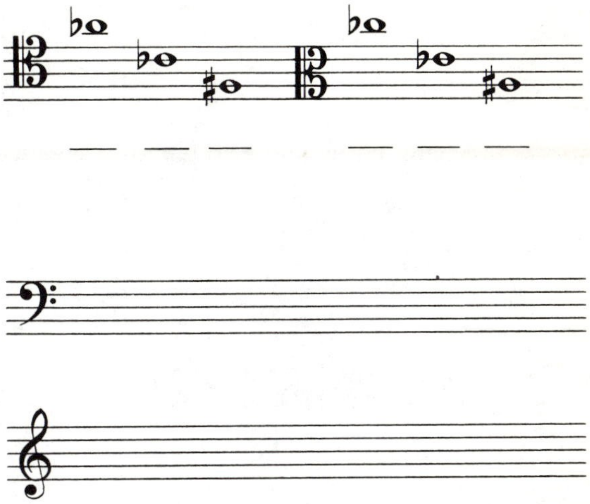

107. It will be useful now to sound at the piano all the notes appearing in frames 94–106.

THE OCTAVE; THE OTTAVA SIGN

Observe that the keyboard is arranged in continuous patterns of seven white keys and five black keys (see below). The order of pitch names within each pattern remains the same.

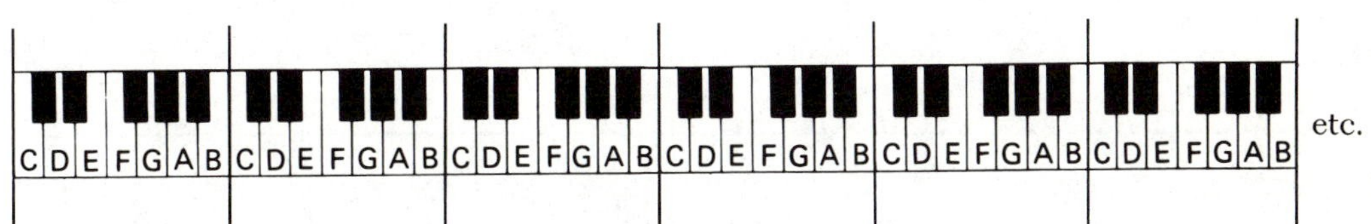

At the keyboard, play all keys corresponding to any one pitch, such as D. As you do this, you will notice that different tones of the same pitch name sound like repetitions of that pitch at higher or lower pitch levels.

These repetitions of pitches at different pitch levels are generally called *octaves*. More exactly, an octave is the difference in pitch between one tone and the next tone higher or lower of the same pitch name.

1. D D 2. A♭ A♭ 3. G♯ G♯

108. Write below the staves the names of these pitches.

C♯

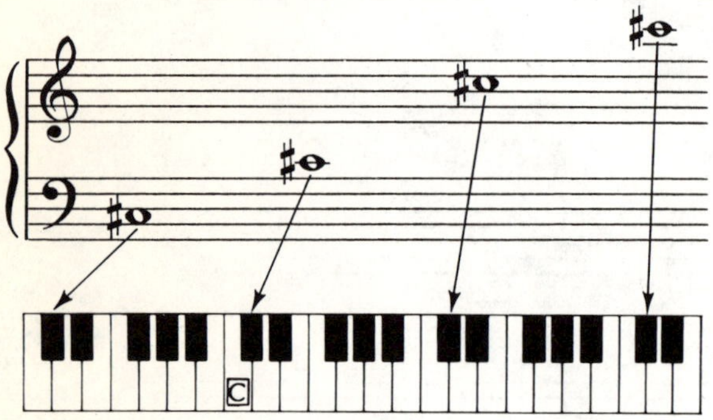

109. The pitch name of each note below is _____.

Draw arrows to the keyboard locations of these notes.

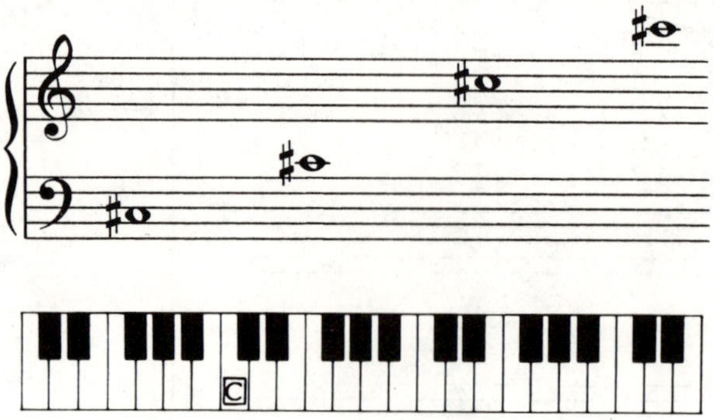

octave

110. The difference in pitch between one tone and the next tone higher or lower of the same pitch name is called a(n) ___________.

1

111. In the example below, D to D is an octave.

Which example below is an octave? _____

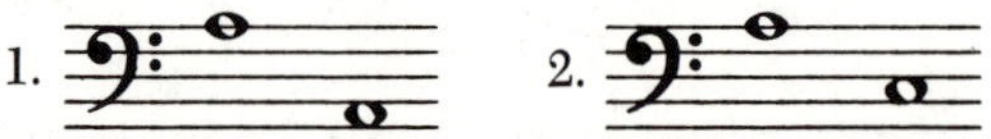

1. 2.

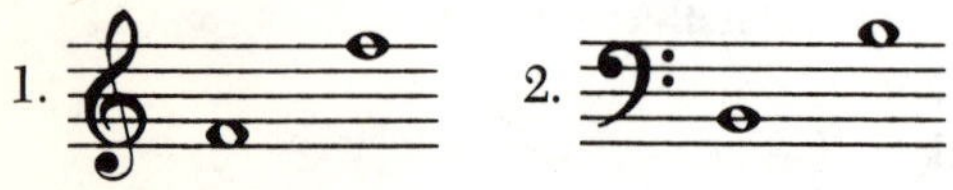

1. 2.

112. Write the note which is an octave higher than each of these pitches.

1. 2.

1. 2.

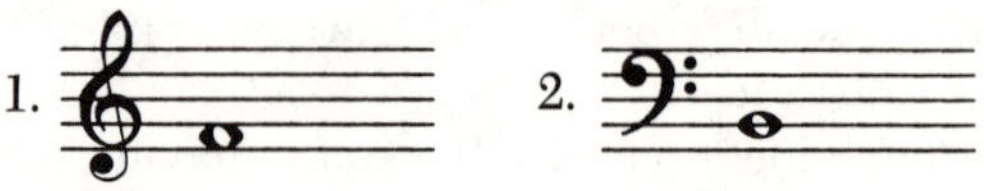

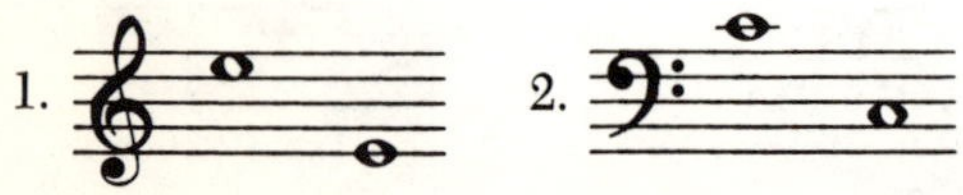

113. Write the note which is an octave lower than each of these pitches.

1. 2.

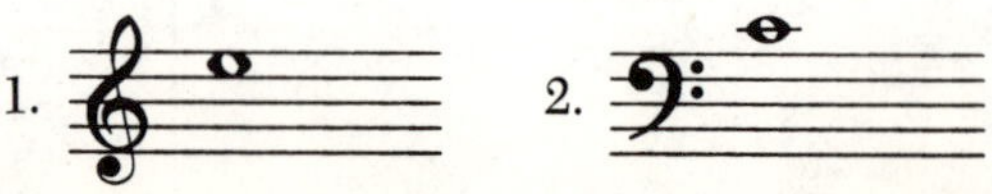

2 3	**114.** Which of the following pairs of notes are octaves? _____ _____
pitch name	**115.** An octave is the difference in pitch between one tone and the next tone higher or lower of the same ___________ ___________.
1. Fb Fb 2. E♯ E♯	**116.** Write the note that is an octave *higher* than each of these pitches, and name each pitch below the staff.
1. Db Db 2. G× G×	**117.** Write the note that is an octave *lower* than each of these pitches, and name each pitch below the staff.
3	**118.** Which example below is *not* an octave? _____
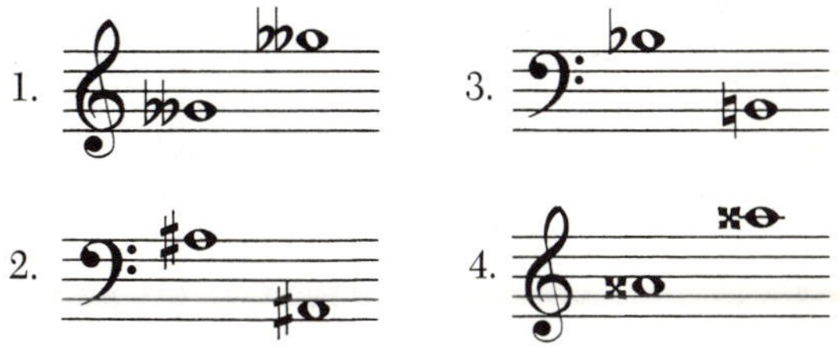	**119.** Now play at the keyboard all pitches in frames 108–18.

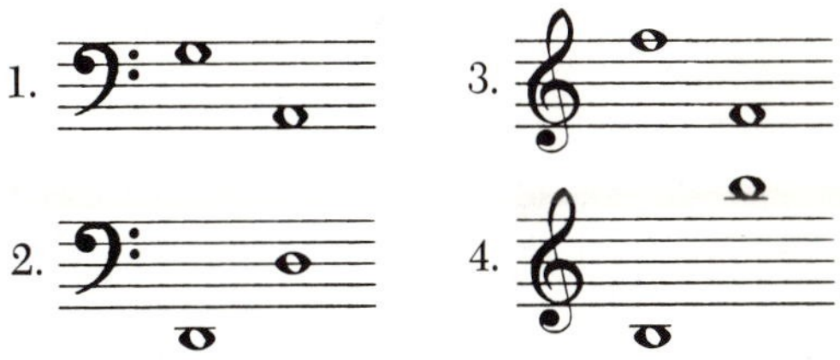

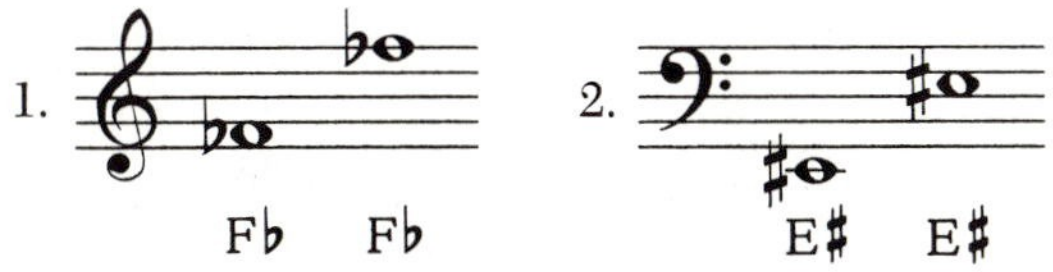

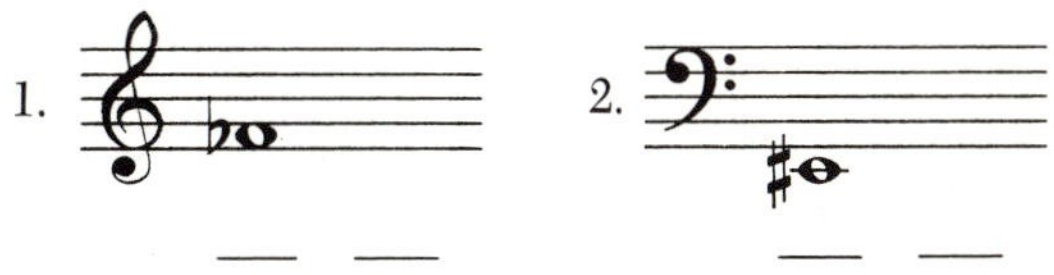

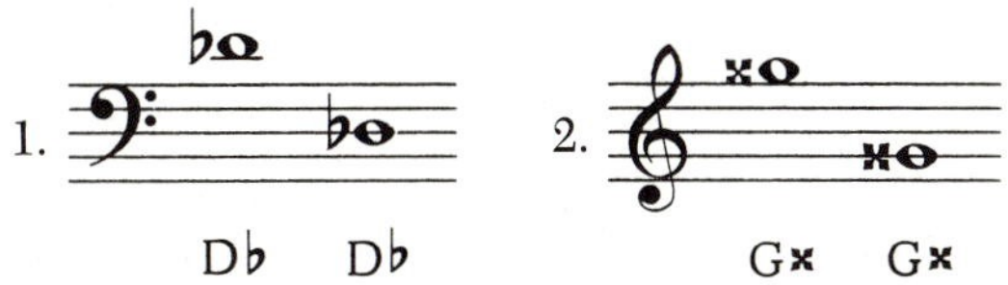

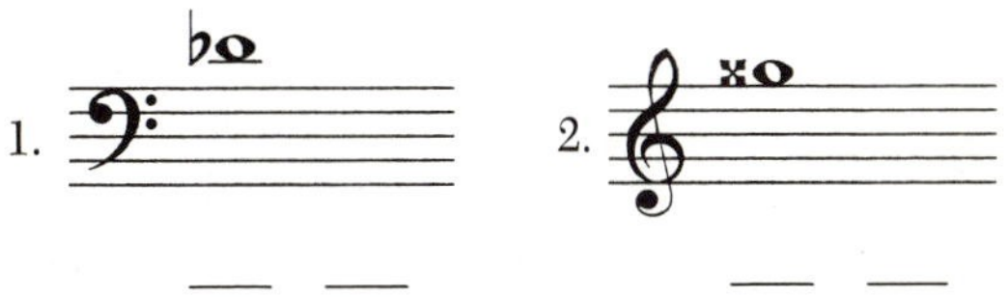

120. In notation, too many leger lines can result in awkwardness and difficulty in reading. A common solution to the problem is to place the *ottava** sign (usually 8va----┐ or 8 ----) above or below a note, indicating that the note will sound an octave higher (if above) or lower (if below) than written.

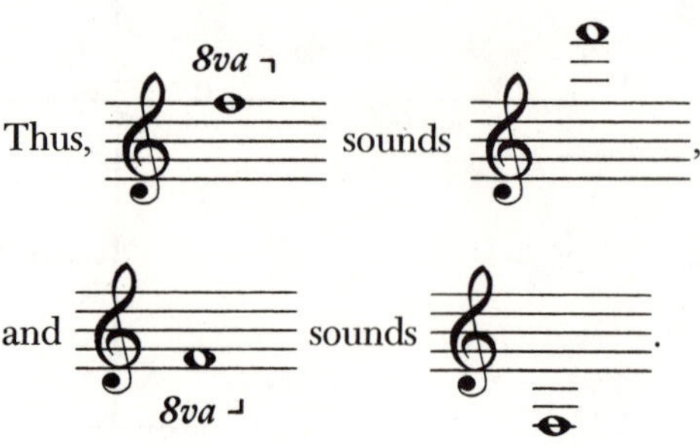

Rewrite this note as it would actually sound, using leger lines.

* *Ottava* is the Italian word for "octave."

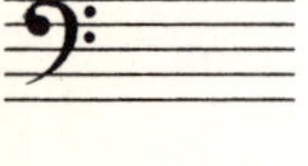

ottava (or 8va or 8)

121. The ________________ sign is used to avoid too many leger lines.

Rewrite these notes as they would actually sound, using leger lines.

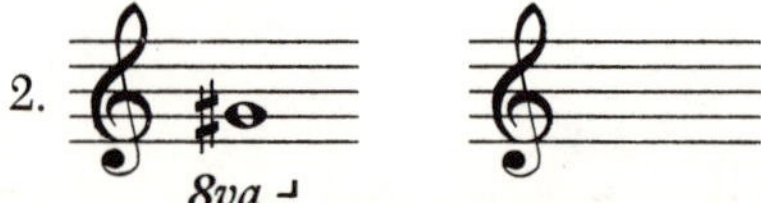

122. The broken line following the ottava sign (8va-----) prolongs its effect until the broken line ends, usually with a short vertical line.

The excessive use of ________ ________ can be avoided by employing the ottava sign.

leger lines

123. Rewrite this example as it actually sounds, using leger lines as necessary.

124. Continue as in frame 123.

125. Using the ottava sign, rewrite this example *without* leger lines so that both will sound identical.

126. Continue as in frame 125.

127. Observing the clef, rewrite this example on the lower staff so that both will sound the same.

128. Continue as in frame 127.

129. Continue as in frame 128.

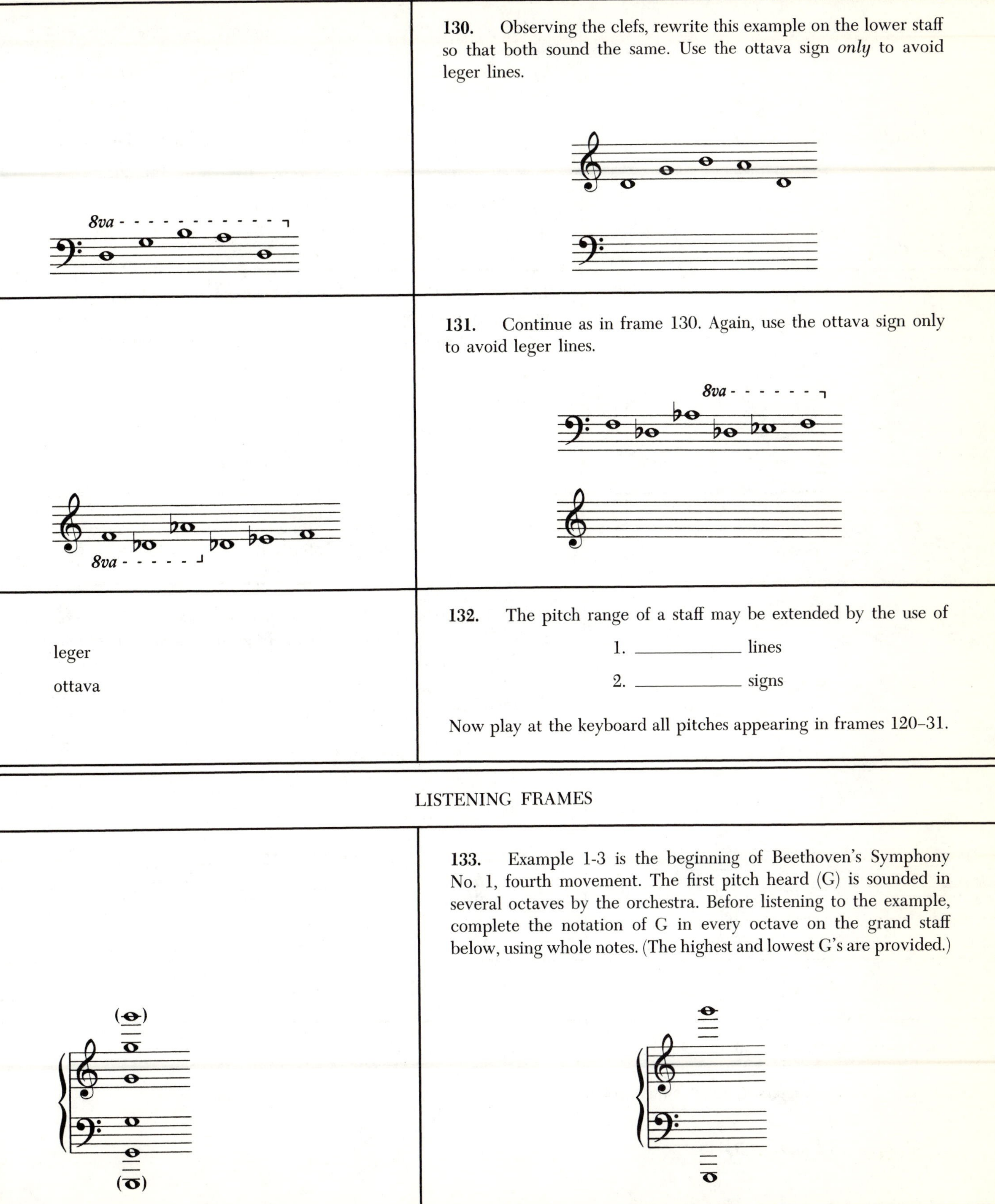

130. Observing the clefs, rewrite this example on the lower staff so that both sound the same. Use the ottava sign *only* to avoid leger lines.

131. Continue as in frame 130. Again, use the ottava sign only to avoid leger lines.

leger

ottava

132. The pitch range of a staff may be extended by the use of

1. ____________ lines
2. ____________ signs

Now play at the keyboard all pitches appearing in frames 120–31.

LISTENING FRAMES

133. Example 1-3 is the beginning of Beethoven's Symphony No. 1, fourth movement. The first pitch heard (G) is sounded in several octaves by the orchestra. Before listening to the example, complete the notation of G in every octave on the grand staff below, using whole notes. (The highest and lowest G's are provided.)

134. Now listen to Example 1-3. The passage continues with violins playing five groups of pitches, each of which is interrupted by a silence. Notice that each group repeats the pitches of the previous group and then adds one more.

higher

The final pitch of each group is __________ (higher/lower) than that of the previous group.

yes

After the octave G's at the beginning, are all of the violins playing the same pitches? _____

135. Listen to Example 1-4, the beginning of the fourth movement of Brahms' Symphony No. 4, paying particular attention to the highest melodic line. Which description below most accurately describes the first *six* tones? _____

1

1. Each tone is successively higher.
2. Each tone is successively lower.
3. The tones move up and down.

136. Within the first *eight* tones of Example 1-4, an octave occurs. Listen until you can identify it.

137. The pitches of the first eight tones are notated here in whole notes. One chromatic sign is missing from the notation where indicated by the arrow.

1. Listen again to the recording, and fill in the appropriate sign: ♭, ♯, or ♮.
2. Below the staff, name each pitch.
3. Draw a circle around the two notes that sound an octave apart.

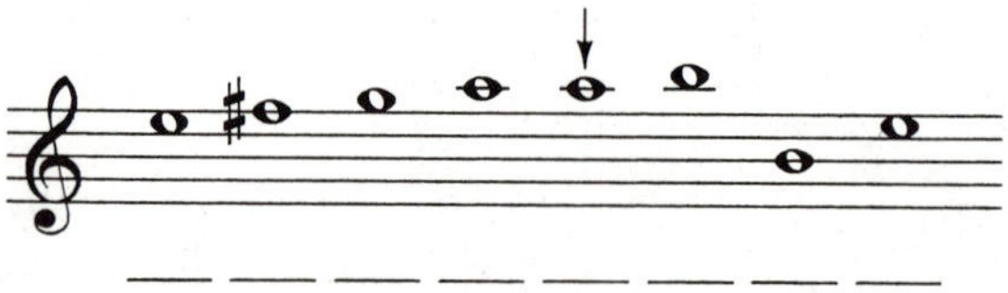

E F♯ G A A♯ B B E

___ ___ ___ ___ ___ ___ ___ ___

SELF-QUIZ I

1. The symbols used in musical __________ represent sounds, silences, and their duration.

2. __________ refers to a tone's highness or lowness.

3. Identify each clef: 1.  𝄢 __________ or __________ 2.  𝄞 __________ or __________.

4. The symbols below are generally called __________________ signs, or __________________.

♮ ♭ × ♭♭ ♯

5. Using whole notes, rearrange these pitches in order from lowest to highest on the adjacent staff.

6. Name these pitches below the staff. Then draw an arrow to their locations on the keyboard.

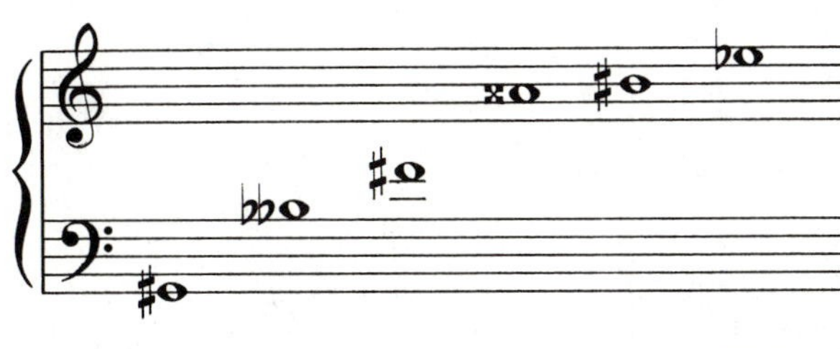

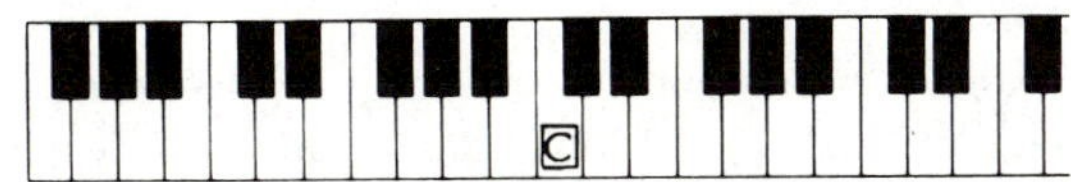

7. The difference in pitch between one tone and the next tone higher or lower of the same pitch name is called a(n) ______________.

8. The symbol 8va--------┐ is known as the __________________ sign.

9. Which of these examples are octaves? __________________

1. 

2. 

3. 

4. 

5. 

10. The pitch range of the staff may be extended by the use of __________________ lines or __________________ signs.

CHAPTER ▪ II ▪ RHYTHM AND METER

Musical time, an essential element in the music of all cultures, has been explored in many directions throughout the history of our own culture. Our traditional system of notation expresses musical time primarily in terms of rhythm, meter, and tempo, and the symbols and terms which visually convey this aspect of music are continuing in their development.

While the notation of pitch has become highly accurate, the more complex notation of time has necessarily progressed through a more intricate route of continuous trial and error. Nevertheless, the basic ideas in the traditional notation of rhythm and meter are generally straightforward, providing a foundation for a more advanced understanding of the rhythmic elements of music in later musical studies.

BASIC PRINCIPLES OF RHYTHM AND METER

Rhythm	**1.** Music consists of sounds and silences of various durations moving through time. This motion of music through time is called *rhythm.* __________ is the motion of music through time.
time Beats	**2.** As music moves through time, regular pulsations occur. These pulsations are called *beats.* Rhythm is the motion of music through __________. __________ are the regular pulsations which occur as music moves through time.
pulsations	**3.** The regular __________ which occur as music moves through time are called beats.

4. Although beats generally divide time into equal portions, some beats are felt more strongly than others. In other words, some beats are *strong* (more heavily stressed) and others are *weak* (less heavily stressed).

Beats have __________ (equal/unequal) duration, and __________ (equal/unequal) stress.

equal

unequal

---

5. Strong and weak beats usually occur in continuous patterns, two of which are represented by the diagrams below.

(⇊ = strong beats; ↓ = weak beats. The time span of each pattern is represented by the horizontal lines.)

1. 1 2 | 1 2 | 1 2 | 1 2 etc.

2. 1 2 3 | 1 2 3 | 1 2 3 etc.

Produce the above patterns by clapping or tapping, making the strong beats louder. Be sure to allow an equal amount of time between all beats.

Each pattern in example 1 contains two beats.

The patterns in example 2 each contain __________ beats.

three

---

6. The organization of beats into patterns of stress is called *meter*.

Rhythm is the __________ of music through time.

__________ is the organization of beats into patterns of stress.

motion

Meter

---

7. The regular pulsations which occur as music moves through time are called __________.

Meter is the organization of beats into patterns of __________.

beats

stress

---

8. In music the usual patterns of strong and weak beats all have a strong first beat and a weak last beat, but they vary in the *number* of beats they contain. Meters are therefore classified according to the number of beats they contain.

All meters have a strong __________ beat and a weak last beat.

first

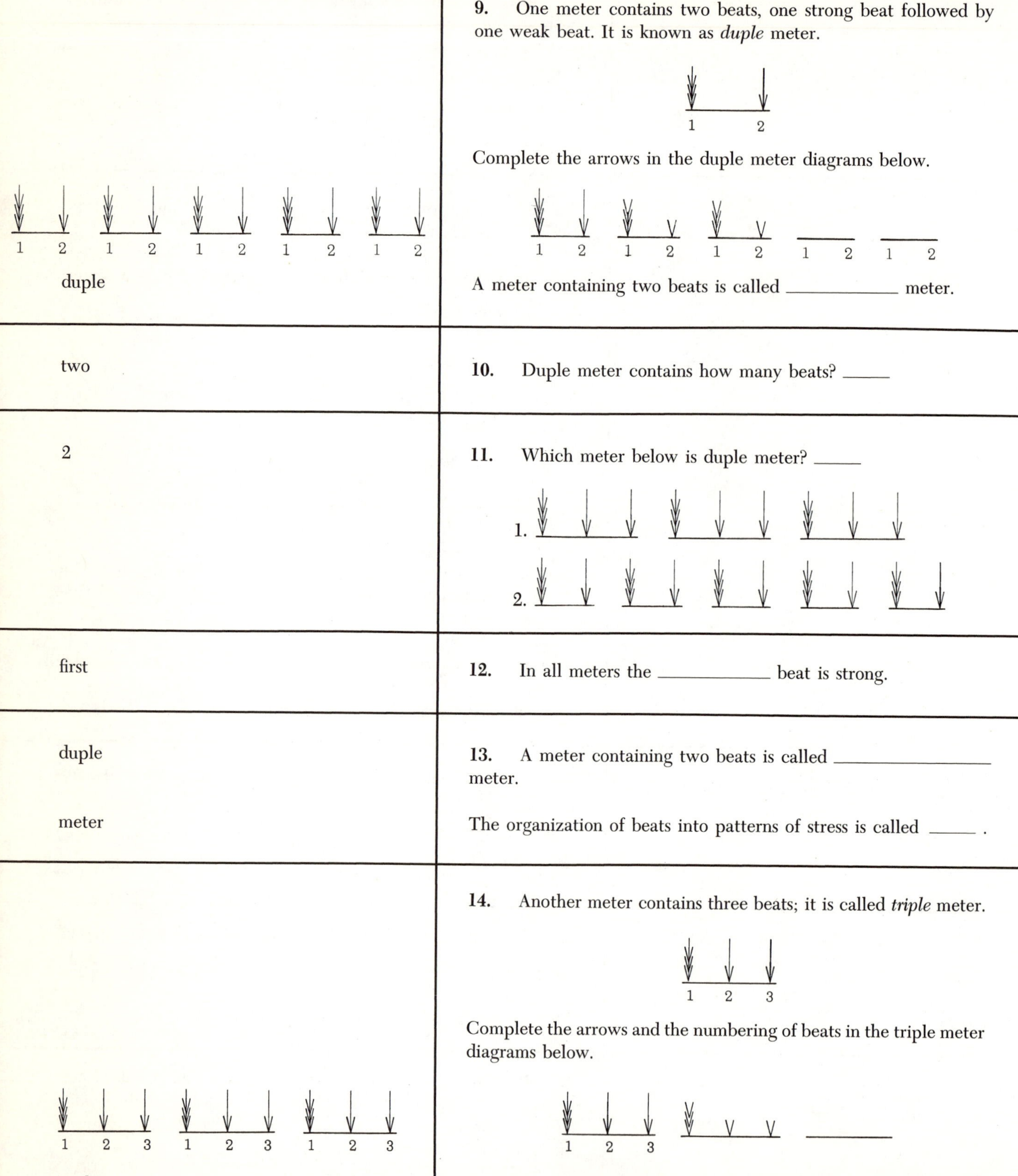

Answers	Frames
	9. One meter contains two beats, one strong beat followed by one weak beat. It is known as *duple* meter. 1 2 Complete the arrows in the duple meter diagrams below. 1 2 1 2 1 2 1 2 1 2
1 2 1 2 1 2 1 2 1 2 duple	A meter containing two beats is called __________ meter.
two	**10.** Duple meter contains how many beats? _____
2	**11.** Which meter below is duple meter? _____ 1. 2.
first	**12.** In all meters the __________ beat is strong.
duple	**13.** A meter containing two beats is called __________ meter.
meter	The organization of beats into patterns of stress is called _____ .
	14. Another meter contains three beats; it is called *triple* meter. 1 2 3 Complete the arrows and the numbering of beats in the triple meter diagrams below. 1 2 3
1 2 3 1 2 3 1 2 3 triple	A meter consisting of three beats is called __________ meter.

1. triple

2. duple

weak

15. Name the meters shown below.

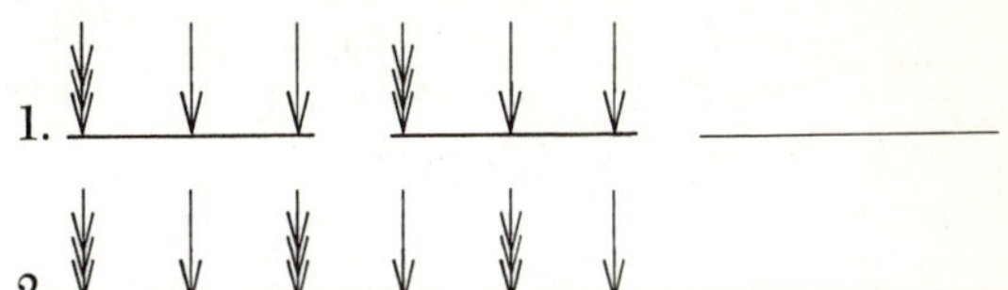

All meters have a strong first beat and a __________ last beat.

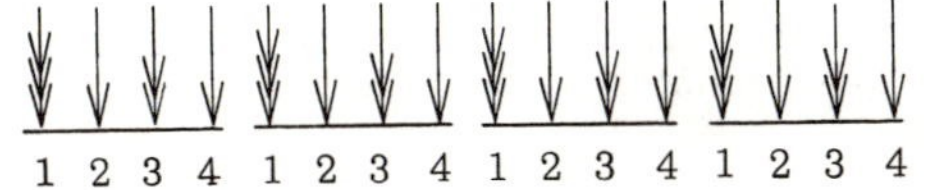

16. A four-beat pattern is called *quadruple* meter. It is a combination of two duple patterns in which the first beat receives more stress than the third. (= strongest beats; = lesser strong beats.)

1 2 + 1 2 = 1 2 3 4

Complete the arrows and the numbering of beats in the quadruple patterns below. (= strongest beats; = lesser strong beats.)

Clap or tap the above quadruple meter diagrams, making the first beat louder than the third. As before, allow an equal amount of time between all beats.

Quadruple

first

1. duple

2. quadruple

3. triple

17. __________ meter contains four beats. Which is the strongest beat? __________

Identify these meters.

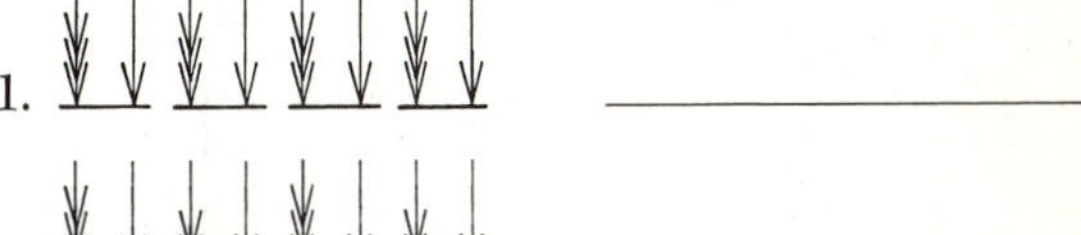

---

two

two four

18. Duple meter contains how many beats? __________

The weak beats in triple meter are two and three. The weakest beats in quadruple meter are __________ and __________.

1. 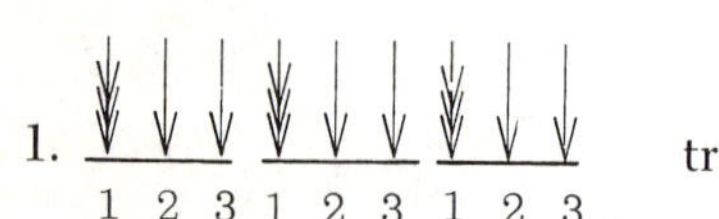

triple

2. 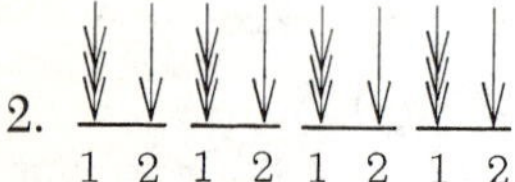

duple

3. 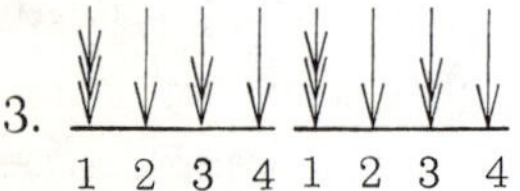

quadruple

19. Complete the diagrams for these meters, using arrows and numbers as before. Include the name of each meter in the space provided.

1. 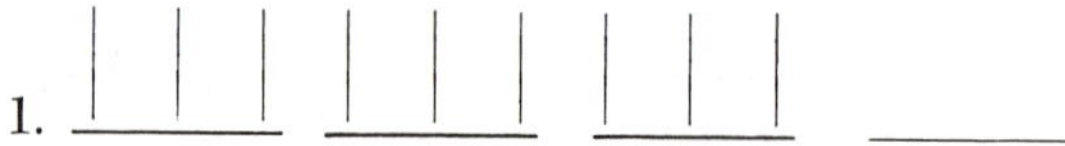 ____________

2.  ____________

3.  ____________

For practice, tap or clap each meter shown above, emphasizing the strong beats. (Remember to make all beats the same duration regardless of difference in stress.)

---

duple, triple, quadruple

(any order)

duration

stress

20. The three meters considered thus far are ____________, ____________, and ____________.

In all meters, beats have equal ____________ but unequal ____________.

---

five

21. Still another meter results from combining a duple pattern and a triple pattern to form a *quintuple,* or five-beat, pattern. The combination may be either duple + triple or triple + duple; either way, however, the first beat receives the greatest degree of stress. It is called quintuple meter.

1 2 + 1 2 3 = 1 2 3 4 5

1 2 3 + 1 2 = 1 2 3 4 5

Quintuple meter contains how many beats? ____________

Quintuple quintuple 1 2 3 4 5 1 2 3 4 5 1 2 3 4 5	**22.** ________________ meter is a combination of either duple + triple or triple + duple meters. Both meters below are ________________. 1. 1 2 3 4 5 1 2 3 4 5 1 2 3 4 5 2. 1 2 3 4 5 1 2 3 4 5 1 2 3 4 5 For practice, tap or clap each meter shown above, emphasizing the strong beats as before.
triple 1 2 3 4 5 1 2 3 4 5 1 2 3 4 5	**23.** Quintuple meter is a combination of duple and ________________ meters. In all meters the first beat is the strongest. Complete the quintuple meter diagrams below, including beat numbers. 1 2 3 4 5 1 3 1 3
1. triple 2. quadruple 3. duple 4. quintuple	**24.** Identify these meters. 1. ________________ 2. ________________ 3. ________________ 4. ________________
1. three 2. four 3. five 4. two	**25.** Give the number of beats in each meter below. 1. triple ________ 2. quadruple ________ 3. quintuple ________ 4. duple ________

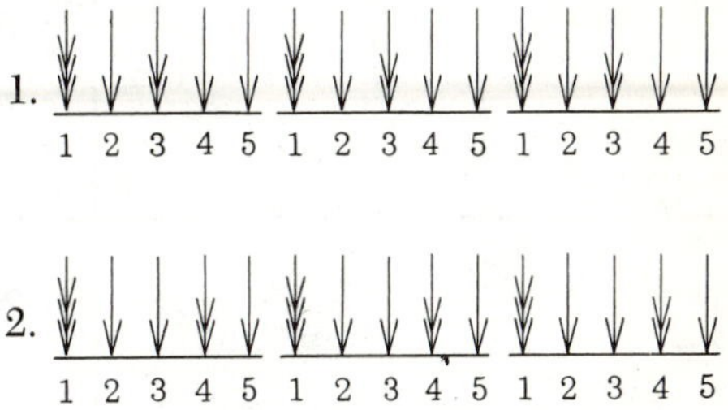

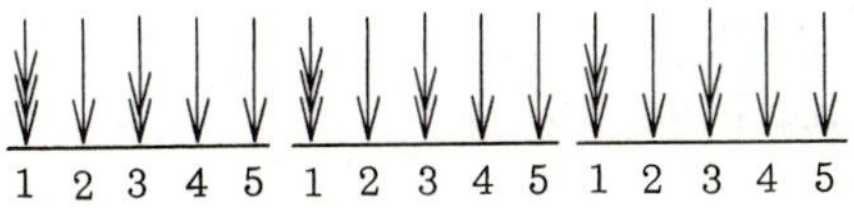

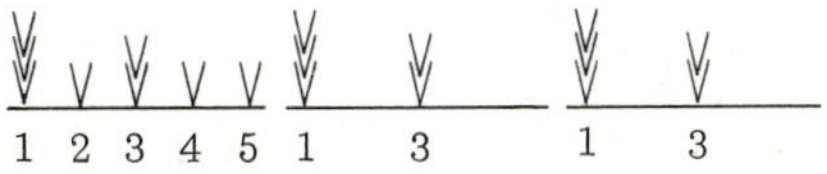

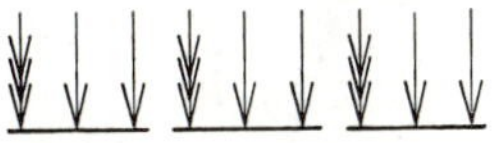

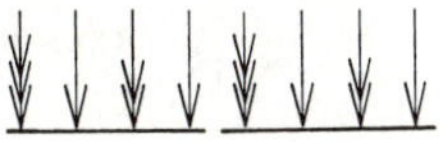

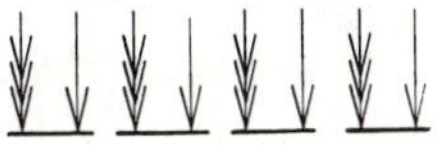

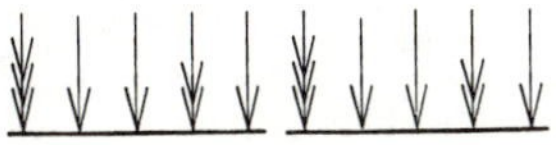

equal Rhythm	**26.** Meters containing other numbers of beats—one, six, seven, ten, for example—sometimes occur in music, but these meters generally involve extensions of the basic principles set forth here and are reserved for further study after completion of this chapter. Beats are of ____________ duration and unequal stress. ____________ is the motion of music through time.
tempo	**27.** The rate of speed with which beats occur is called *tempo.* In music of a quick tempo, the beat rate is faster than in music of a slow ____________.
tempo	**28.** The rate of speed with which beats occur is called ____________.
beats	**29.** The tempo of a piece of music is usually indicated at the beginning by words or symbols denoting various degrees of speed, such as *Presto* (very fast), *Allegro* (fast), *Adagio* (slow), and many others in various languages. Tempo refers to the rate of speed with which ____________ occur.
Tempo	**30.** Extremely fast or slow tempos may affect the treatment of the beat in performance. In a very fast tempo the beats may proceed so quickly that it is necessary to combine two or more beats into a single beat. In a very slow tempo, the beats sometimes move so slowly that it may be practical to divide each beat to facilitate conducting or performance. In this book, meter names refer to the *basic* number of beats in each meter as described in this chapter, independent of extremes of tempo as discussed in this frame. ____________ is the rate of speed at which beats occur.
Rhythm Beats	**31.** ____________ is the motion of music through time. ____________ are the regular pulsations that occur as music moves through time.
Tempo Meter	**32.** ____________ is the rate of speed at which beats occur. ____________ is the organization of beats into patterns of stress.

LISTENING FRAMES

quadruple (If your answer was "triple," listen to the excerpt again. Observe that the beats occur in stress patterns of four rather than three.)	**33.** Example 2-1 is the opening melody of Beethoven's "Archduke" Trio, first movement. As you listen, determine the meter by tapping the beats while counting them aloud. (Your counting should return to "one" each time you hear the stress pattern beginning again.) The meter in this passage is __________ (quadruple/triple).
eight	**34.** Listen to Example 2-1 again, carefully counting each quadruple pattern. How many times does the quadruple pattern occur? __________
triple first	**35.** Example 2-2 has excerpts from two compositions. Again, as you listen tap and count the beats to determine the meter of each. Both excerpts are in __________ meter. Which excerpt employs the faster tempo __________ (first/second)? (The first passage is the beginning of Mozart's Symphony No. 41, third movement. The second passage is the opening of Brahms' Symphony No. 1, second movement.)
sixteen	**36.** Listen again to the first excerpt in the previous example, counting each triple pattern. How many times does the triple pattern occur? __________
quintuple (If your answer was incorrect, listen to the passage again. Remember that beats are of *equal* duration.)	**37.** Listen to Example 2-3, from Dave Brubeck's "Take Five." Count the beats carefully. The meter in this passage is __________ (quadruple/quintuple).

DURATIONAL SYMBOLS FOR SOUNDS AND SILENCE

whole

38. This form of note (𝅝) is called a __________ note.

The relative duration of a note is indicated variously by filling in the note or leaving it open (• or 𝅝), by attaching stems (♩), flags (♪), and beams (♫), and by appending dots (♩.). These will be explained in the following frames.

(𝅝 = 𝅗𝅥 𝅗𝅥)
𝅝 = 𝅗𝅥 𝅗𝅥
𝅝 = 𝅗𝅥 𝅗𝅥

39. One form of note is the *half note* (𝅗𝅥), which resembles a whole note with a *stem* attached.

The half note (𝅗𝅥) lasts half as long in time as the whole note. Thus the duration of two half notes equals the duration of one whole note.

Draw two half notes for each whole note below, following the given example.

𝅝 = 𝅗𝅥 𝅗𝅥
𝅝 =
𝅝 =

---

1. (𝅗𝅥) 𝅗𝅥 = 𝅝
2. 𝅗𝅥 (𝅗𝅥) = 𝅝
3. 𝅗𝅥 𝅗𝅥 = 𝅝

40. Add the correct number of half notes to equal each whole note below.

1. 𝅗𝅥 _____ = 𝅝
2. _____ 𝅗𝅥 = 𝅝
3. _____ _____ = 𝅝

---

one

(𝅝) = ♩ ♩ ♩ ♩

41. Two half notes (𝅗𝅥 𝅗𝅥) are equal in duration to __________ (how many?) whole note(s) (𝅝).

The *quarter note* (♩) resembles a *filled-in* half note. Four of them (♩ ♩ ♩ ♩) are equal in duration to one whole note (𝅝).

Draw four quarter notes following the given whole note.

𝅝 =

42. Since a whole note (𝅝) lasts as long as two half notes (𝅗𝅥 𝅗𝅥) or four quarter notes (♩ ♩ ♩ ♩), simple mathematical calculation will reveal the following relationships.

Four quarter notes (♩ ♩ ♩ ♩) equal the duration of one whole note (𝅝). How many half notes (𝅗𝅥) equal one whole note (𝅝)? _____

Four quarter notes (♩ ♩ ♩ ♩) equal the duration of _____ (how many?) half notes (𝅗𝅥).

One half note (𝅗𝅥) is equal in duration to _____ (how many?) quarter notes (♩).

two

two

two

43. The *eighth note* (♪) resembles a quarter note with a *flag* added to the right side of the stem.

Eight eighth notes (♪ ♪ ♪ ♪ ♪ ♪ ♪ ♪) equal one whole note (𝅝).

How many eighth notes (♪) equal one whole note (𝅝)? _____

How many eighth notes equal one half note (𝅗𝅥)? _____

Draw two quarter notes and four eighth notes.

eight

four

♩ ♩ ♪ ♪ ♪ ♪

44. Shown below are the relative values of the note forms we have studied thus far. Write in the space provided the name of each form of note.

1. 𝅝 whole
2. 𝅗𝅥 𝅗𝅥 _____
3. ♩ ♩ ♩ ♩ _____
4. ♪♪♪♪♪♪♪♪ _____

1. (whole)
2. half
3. quarter
4. eighth

45. A stemmed note with two flags is a *sixteenth note* (𝅘𝅥𝅯), sixteen of which equal one whole note (𝅝).

A third flag produces a *thirty-second note* (𝅘𝅥𝅰), thirty-two of which equal the duration of one whole note (𝅝). Some notes have four, five, or six flags, and their durational values lessen correspondingly.

One whole note equals ________________ (how many?) sixteenth notes.

One half note equals __________ (how many?) sixteenth notes.

sixteen

eight

---

46. Draw these notes.

1. quarter ____
2. half ____
3. sixteenth ____
4. whole ____
5. eighth ____

1. ♩
2. 𝅗𝅥
3. 𝅘𝅥𝅯
4. 𝅝
5. ♪

---

47. Rhythm is the motion of music through __________.

How many 𝅘𝅥𝅯's equal one 𝅝? __________

How many 𝅘𝅥𝅰's equal one 𝅝? __________

time

sixteen

thirty-two

---

48. A *fourth* flag produces a *sixty-fourth note* (𝅘𝅥𝅱), sixty-four of which equal the duration of one whole note (𝅝).

One 𝅝 equals how many 𝅘𝅥𝅱's? ________________

One 𝅗𝅥 equals how many 𝅘𝅥𝅱's? ________________

__________ are the regular pulsations that occur as music moves through time.

sixty-four

thirty-two

Beats

1. half 2. sixteenth 3. sixty-fourth 4. thirty-second two	**49.** Name each form of note below. 1. 𝅗𝅥 ________ 2. 𝅘𝅥𝅯 ________ 3. 𝅘𝅥𝅱 ________ 4. 𝅘𝅥𝅰 ________ Duple meter contains how many beats? ____
two four eight beats	**50.** One ♩ equals how many ♪'s? ________ One ♩ equals how many 𝅘𝅥𝅯's? ________ One ♩ equals how many 𝅘𝅥𝅰's? ________ Meter is the organization of ________ into patterns of stress.
sixteen thirty-two ♩ triple	**51.** One ♩ equals how many 𝅘𝅥𝅱's? ________ One 𝅗𝅥 equals how many 𝅘𝅥𝅰's? ________ One ____ equals four 𝅘𝅥𝅯's. A meter containing three beats is called ________ meter.
two 𝅜 𝅜 𝅜 𝅜 𝅜	**52.** The only note form of longer relative durational value than the whole note (𝅝) is the *double whole note* (𝅜),* which lasts twice as long as one whole note. Thus, one 𝅜 equals how many 𝅝's? ________ Draw five double whole notes below. * Variants in the shape of this note are ‖𝅜‖ and ▭. These variants are not used in this book.
double whole one two four	**53.** This form of note (𝅜) is called a ________ ________ note. Two 𝅝's equal how many 𝅜's? ________ Four 𝅝's equal how many 𝅜's? ________ One 𝅜 equals how many 𝅗𝅥's? ________

Quadruple

first

128

(𝅝 = 64 𝅘𝅥𝅱's; 𝅜 = 64 x 2 = 128 𝅘𝅥𝅱's)

54. ______________ meter contains four beats.

Which is the strongest beat? ________

The double whole note (𝅜) and the sixty-fourth note (𝅘𝅥𝅱) represent the extremes of relative duration studied thus far.

One 𝅜 equals how many 𝅘𝅥𝅱's? ____

---

55. A curved line connecting two or more note heads* of the same pitch, called a *tie*, has the effect of extending the duration of the pitch through the last tied note. (When the stems are attached below the note heads, the tie is placed above them, and vice versa.) For example:

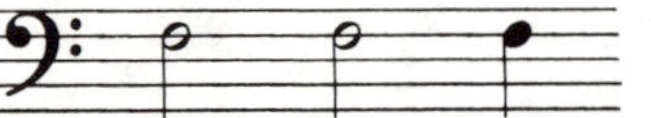

Connect these notes with ties.

* The term "note head" is sometimes used in reference to the oval portion of the note to which stems are attached.

---

tie

1. 𝅗𝅥 2. 𝅘𝅥

56. The symbol indicated by the arrow is called a ____.

Draw the single note that equals the duration of the tied notes below.

1. 𝅘𝅥 𝅘𝅥 = 2. 𝅘𝅥𝅮 𝅘𝅥𝅮 =

---

1. 𝅘𝅥𝅮 2. 𝅝

57. A curved line resembling the tie sometimes fulfills other notational functions, including phrasing, slurs, articulations, and bowings for stringed instruments. These additional functions, however, will not be dealt with here.

Draw the single note that equals the duration of the tied notes below.

1. 𝅘𝅥𝅯 𝅘𝅥𝅯 = 2. 𝅘𝅥 𝅘𝅥 𝅘𝅥 𝅘𝅥 =

58. A *dot* placed after a note (𝅗𝅥.) adds half of the note's value to its duration.

𝅗𝅥. = ♩‿♩‿♩ or 𝅗𝅥‿♩

♩. = ♪‿♪‿♪ or ♩‿♪

♪. = 𝅘𝅥𝅯‿𝅘𝅥𝅯‿𝅘𝅥𝅯 or ♪‿𝅘𝅥𝅯

𝅝. = 𝅗𝅥‿𝅗𝅥‿𝅗𝅥 or 𝅝‿𝅗𝅥

Place a dot after each of the following notes: 𝅝 ♩ 𝅗𝅥

𝅝. ♩. 𝅗𝅥.

59. Draw the single dotted note which is equivalent to each of the following examples. (Refer to the preceding frame if necessary.)

1. ♩‿♩‿♩ = _____
2. ♩‿♪ = _____
3. 𝅗𝅥‿♩ = _____

1. 𝅗𝅥.
2. ♩.
3. 𝅗𝅥.

60. On the lower staff, draw the single dotted note that is the equivalent of each of the tied-note groups.

61. Stemmed notes lying *below* the third (middle) line of the staff usually have stems drawn *upward* from the right side of the note.

Add stems to the last four notes below. In general, stems should be approximately one octave in length.

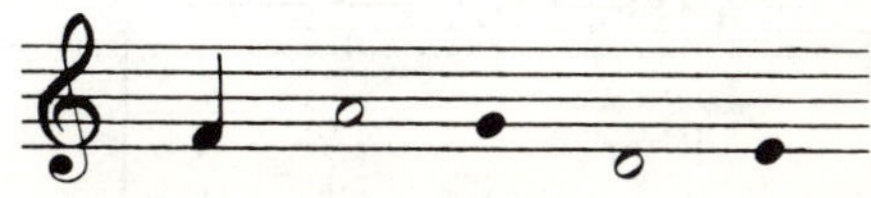

octave

62. Notes lying *above* the third line usually have stems drawn *downward* from the left side of the note.

Add stems to the last four notes below.

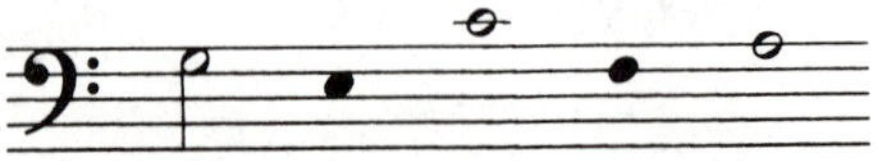

Stems are ordinarily one ______ in length.

either

63. Stems of notes lying *on* the middle line may point in *either direction.* Upward stems are always drawn from the right side of the note and downward stems from the left.

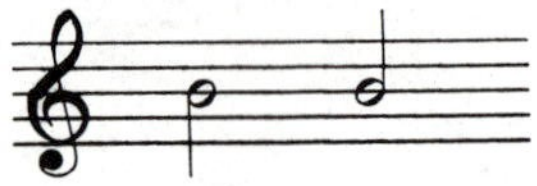

Add stems to the notes below. Refer to frames 61–63 as necessary.

1 4

64. Under certain conditions stem directions are variable, but the rules given in frames 61–63 follow general practice and should be used consistently for now.

Which stem directions are correct? ____ ____

1. 2. 3. 4. 5.

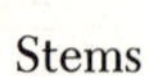

65. ______ are drawn about one octave in length.

Add stems to the notes below. In addition, identify each pitch below the staff.

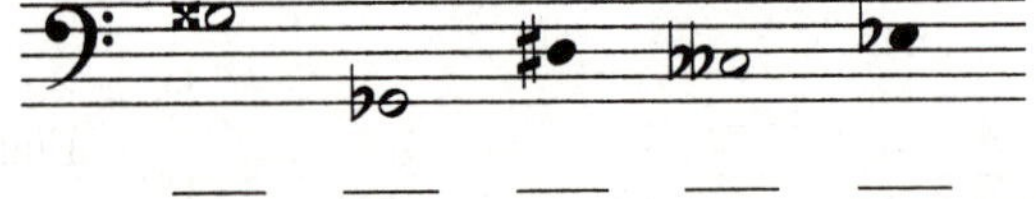

____ ____ ____ ____ ____

66. Flags and dots are always drawn to the *right.* Notice that flags on upward stems point down while those on downward stems point up. Also observe that dots following notes on a line are placed in the next space above.

Add a stem, one flag, and a dot to each of these notes.

either

67. Correct the following examples. There are two errors in each.

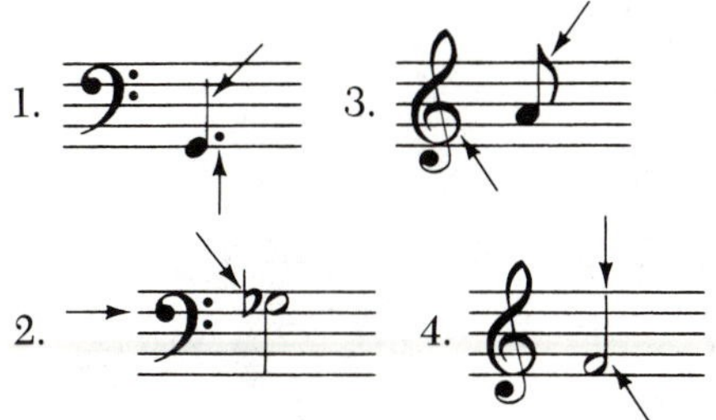

right

68. Correct these examples. Again, each contains two errors.

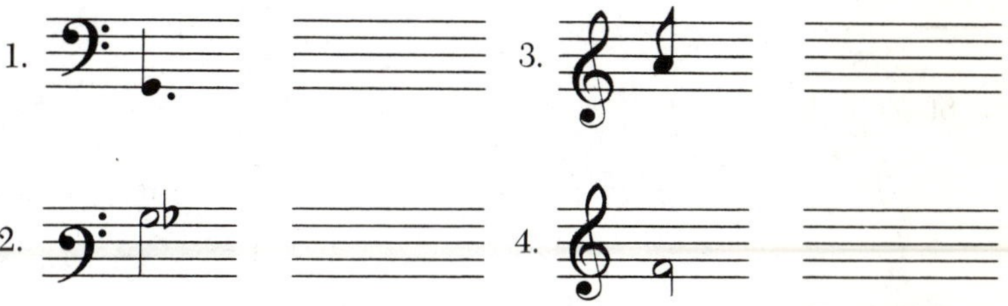

Flags and dots are always drawn to the __________ (right/left).

69. Lines called *beams* often replace flags in a series of flagged notes.

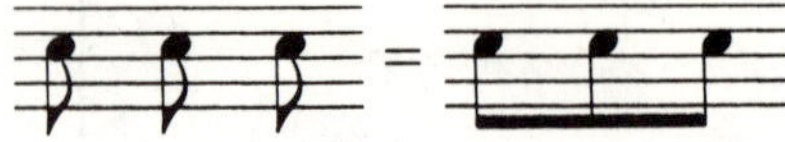

The number of beams used is the same as the number of flags replaced. Notice that the beams are straight lines.

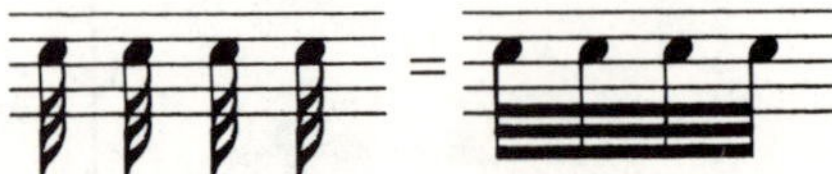

Connect these notes with the correct number of beams.

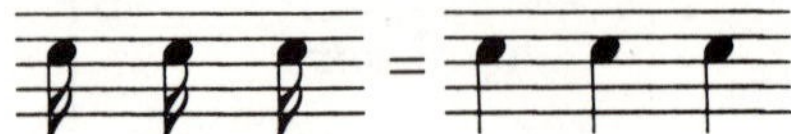

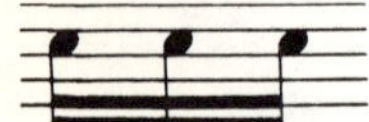

70. Beams may also connect flagged notes of different durations.

Rewrite the following with flags instead of beams.

71. Beams connect notes of different pitches as well as notes of the same pitch. Notice that the beams slant in the overall pitch direction of the note group.

Notate these examples with flags instead of beams.

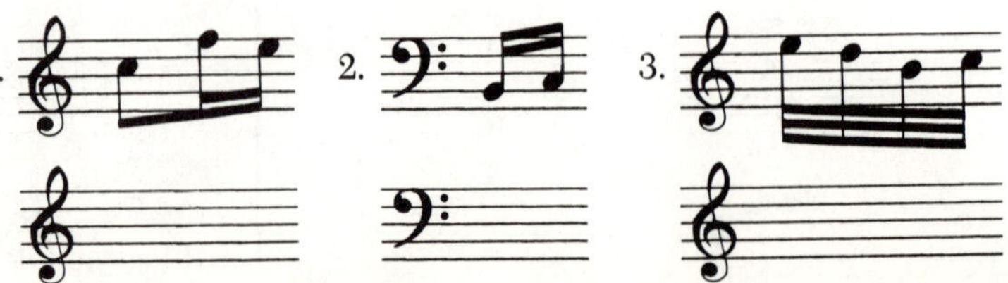

1. 2.

72. The usual stem directions may be altered when beams connect notes *both* above and below the third staff line. If most of the notes in the beamed group lie *above* the third line, the stems point downward; if *below* the third line, the stems point upward.

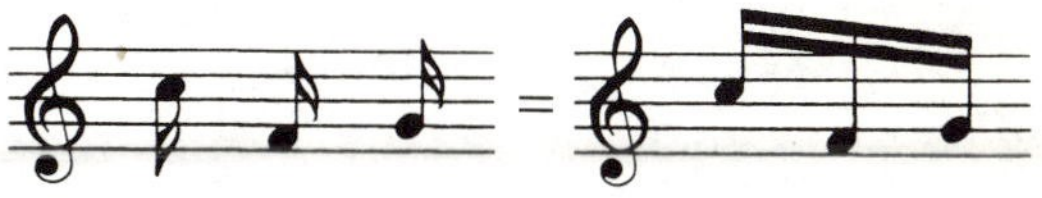

=

Rewrite these note groups with beams instead of flags according to the directions given above.

1. 2.

---

1. 3. 2.

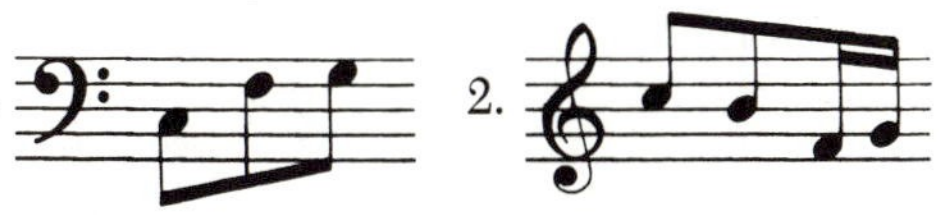

73. Rewrite these note groups with flags instead of beams, altering the stem directions when necessary.

1. 2. 3.

---

rests

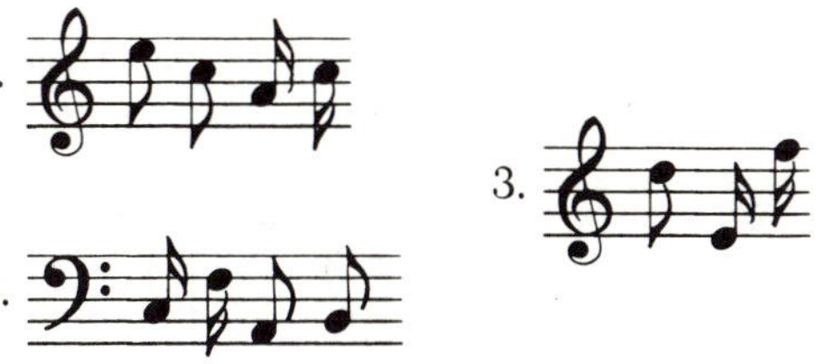

74. Silences in music usually have definite durational value, just as tones do. They are represented in musical notation by symbols called *rests.*

Symbols called ____________ represent silences in musical notation.

---

75. Each durational note value has its equivalent rest, three of which are shown below.

	NOTE	REST
whole		
half		
quarter		

Note that the whole rest hangs from the fourth line, while the half rest lies on the third line. The position of rests on the staff remains the same, regardless of the clef used.

Draw the equivalent rest to the right of each of these notes.

76. Eighth, sixteenth, thirty-second, and sixty-fourth rests are shown below. Note that the hooks on the rests agree in number with the flags on the corresponding notes.

	NOTE	REST
eighth		
sixteenth		
thirty-second		
sixty-fourth		

Draw the equivalent rest to the right of each of these notes.

77. Draw the equivalent rest to the right of each of these notes. (Refer to preceding frames if necessary.)

78. The double whole rest occupies the entire third space of the staff.*

NOTE REST

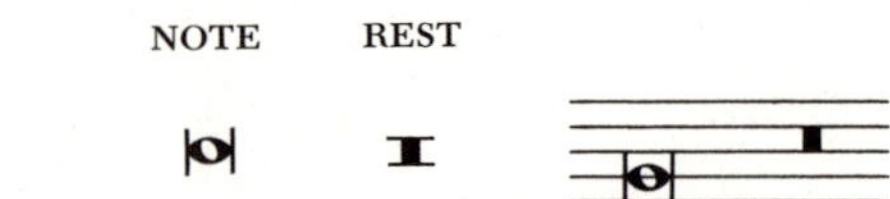

Draw the equivalent rest to the right of each note below.

* The 8va sign is not used with rests, since rests do not represent pitch.

* Variants in the shape of this rest are , , , and others.

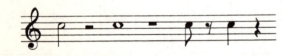

1. (whole) (𝅝)
2. quarter 𝅘𝅥
3. eighth 𝅘𝅥𝅮
4. half 𝅗𝅥
5. thirty-second 𝅘𝅥𝅰

79. Name these rests and draw the equivalent note value of each.

1. whole 𝄻 𝅝
2. ________ 𝄽 ____
3. ________ 𝄾 ____
4. ________ 𝄼 ____
5. ________ 𝅀 ____

---

1. sixteenth 𝅘𝅥𝅯
2. double whole 𝅜
3. sixty-fourth 𝅘𝅥𝅱

80. Continue as in frame 79.

1. ________ 𝄿 ____
2. ________ 𝄺 ____
3. ________ 𝅁 ____

---

1. (𝄾 𝄾 𝄾) (𝄽 𝄾)
2. 𝄽 𝄽 𝄽 𝄼 𝄽
3. 𝄼 𝄼 𝄼 𝄻 𝄼
4. 𝄿 𝄿 𝄿 𝄾 𝄿

81. A dot after a rest has the same effect as a dot after a note, adding half of the rest's value to its duration.

Complete these examples. Never use ties to connect rests.

1. 𝄽. = 𝄾 𝄾 𝄾 or 𝄽 𝄾
2. 𝄼. = ________ or ________
3. 𝄻. = ________ or ________
4. 𝄾. = ________ or ________

---

1. 𝄼. 3. 𝅘𝅥.
2. 𝄼. 4. 𝅝.

82. Provide the appropriate dotted note or rest in the following.

1. 𝅗𝅥. = ____ (rest)
3. 𝄽. = ____ (note)
2. 𝄼 𝄽 = ____ (rest)
4. 𝄻 𝄼 = ____ (note)

---

1. 𝄽. 3. 𝅝.
2. 𝄻. 4. 𝅘𝅥𝅮.

83. Continue as in frame 82.

1. 𝅘𝅥. = ____ (rest)
3. 𝄻. = ____ (note)
2. 𝅜. = ____ (rest)
4. 𝄾 𝄿 = ____ (note)

1. 𝄼. 4. 𝄽. 2. 𝅝. 5. ♩. 3. 𝄼. 6. ♪.	**84.** Draw the dotted note or rest equivalent to each given value. NOTE REST NOTE REST 1. 𝅗𝅥 ♩ (tied) = ____ 4. ♪ ♪ ♪ (tied) = ____ 2. ____ = 𝄼. 5. ____ = 𝄽. 3. 𝅗𝅥. = ____ 6. ____ = 𝄾 𝄿
1. 𝅗𝅥. 4. 𝄻. 2. 𝄽. 5. ♪. 3. ♩. 6. 𝄻.	**85.** Continue as in frame 84. NOTE REST NOTE REST 1. ____ = 𝄽 𝄽 𝄽 4. 𝅝 𝅗𝅥 (tied) = ____ 2. ♩ ♪ (tied) = ____ 5. ____ = 𝄿 𝄿 𝄿 3. ____ = 𝄽 𝄾 6. 𝅝 𝅝 𝅝 (tied) = ____
Rhythm tempo four	**86.** ________ is the motion of music through time. The rate of speed at which beats occur is called ________. One 𝅝 equals how many ♩'s? ________

LISTENING FRAMES

2

87. Listen again to Example 2-1, the opening of Beethoven's "Archduke" Trio, counting and tapping the beats as you listen. (Remember that it is in quadruple meter.) Which of the following most closely resembles the durations of the first *five* tones? ____

1. 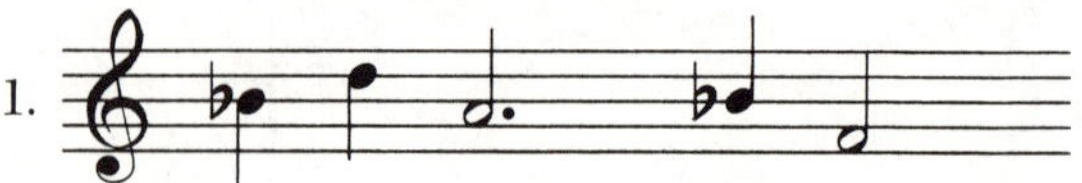

2. 

3. 

88. Continuing with Example 2-1, listen to the background rhythm that accompanies this melody. The melody is here notated in correct pitches and rhythmic values. Again, count and tap the beats as you listen.

3

Which line below the melody is the correct background rhythm? _____

1.

2.

3.

2

89. Now listen again to the first portion of Example 2-2, the beginning of Mozart's Symphony No. 41, third movement. Tap and count the beats as you listen. Which of the following best describes the durations of the first *eight* tones? _____

1. The durations are all the same.
2. The first tone is the longest; the next four are shorter, and the last three are even shorter.
3. The first three tones are the shortest, and the last five are longer.

1

90. The notation below that corresponds to the durations of the first *ten* tones in Example 2-2 is _____.

1.

2.

3.

FURTHER PRINCIPLES OF RHYTHMIC NOTATION

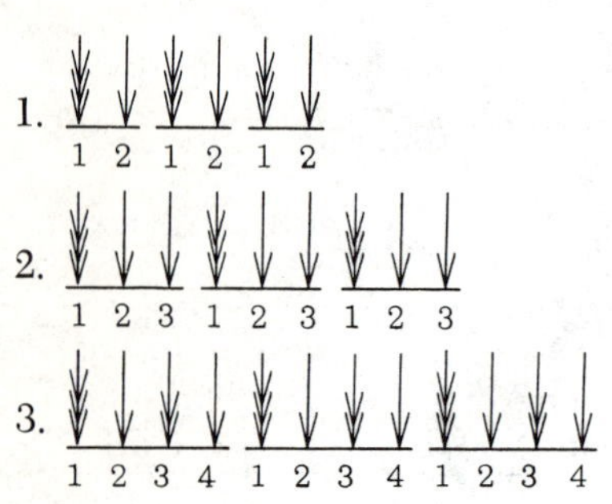

91. Complete the arrows and the numbering of beats in these meter diagrams.

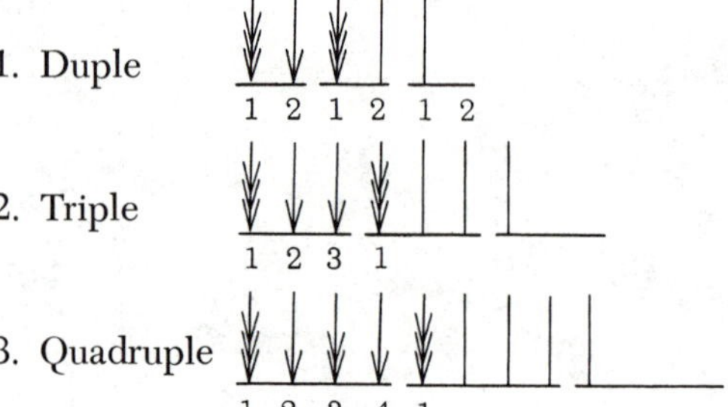

Tap or clap each meter above, emphasizing the strong beats. (Remember to make all beats the same duration.)

---

beat unit

92. In musical notation, the beat is represented by a note of definite durational value. In the example of duple meter below, each beat is represented by a quarter note.

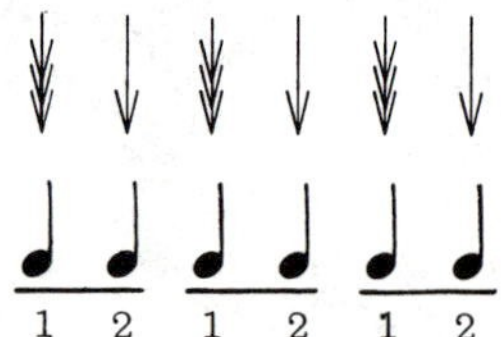

The note which represents the beat is called the *beat unit.*

In the above example, the quarter note is the ________ ________.

---

beat

1. quarter 2. half 3. eighth

triple

93. The note representing the __________ is called the beat unit.

Name the beat unit in each of the following examples.

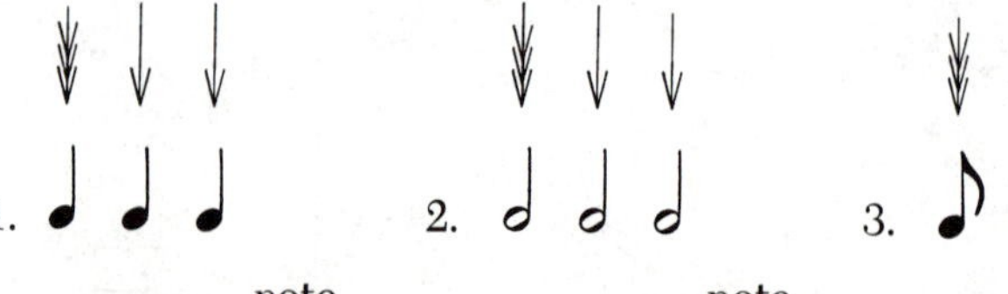

________ note ________ note ________ note

Each pattern above is an example of __________ meter.

longer	**94.** The *exact* duration of the beat is determined by the tempo and the musical context. In a fast tempo, a ♩ beat unit is *shorter* in duration than in a slow tempo. A 𝅗𝅥 beat unit lasts ________ (shorter/longer) in a slow tempo than in a fast tempo.
1. triple 2. duple 3. quadruple ♪ ♪ ♪ 𝅗𝅥 𝅗𝅥 ♩ ♩ ♩ ♩	**95.** Once established, the beat unit remains the same throughout a given meter. In the examples below, identify each meter. Then provide one note for each beat according to the indicated beat unit. (♪) ↓ ↓ ↓ (𝅗𝅥) ↓ ↓ (♩) ↓ ↓ ↓ ↓ 1. ________ 2. ________ 3. ________ (notes) ________ ________ ________
1. 𝅗𝅥 triple 2. ♪ quintuple 3. 𝅝 quadruple	**96.** Draw the beat unit and identify the meter corresponding to each example below. BEAT UNIT METER 1. 𝅗𝅥 𝅗𝅥 𝅗𝅥 ____ ________ 2. ♪ ♪ ♪ ♪ ♪ ____ ________ 3. 𝅝 𝅝 𝅝 𝅝 ____ ________
1. ♪♪ 2. ♪.♪. 3. ♩.♩. duple	**97.** The beat unit is a note that may be of any durational value. Notate the beats in each example below according to the indicated beat unit. (♪) ↓ ↓ (♪.) ↓ ↓ (♩.) ↓ ↓ 1. ________ 2. ________ 3. ________ Each of these patterns is an example of ________ meter.

note	**98.** The beat unit is the ________ that represents the beat.
1. ♪♪ 3. 𝅗𝅥𝅗𝅥 2. 𝅘𝅥𝅯𝅘𝅥𝅯 4. 𝅘𝅥𝅰𝅘𝅥𝅰	**99.** The beat in music is often divided into notes of shorter duration, although the beat unit continues to represent the overall pulsation pattern in the meter. Beats may be divided into two or more notes equaling the duration of the beat unit. Divide each note below into two *equal* notes of shorter duration, following the given example. 𝅗𝅥 = ♩ ♩ 1. ♩ = ____ ____ 3. 𝅝 = ____ ____ 2. ♪ = ____ ____ 4. 𝅘𝅥𝅯 = ____ ____
𝅝 = 𝅗𝅥𝅗𝅥 = ♩♩♩♩	**100.** A note that divides into two equal parts (𝅗𝅥 = ♩♩) can be divided further (or sub-divided) into four parts: 𝅗𝅥 = ♩♩ = ♪♪♪♪, into eight parts: 𝅗𝅥 = ♩♩ = ♪♪♪♪ = 𝅘𝅥𝅯𝅘𝅥𝅯𝅘𝅥𝅯𝅘𝅥𝅯𝅘𝅥𝅯𝅘𝅥𝅯𝅘𝅥𝅯𝅘𝅥𝅯, sixteen parts, thirty-two, sixty-four, etc. Divide and sub-divide the whole note below. 𝅝 = ____ ____ = ____ ____ ____ ____ (division) (sub-division)
𝅗𝅥 = ♩♩ = ♪♪♪♪	**101.** Divide and sub-divide the half note below. Refer to the previous frame if necessary. 𝅗𝅥 = ____ ____ = ____ ____ ____ ____ (division) (sub-division)
♩ = ♪♪ = 𝅘𝅥𝅯𝅘𝅥𝅯𝅘𝅥𝅯𝅘𝅥𝅯	**102.** Continue as in frame 101. ♩ = ____ ____ = ____ ____ ____ ____ (division) (sub-division)
unit two three	**103.** The beat ________ is a note that may be of any durational value. One 𝅗𝅥 equals how many ♩'s? ____ One 𝅗𝅥. equals how many ♩'s? ____

104. A *dotted* note as a beat unit divides equally into three parts (𝅗𝅥. = ♩ ♩ ♩) and sub-divides into six parts:

𝅗𝅥. = ♩ ♩ ♩ = ♪ ♪ ♪ ♪ ♪ ♪,

twelve parts, twenty-four, forty-eight, etc.*

Divide and sub-divide the dotted quarter note below.

♩. = ____ ____ ____ (division) = ____ ____ ____ ____ ____ ____ (sub-division)

* It is possible to divide dotted-note beat units into two equal parts and nondotted-note beat units into three equal parts, but this involves notation unrelated to the present discussion.

♩. = ♪ ♪ ♪ = 𝅘𝅥𝅯 𝅘𝅥𝅯 𝅘𝅥𝅯 𝅘𝅥𝅯 𝅘𝅥𝅯 𝅘𝅥𝅯

---

105. Divide and sub-divide these dotted notes.

𝅗𝅥. = ____ ____ ____ (division) = ____ ____ ____ ____ ____ ____ (sub-division)

♪. = ____ ____ ____ (division) = ____ ____ ____ ____ ____ ____ (sub-division)

𝅗𝅥. = ♩ ♩ ♩ = ♪ ♪ ♪ ♪ ♪ ♪

♪. = 𝅘𝅥𝅯 𝅘𝅥𝅯 𝅘𝅥𝅯 = 𝅘𝅥𝅰 𝅘𝅥𝅰 𝅘𝅥𝅰 𝅘𝅥𝅰 𝅘𝅥𝅰 𝅘𝅥𝅰

---

106. All beat units are either *dotted* notes (which divide equally into threes) or *nondotted* notes (which divide equally into ________).

Divide each note below into either two or three parts of equal duration.

1. ♩ = ____ ____
2. ♩. = ____ ____ ____
3. 𝅗𝅥. = ____ ____ ____
4. 𝅗𝅥 = ____ ____

twos

1. ♪ ♪
2. ♪ ♪ ♪
3. ♩ ♩ ♩
4. ♩ ♩

---

107. Divide each note into either two or three parts of equal duration. Refer to previous frames if necessary.

1. ♪ =
2. ♪. =
3. 𝅝 =
4. 𝅗𝅥. =

1. 𝅘𝅥𝅯 𝅘𝅥𝅯
2. 𝅘𝅥𝅯 𝅘𝅥𝅯 𝅘𝅥𝅯
3. 𝅗𝅥 𝅗𝅥
4. ♩ ♩ ♩

---

108. All beat units divide into either twos or threes. Therefore, there are two *beat types:*

1. *Simple* beats (which divide equally into twos)
2. *Compound* beats (which divide equally into threes)

The two beat types are ________ and ________.

simple compound
(either order)

Answers	Frames
twos threes simple	**109.** The simple beat divides equally into ________. The compound beat divides equally into ________. Dotted beat units are compound beat types. ♩. = ♪♪♪ (beat unit) (division) Nondotted beat units are ________ beat types. ♩ = ♪♪ (beat unit) (division)
1 4 Simple	**110.** Which of these beat units are *simple* beat types? ____ ____ 1. ♩ 2. ♩. 3. 𝅗𝅥. 4. ♪ 5. ♪. ________ beat types are represented by nondotted beat units.
1 4 5 units	**111.** Which of these beat units are *compound* beat types? ____ ____ ____ 1. 𝅗𝅥. 2. 𝅘𝅥𝅯 3. 𝅜 4. ♪. 5. 𝅘𝅥𝅯. Compound beat types are represented by dotted beat ________.
1. simple 3. simple 2. compound 4. compound	**112.** Name the beat type in each meter below. (Beat units are shown by arrows.) 1. ♩ ♩ ________ 3. ♪ ♪ ♪ ________ 2. ♩. ♩. ________ 4. ♩. ♩. ♩. ________

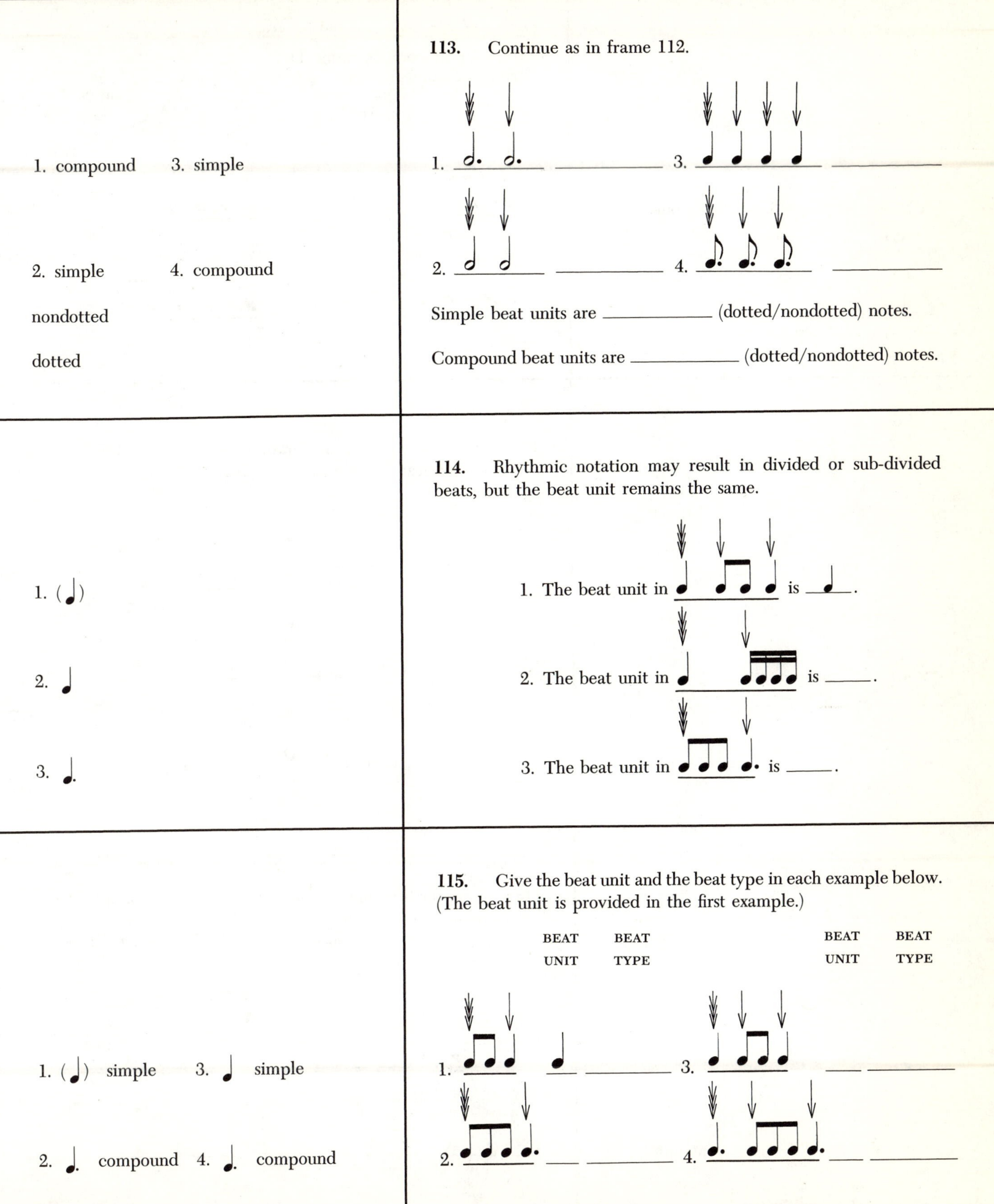

1. compound 3. simple

2. simple 4. compound

nondotted

dotted

113. Continue as in frame 112.

1. ______ ______ 3. ______ ______

2. ______ ______ 4. ______ ______

Simple beat units are ______ (dotted/nondotted) notes.

Compound beat units are ______ (dotted/nondotted) notes.

1. ( )

2.

3.

114. Rhythmic notation may result in divided or sub-divided beats, but the beat unit remains the same.

1. The beat unit in ______ is ______.

2. The beat unit in ______ is ______.

3. The beat unit in ______ is ______.

1. ( ) simple 3. simple

2. compound 4. compound

115. Give the beat unit and the beat type in each example below. (The beat unit is provided in the first example.)

	BEAT UNIT	BEAT TYPE		BEAT UNIT	BEAT TYPE
1.		______	3.	______	______
2.	______	______	4.	______	______

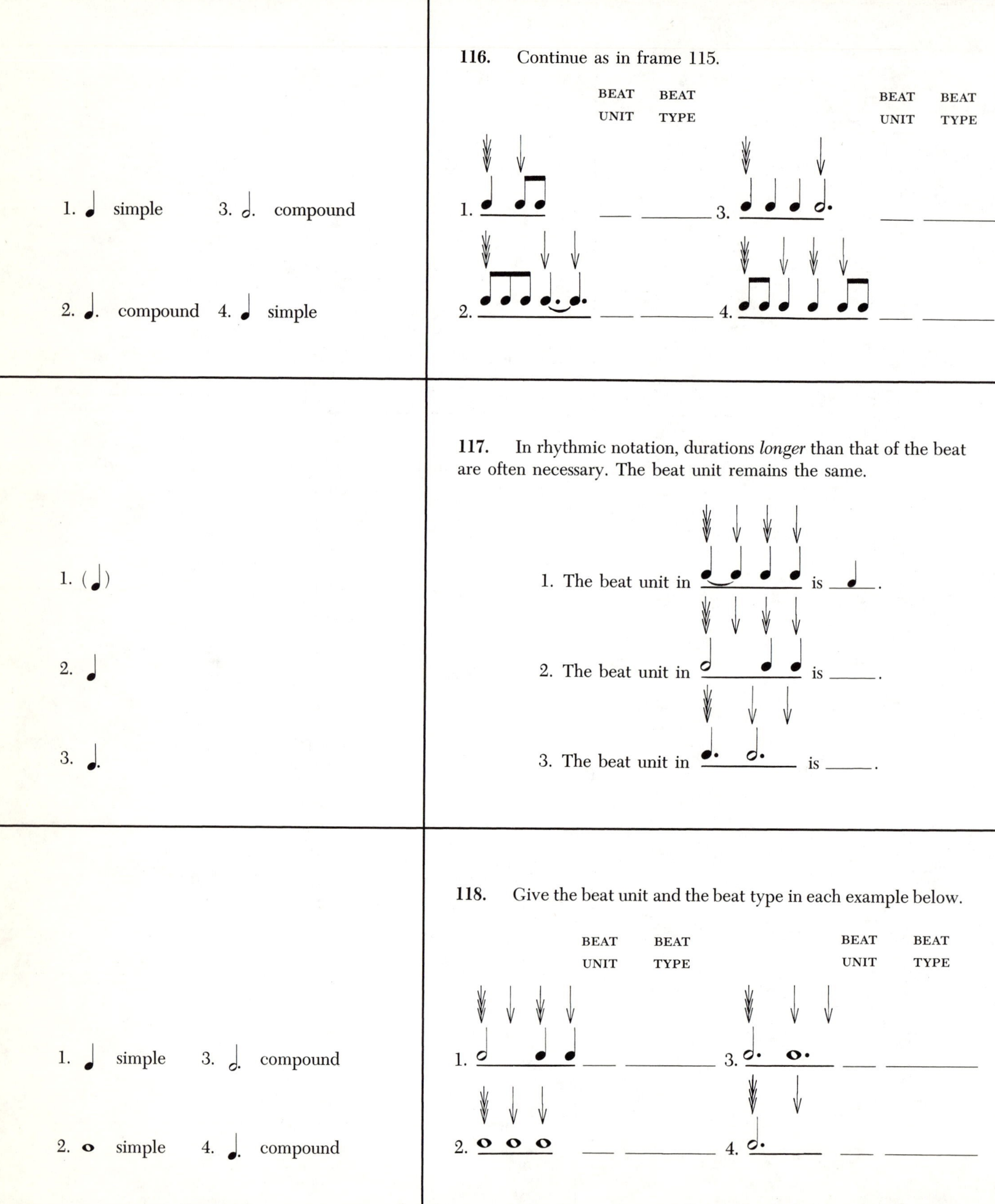

1. ♩ simple 3. 𝅗𝅥. compound

2. ♩. compound 4. ♩ simple

116. Continue as in frame 115.

	BEAT UNIT	BEAT TYPE		BEAT UNIT	BEAT TYPE
1.	___	______	3.	___	______
2.	___	______	4.	___	______

1. (♩)

2. ♩

3. ♩.

117. In rhythmic notation, durations *longer* than that of the beat are often necessary. The beat unit remains the same.

1. The beat unit in ______ is ♩.

2. The beat unit in ______ is ____.

3. The beat unit in ______ is ____.

1. ♩ simple 3. 𝅗𝅥. compound

2. 𝅝 simple 4. ♩. compound

118. Give the beat unit and the beat type in each example below.

	BEAT UNIT	BEAT TYPE		BEAT UNIT	BEAT TYPE
1.	___	______	3.	___	______
2.	___	______	4.	___	______

1. ♪ simple 3. 𝅗𝅥. compound

2. ♩ simple 4. ♩. compound

triple

119. Continue as in frame 118.

		BEAT UNIT	BEAT TYPE			BEAT UNIT	BEAT TYPE
1. 	♪‿♬♪	___	___	3. 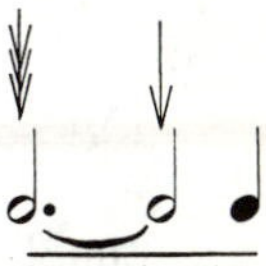	𝅗𝅥.‿𝅗𝅥 ♩	___	___
2. 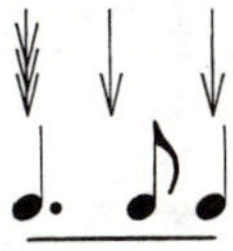	♩. ♪♩	___	___	4. 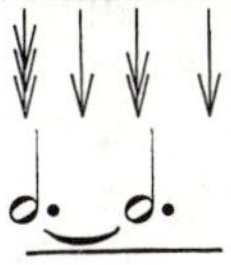	𝅗𝅥.‿𝅗𝅥.	___	___

No. 1 above is an example of ________ meter.

Beats

simple compound
(either order)

120. ________ are the regular pulsations that occur as music moves through time.

Two beat types are ________ and ________.

---

duple triple
quadruple quintuple
(any order)

121. Four meters are ________, ________, ________, and ________.

---

triple

unit

type

122. A meter containing three beats is called ________ meter.

The beat ________ is the note that represents each beat.

"Compound" is one beat ________.

---

1. meter
2. unit
3. beat

123. Three factors in the notation of rhythm and meter are:

1. ________
2. beat ________
3. ________ type

124. Supply the missing information as indicated below.

	METER	BEAT UNIT	BEAT TYPE
1.	______	♩	______
2.	______	___	compound
3.	triple	___	______

Answers: 1. duple (♩) simple; 2. triple ♩. (compound); 3. (triple) ♪ simple

125. Continue as in frame 124.

	METER	BEAT UNIT	BEAT TYPE
1.	duple	___	______
2.	______	___	simple
3.	______	♩	______

Answers: 1. (duple) 𝅗𝅥. compound; 2. quadruple 𝅗𝅥 (simple); 3. triple (♩) simple

126. In the examples below, the beat unit is provided. Name the meter and the beat type for each.

	BEAT UNIT	METER	BEAT TYPE
1.	♩.	______	______
2.	♩.	______	______
3.	♩	______	______

Answers: 1. duple compound; 2. triple compound; 3. quadruple simple

three

127. The beat groups that form the meter are organized on the staff in *measures.* Each measure is contained within two vertical lines on the staff, called *bar lines.*

The staff below has two measures and ________ bar lines.

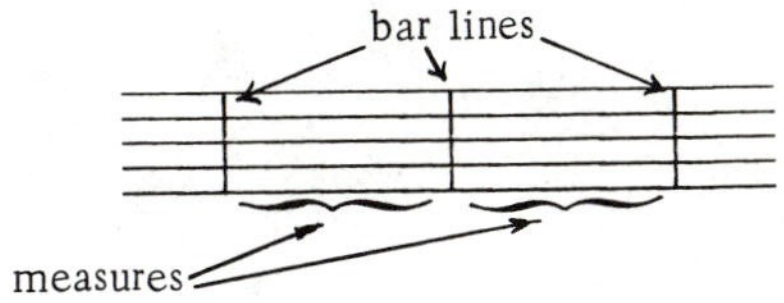

bar lines

measures

four

triple

128. How many measures are on this staff? ________

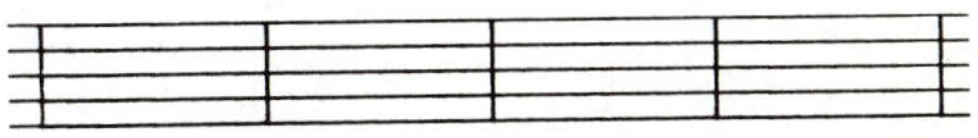

Name the meter shown in the measure below. ________

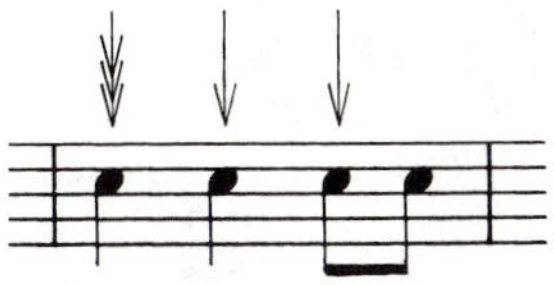

1. (triple) (♩) 3. quadruple 𝅗𝅥

2. duple ♩ 4. duple ♩

129. Name the meter and draw the beat unit in each of the measures below.

	METER	BEAT UNIT		METER	BEAT UNIT
1. 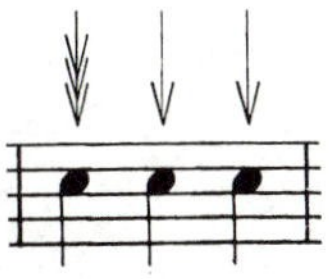	triple	♩	3. 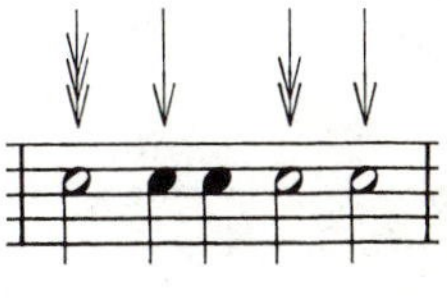	________	____
2. 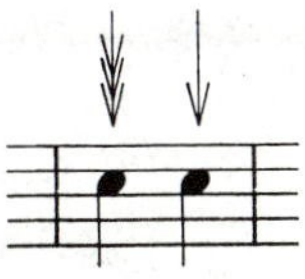	________	____	4. 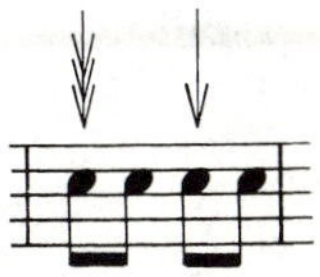	________	____

1. duple 𝅗𝅥 simple
2. duple ♩. compound
3. triple ♩ simple
4. triple ♪. compound

130. Give the meter, beat unit, and beat type in each of these measures.

	METER	BEAT UNIT	BEAT TYPE
1. 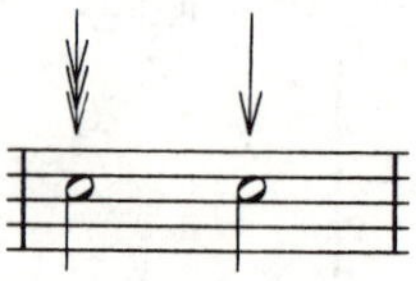	________	____	________
2. 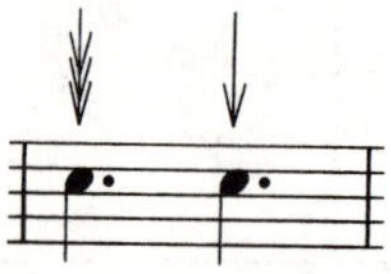	________	____	________
3. 	________	____	________
4. 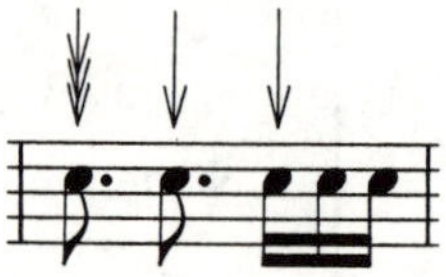	________	____	________

---

triple

triple

131. Music containing two beats in each measure is said to be in *duple meter.*

Music containing three beats in each measure is in ____________ meter.

The passage below is in ____________ meter.

---

simple compound
(either order)
simple

compound

132. The two beat types are ____________ and ____________.

The ____________ beat divides equally into twos.

The ____________ beat divides equally into threes.

duple

♩

simple

133.

The above rhythmic passage is in ____________ meter.

The beat unit is ____.

The beat type is ____________.

meter beat unit

beat type
(any order)

134. Thus there are three basic elements in the notation of rhythm and meter: ____________, ____________, and ____________.

triple

unit

beat type

135.

The above passage is in ____________ meter.

♩. is the beat ____________.

The ____________ ____________ is compound.

meter

beat unit

beat type(s)

136. The grouping of beats according to stress patterns is called ____________.

The note representing the beat is the ____________ ____________.

Simple and *compound* are two ____________ ____________s.

duple compound

triple simple

137. For convenience, we may refer to any meter using a simple beat type as a *simple meter,* while any meter using a compound beat type is called a *compound meter.*

Thus, duple meter using a simple beat type is called *duple simple meter,* while duple meter using a compound beat type is called *duple compound meter.*

Answer the following from the above information.

	METER	BEAT TYPE
1. Duple compound meter =	______	______
2. Triple simple meter =	______	______

---

triple

simple

triple simple

138.

The above rhythmic passage is in ______ meter.

The beat type is ______.

Therefore, the passage uses ______ ______ meter.

---

triple simple

♩.

139.

The above passage uses ______ ______ meter.

The beat unit is ______.

140.

1.

2.

No. 1 above is in ____________ ____________ meter. Its beat unit is _____.

No. 2 above is in ____________ ____________ meter. Its beat unit is _____.

quadruple simple

𝅗𝅥

duple compound

♪.

LISTENING FRAMES

141. In previous listening frames discussing Example 2-1, Beethoven's "Archduke" Trio, you identified the meter (quadruple) and the background rhythm. As you hear the excerpt again, count and tap the beats to determine whether the beat is divided into twos or threes, thus revealing the beat type.

The beat type is ____________.

Therefore, this example uses ____________ ____________ meter.

simple

quadruple simple

142. Listen to Example 2-4, the beginning of Mozart's Piano Concerto No. 27, last movement. The meter is *duple.* Count and tap the beats as you listen, to determine whether the beat is divided into twos or threes. (Listen to the entire passage before you answer.)

The beat type is ____________.

This excerpt therefore uses ____________ ____________ meter.

compound

duple compound

143. Example 2-5, a portion of John Philip Sousa's "El Capitan March," changes directly from one beat type to the other without pause. Count and tap the beats as you listen. The entire excerpt is in duple meter.

compound

1. The first part of the excerpt uses duple ________ meter.

simple

2. The second part of the excerpt uses duple ________ meter.

the same

3. The tempo of the two passages is ________ (the same/ different).

THE METER SIGNATURE

The three basic elements in the notation of rhythm and meter—meter, beat unit, and beat type—are all expressed in the two numbers that appear at the beginning of a piece of music and wherever changes in meter occur. This set of numbers is known as the *meter signature,* also called the *time signature.* With the meter signature, we no longer need the arrows and lines we have been using to indicate beats.

144. The three elements of rhythmic notation—meter, beat unit, and beat type—are expressed in the two numbers that appear at the beginning of a piece of music and wherever changes in meter occur.

$\frac{2}{4}$

These two numbers are known as the *meter signature.*

two

The meter signature consists of how many numbers? ________

145. The meter signature expresses three elements.

1. meter
2. beat unit
3. beat type
(any order)

1. ________
2. ________
3. ________

signature	**146.** Meter signatures for simple meters are constructed in a different way from those for compound meters. The construction of *simple* meter signatures will be considered first. The meter ________________ is found at the beginning of a piece of music.
1. $\frac{2}{4}$ 2. $\frac{3}{8}$	**147.** In simple meter signatures, the *top* number indicates the fundamental number of beats in the meter. → $\frac{2}{4}$ = two beats = duple meter Supply the top number of these meter signatures as indicated by the given meter. 1. duple $\frac{\ }{4}$ 2. triple $\frac{\ }{8}$
1. triple 2. duple 3. quadruple	**148.** Derive the meter from the meter signatures below. 1. $\frac{3}{4}$ ________________ 2. $\frac{2}{8}$ ________________ 3. $\frac{4}{2}$ ________________
1. $\frac{2}{4}$ 2. $\frac{3}{2}$ 3. $\frac{3}{8}$	**149.** The *bottom* number of a simple meter signature indicates the durational value that represents the beat, or beat unit. **1** means whole note (rare) **2** means half note **4** means quarter note **8** means eighth note **16** means sixteenth note → $\frac{2}{4}$ indicates that a quarter note, or ♩ note, is the beat unit. Supply the bottom number of these meter signatures as indicated by the given beat unit. 1. ♩ $\frac{2}{\ }$ 2. 𝅗𝅥 $\frac{3}{\ }$ 3. ♪ $\frac{3}{\ }$

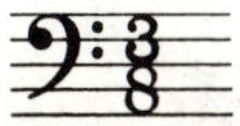

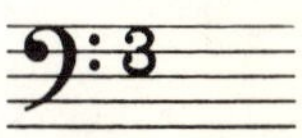

1. 𝅗𝅥 2. ♪ 3. ♩

150. Derive and draw the beat units from the given meter signatures.

1. $\genfrac{}{}{0pt}{}{2}{2}$ ____ 2. $\genfrac{}{}{0pt}{}{4}{8}$ ____ 3. $\genfrac{}{}{0pt}{}{5}{4}$ ____

---

meter

beat unit

151. The top number of a simple meter signature indicates the __________.

The bottom number of a simple meter signature indicates the __________ __________.

---

1. quadruple 𝅗𝅥

2. triple 𝅘𝅥𝅯

152. Name the meter and draw the beat unit expressed by each of these meter signatures.

METER SIGNATURE	METER	BEAT UNIT
1. $\genfrac{}{}{0pt}{}{4}{2}$	__________	____
2. $\genfrac{}{}{0pt}{}{3}{16}$	__________	____

---

1. $\genfrac{}{}{0pt}{}{3}{2}$

2. $\genfrac{}{}{0pt}{}{4}{8}$

153. Construct meter signatures from the given information.

METER SIGNATURE	METER	BEAT UNIT
1.	triple	𝅗𝅥
2.	quadruple	♪

---

1 3 5

154. A meter signature is *not* a fraction. Writing a meter signature as a fraction is therefore incorrect.

Thus $\genfrac{}{}{0pt}{}{2}{4}$, not $\frac{2}{4}$ or 2/4

Which of the following are correct? ____ ____ ____

1. $\genfrac{}{}{0pt}{}{3}{4}$ 2. 3/4 3. $\genfrac{}{}{0pt}{}{4}{2}$ 4. $\frac{2}{2}$ 5. $\genfrac{}{}{0pt}{}{4}{8}$

1. triple 𝅘𝅥𝅯
2. quintuple 𝅘𝅥𝅮

155. Name the meter and draw the beat unit for each of these meter signatures.

METER SIGNATURE	METER	BEAT UNIT
1. $\genfrac{}{}{0pt}{}{3}{16}$	____________	____
2. $\genfrac{}{}{0pt}{}{5}{8}$	____________	____

1. simple
2. compound
3. compound
4. simple

156. Four possible beat units are shown below. Name the beat type of each.

1. 𝅗𝅥 ____________
2. 𝅘𝅥𝅮. ____________
3. 𝅝. ____________
4. 𝅘𝅥𝅯 ____________

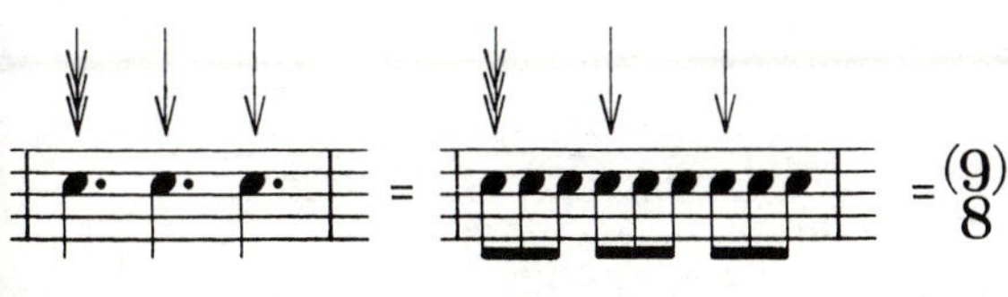

157. Compound meter signatures express the *division* of the beat: the *top* number indicates the number of divisions in the entire pattern, while the *bottom* number indicates the durational value of each division.

= = six eighth notes = $\genfrac{}{}{0pt}{}{6}{8}$

Using the above procedure as a guide, divide each beat unit and supply the bottom number in the example below.

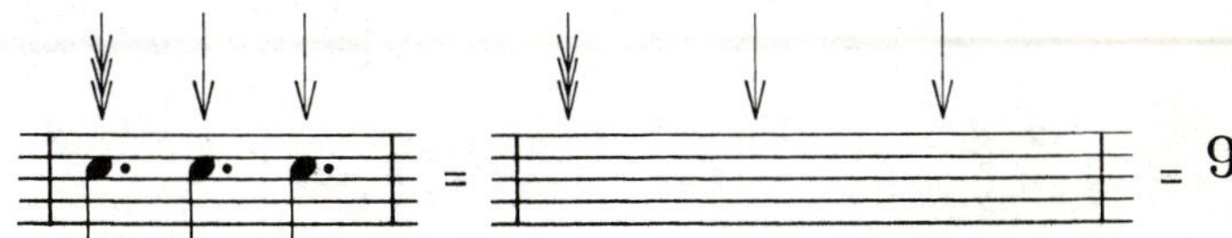

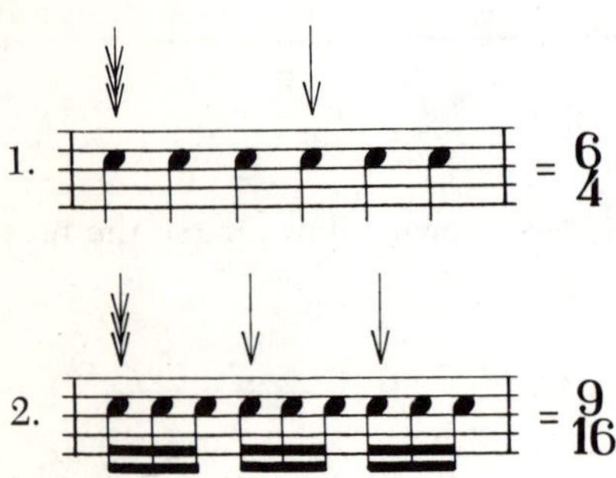

158. Following the given example, derive these compound meter signatures:

1. Divide the beat units to arrive at the bottom number. (Be sure to include the arrows.)
2. Count the divisions to arrive at the top number.

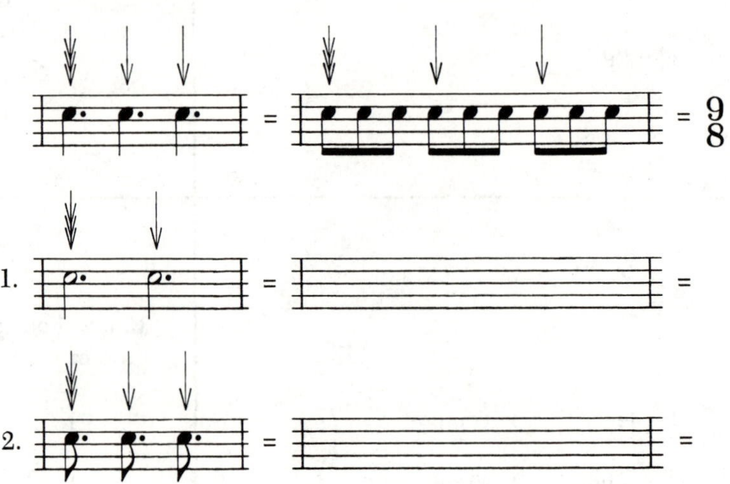

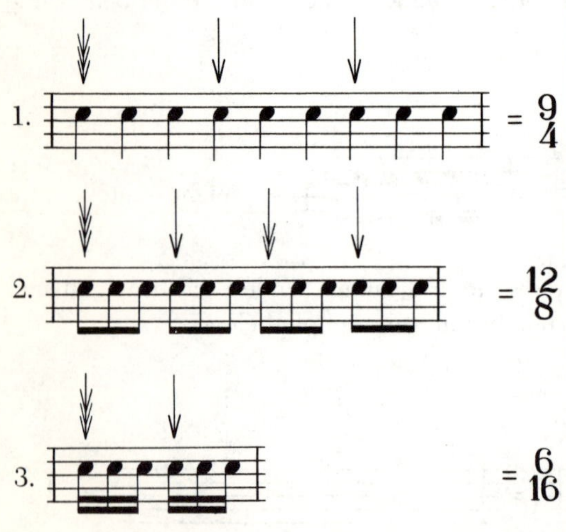

159. Continue as in frame 158.

160. Construct meter signatures for the measures below by *mentally* dividing the beat units and then counting the divisions. (Review frames 157–159 if necessary.)

1. ______

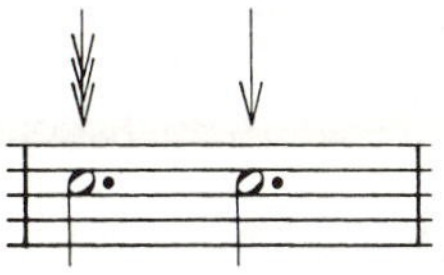

2. ______

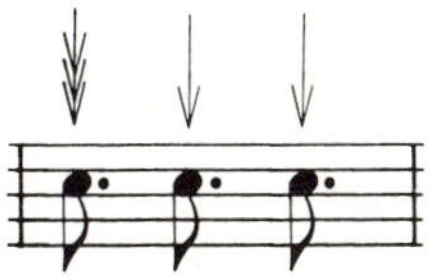

Answers: 1. $\frac{6}{4}$ 2. $\frac{9}{16}$

161. Continue as in frame 160.

1.  ______ 3. ______

2.  ______ 4. ______

Answers: 1. $\frac{6}{8}$ 3. $\frac{9}{64}$ 2. $\frac{6}{32}$ 4. $\frac{12}{4}$

162. In compound meter signatures, the top number is always divisible by *three.* The number that results from this division reveals the meter.

$\frac{6}{8}$ Six (top number) divided by three is two, indicating duple meter.

Divide the *top* number of each compound meter signature below by three, and name the meter in each.

1. $\frac{6}{4}$ ______ 2. $\frac{9}{8}$ ______

Answers: 1. duple 2. triple

163. Derive the meters from these given compound meter signatures by dividing the top number by ______.

1. $\frac{9}{4}$ ______

2. $\frac{12}{16}$ ______

3. $\frac{6}{4}$ ______

Answers: three

1. triple

2. quadruple

3. duple

1. triple ♩.

2. quadruple 𝅗𝅥.

164. Name the meter and draw the beat unit in each of these compound signatures. (Remember that dividing the top number by three provides the meter. Derive the beat unit by combining *three* of the notes represented by the bottom number to produce one dotted note.)

METER SIGNATURE	METER	BEAT UNIT
1. 9/8	____________	____
2. 12/4	____________	____

1. duple 𝅗𝅥.

2. duple 𝅝.

3. quadruple ♩.

165. Continue as in frame 164.

METER SIGNATURE	METER	BEAT UNIT
1. 6/4	____________	____
2. 6/2	____________	____
3. 12/8	____________	____

1. 6/4

2. 9/16

3. 15/8

166. Construct compound meter signatures from the given information.

METER SIGNATURE	METER	BEAT UNIT
1.	duple	𝅗𝅥.
2.	triple	♪.
3.	quintuple	♩.

meter

compound

167. All __________ signatures are either simple or compound.

In __________ (simple/compound) meter signatures, the top number is always divisible by three.

168. The top number quickly reveals whether a meter signature is simple or compound:

1. If the top number is a multiple of three (6, 9, 12, 15, 18, etc.) the signature is compound.
2. If the top number is *not* a multiple of three (2, 4, 5, 7, 8, etc.) the signature is simple.*

2/4 9/8 6/4 4/8 5/2 12/4 7/16 15/32

Circle the meter signatures above that are *compound.* The others are __________.

**Three* as a top number may indicate either a simple or compound signature, depending largely on the tempo. In most cases, however, *three* is associated with *simple* signatures. Since its use with compound signatures requires more advanced study, three as a top number is employed only in simple signatures throughout this book.

(9/8) (6/4) (12/4) (15/32)

simple

169. Circle the compound signatures below. Refer to the previous frame if necessary.

4/16 5/8 3/4 2/1 9/32 3/8 4/32 6/16

In *simple* signatures, the top number __________ (is/is not) a multiple of three.

(9/32) (6/16)

is not

170. The *beat unit* in a meter signature also reveals whether a signature is simple or compound: nondotted notes are simple beat types, while dotted notes are compound beat types.

Draw the beat unit and give the beat type in each of these signatures.

METER SIGNATURE	BEAT UNIT	BEAT TYPE
1. 3/4	____	________
2. 6/8	____	________

1. ♩ simple
2. ♩. compound

171. Circle the signatures below that express triple simple meter.

6/4 3/4 5/8 9/2 12/8 3/2 3/16

(3/4) (3/2) (3/16)

(circled:) $\genfrac{}{}{0pt}{}{9}{8}$ $\genfrac{}{}{0pt}{}{9}{2}$ $\genfrac{}{}{0pt}{}{9}{16}$

172. Circle the signatures below that express triple compound meter.

$\genfrac{}{}{0pt}{}{9}{8}$ $\genfrac{}{}{0pt}{}{5}{2}$ $\genfrac{}{}{0pt}{}{3}{4}$ $\genfrac{}{}{0pt}{}{12}{2}$ $\genfrac{}{}{0pt}{}{9}{2}$ $\genfrac{}{}{0pt}{}{3}{2}$ $\genfrac{}{}{0pt}{}{2}{1}$ $\genfrac{}{}{0pt}{}{9}{16}$

---

1. triple compound
2. quadruple simple
3. quadruple compound

173. Complete the descriptions of these meter signatures, following the given example.

$\genfrac{}{}{0pt}{}{6}{8}$ = duple compound meter

1. $\genfrac{}{}{0pt}{}{9}{4}$ = ________ ________ meter
2. $\genfrac{}{}{0pt}{}{4}{8}$ = ________ ________ meter
3. $\genfrac{}{}{0pt}{}{12}{8}$ = ________ ________ meter

---

1. quadruple simple
2. duple compound
3. triple simple

174. Continue as in frame 173.

1. $\genfrac{}{}{0pt}{}{4}{4}$ = ________ ________ meter
2. $\genfrac{}{}{0pt}{}{6}{4}$ = ________ ________ meter
3. $\genfrac{}{}{0pt}{}{3}{2}$ = ________ ________ meter

---

1. (triple) (♩) simple ($\genfrac{}{}{0pt}{}{3}{4}$)
2. (quadruple) ♪ (simple) ($\genfrac{}{}{0pt}{}{4}{8}$)
3. duple (𝅗𝅥.) (compound) ($\genfrac{}{}{0pt}{}{6}{4}$)

175. Supply the missing information below.

	METER	BEAT UNIT	BEAT TYPE	METER SIGNATURE
1.	triple	♩	________	$\genfrac{}{}{0pt}{}{3}{4}$
2.	quadruple	____	simple	$\genfrac{}{}{0pt}{}{4}{8}$
3.	________	𝅗𝅥.	compound	$\genfrac{}{}{0pt}{}{6}{4}$

1. simple $\frac{2}{2}$
2. compound $\frac{6}{16}$
3. simple $\frac{4}{2}$

176. Continue as in frame 175.

	METER	BEAT UNIT	BEAT TYPE	METER SIGNATURE
1.	duple	𝅗𝅥	______	
2.	duple	♪.	______	
3.	quadruple	𝅗𝅥	______	

♩

(treble clef staff with **C**)

177. The symbol **C** is sometimes used as a meter signature to represent $\frac{4}{4}$. It is placed between the second and fourth lines of the staff. It is called *common time.*°

The unit of beat in the following signature is _____.

(bass clef staff with **C**)

Draw on the staff below the symbol that means $\frac{4}{4}$.

(treble clef staff)

° Although popularly referred to as "common time," the symbol **C** is *not* an abbreviation for "common," but has historical origins.

1. triple
2. quadruple
3. quintuple

178. Identify the meter in each meter signature below.

1. (bass clef, $\frac{3}{2}$) ______________
2. (treble clef, **C**) ______________
3. (bass clef, $\frac{5}{4}$) ______________

𝅗𝅥

179. The "common time" symbol (C) with a line through it (¢) is frequently used to replace the meter signature $\frac{2}{2}$. It is called *alla breve.*

The beat unit in the following signature is ____.

[Treble clef staff with ¢]

Draw on the staff below the symbol which means $\frac{2}{2}$.

[Bass clef staff]

[Answer: bass clef staff with ¢]

1. duple simple
2. quadruple simple

180. Identify the meter and beat type in each meter signature below.

	METER	BEAT TYPE
1.  [Treble clef, ¢]	____________	____________
2. 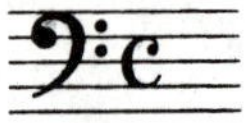 [Bass clef, C]	____________	____________

1. quadruple 𝅗𝅥 simple
2. triple ♩. compound
3. quadruple 𝅗𝅥. compound

181. Derive the missing information from the given meter signatures.

	METER	BEAT UNIT	BEAT TYPE
1. $\frac{4}{2}$	____________	____	____________
2. $\frac{9}{8}$	____________	____	____________
3. $\frac{12}{4}$	____________	____	____________

common time

182. This signature [Treble clef, C] is called ________ ________.

Draw on the staff below the signature known as *alla breve.*

[Bass clef staff]

[Answer: bass clef staff with ¢]

1. $\frac{6}{8}$ 3. ¢

2. $\frac{3}{8}$ 4. $\frac{3}{8}$

183. Complete the meter signatures below. The meter is provided for each.

1.  6 — duple 3. 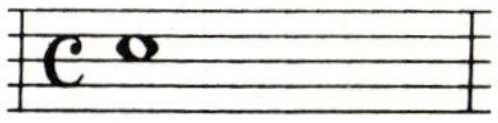 C — duple

2.  3 — triple 4.  3 — triple

---

1. quadruple (♪) simple (4)/8

2. (triple) 𝅘𝅥𝅯 (simple) 3/(16)

184. Complete the meter signature and supply the missing information in each of the following.

	METER	BEAT UNIT	BEAT TYPE		METER SIGNATURE
1.	________	♪	________	=	4
2.	triple	____	simple	=	16

---

1. compound 6/(4)

2. simple 5/(2)

185. Continue as in frame 184.

	METER	BEAT UNIT	BEAT TYPE		METER SIGNATURE
1.	duple	𝅗𝅥.	________	=	4
2.	quintuple	𝅗𝅥	________	=	2

---

1.  (C)

2.  (9/8)

186. Complete these measures by adding one note of the necessary value to each.

1.  (C) 2.  (9/8)

---

1.  (5/8)

2.  (12/4)

187. Continue as in frame 186.

1.  (5/8) 2.  (12/4)

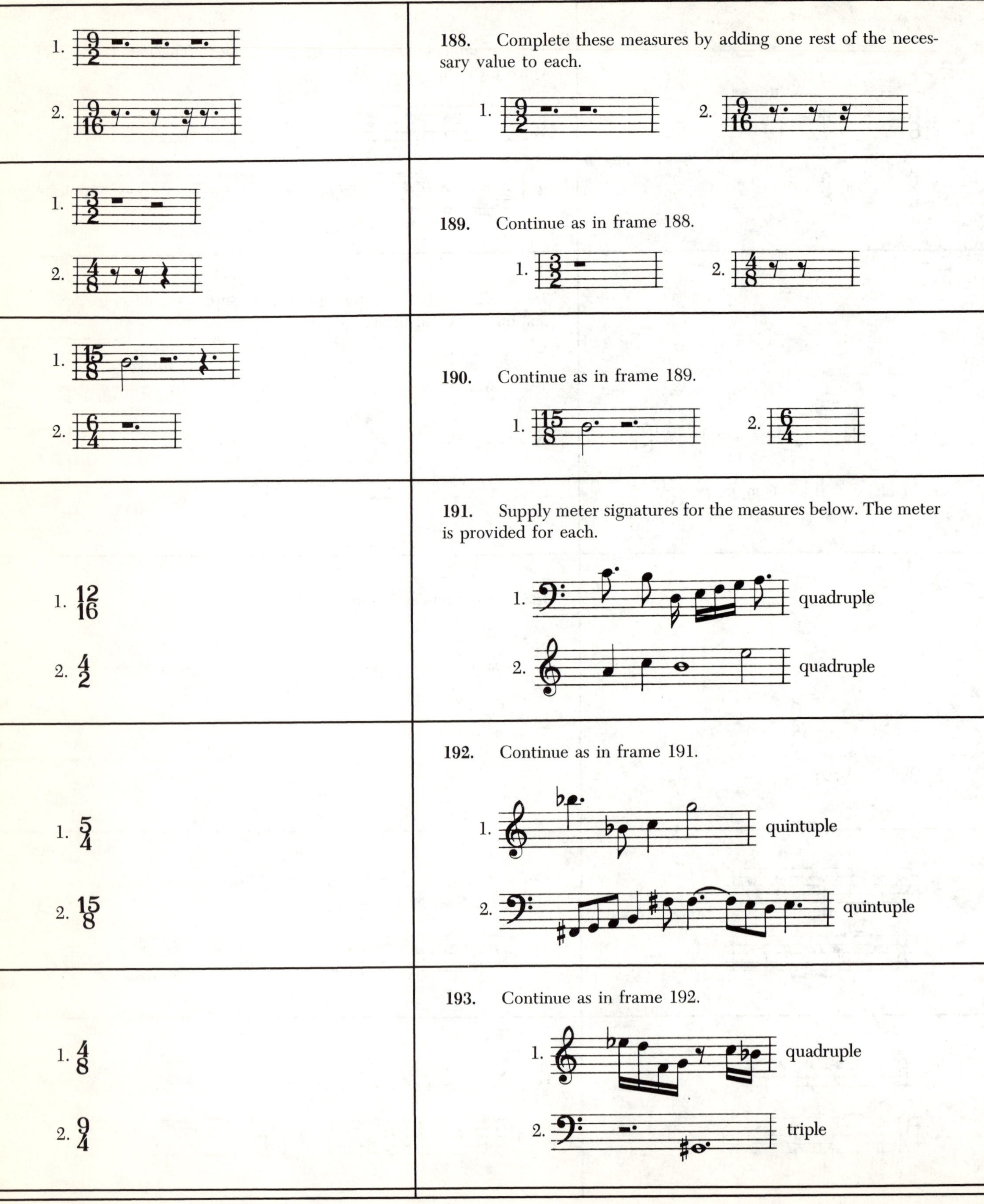

1. $\frac{9}{2}$

2. $\frac{9}{16}$

188. Complete these measures by adding one rest of the necessary value to each.

1. $\frac{9}{2}$ 2. $\frac{9}{16}$

---

1. $\frac{3}{2}$

2. $\frac{4}{8}$

189. Continue as in frame 188.

1. $\frac{3}{2}$ 2. $\frac{4}{8}$

---

1. $\frac{15}{8}$

2. $\frac{6}{4}$

190. Continue as in frame 189.

1. $\frac{15}{8}$ 2. $\frac{6}{4}$

---

1. $\frac{12}{16}$

2. $\frac{4}{2}$

191. Supply meter signatures for the measures below. The meter is provided for each.

1. quadruple

2. quadruple

---

1. $\frac{5}{4}$

2. $\frac{15}{8}$

192. Continue as in frame 191.

1. quintuple

2. quintuple

---

1. $\frac{4}{8}$

2. $\frac{9}{4}$

193. Continue as in frame 192.

1. quadruple

2. triple

LISTENING FRAMES

2 (If your answer was incorrect, listen to the example again. You may be counting *divisions* of the beat rather than the beat itself.)

194. Listen to Example 1-2, from Purcell's "Thy Hand, Belinda!" Count and tap the beats as you listen. Which of the following best describes the meter? (Listen to the entire excerpt before you answer, observing the slow tempo.) _____

1. The meter is quadruple compound.
2. The meter is triple simple.
3. The meter is triple compound.

1

195. The meter signature used in the notation of Example 1-2 is $\frac{3}{2}$. Listen to the excerpt again. Which of the following most closely resembles the rhythm of the first *five* measures? (Notice that the first four measures are the same, but the fifth measure differs.)

_____

1. $\frac{3}{2}$
2. $\frac{3}{2}$
3. $\frac{3}{2}$

3

196. Example 2-4, from Mozart's Piano Concerto No. 27 (last movement), was identified earlier as employing duple compound meter. The actual meter signature used is $\frac{6}{8}$. Listen again to the excerpt, counting and tapping beats as before. Which of the following most accurately resembles the rhythmic notation of the first four measures? _____

1 (If your answer was incorrect, listen to the passage again. Notice that each group of two or three begins on a strong beat.)

197. Example 2-3, from Brubeck's "Take Five," combines beat groups of twos and threes to produce quintuple simple meter. As you listen to the excerpt, count the beats as before. Which of the following most accurately describes the combinations of twos and threes used in the first four measures? _____

1. Every measure combines three beats plus two beats.
2. Every measure combines two beats plus three beats.
3. The first two measures are two beats plus three beats, while the next two measures are three beats plus two beats.

SELF-QUIZ II

1. The organization of beats into patterns of stress is called __________.

2. __________ meter is a combination of duple plus triple, or triple plus duple meters.

3. Draw the equivalent rest to the right of each given note.

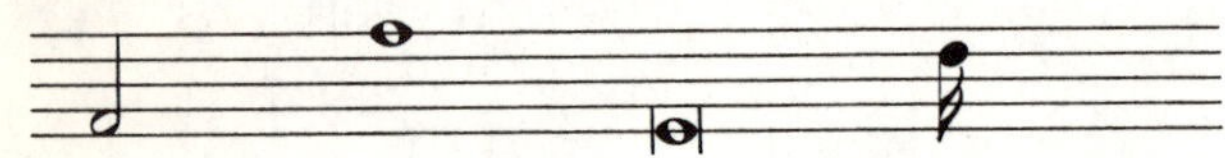

4. Draw the dotted note that is the equivalent of each example below.

1. = _____ 2. = _____ 3. _____ 4. = _____

5. Divide and sub-divide each note below.

1. = _____ _____ = _____ _____ _____ _____
(division) (sub-division)

2. = _____ _____ = _____ _____ _____ _____ _____ _____
(division) (sub-division)

6. 

1. The simple beat units above are _____ _____ _____.
(notes)

2. The compound beat units above are _____ _____ _____.
(notes)

7. The three basic elements in the notation of rhythm and meter are __________, __________, and __________.

8. Derive the missing information from the given meter signatures.

	METER	BEAT UNIT	BEAT TYPE
1. $\frac{3}{4}$	____________	_____	_____
2. $\frac{9}{16}$	____________	_____	_____
3. $\frac{5}{8}$	____________	_____	_____

9. The top number in all compound signatures is a multiple of ____________.
(number)

10. Correctly re-notate this example on the lower staff. The given passage contains seven notation errors.

11.

The above passage uses ____________ ____________________ meter.

The beat unit is _____.

The beat type is ____________.

CHAPTER ▪ III ▪ SCALES AND MODES

As used in music, the word *scale* derives from the Latin word *scala*, meaning "ladder" or "staircase." Just as a staircase leads up or down by means of adjacent steps, so do the tones of a scale proceed up or down in the order of its fixed "staircase" of pitches.

A scale is any division of an octave into a series of tones, arranged in ascending or descending order of pitch, that provides the basic pitch material for a composition or a section of a composition. The octave may be divided into any number of segments: common divisions are five, which results in the *pentatonic* scale; seven (*diatonic*); and twelve (*chromatic*). During the past three hundred years, however, the music of Western civilization has drawn upon only two scales for most of its basic tonal material: the major scale, and the minor scale in its three related forms. Both are *diatonic* scales; that is, they both contain seven tones, plus the octave of the first. These two basic scales are the subject of the first portion of this chapter. The remainder of the chapter is devoted to other scale forms called *modes,* which were in common use long before major and minor scales became prevalent, and which are still frequently employed today.

As with Chapter I, it will be extremely helpful to work through this chapter near a keyboard or other instrument in order to be able to play the various scales and hear the differences between them. The added dimension of *hearing* the scales as you work with them on paper will greatly enhance your understanding of them.

MAJOR SCALES

octave	**1.** In each of these scales, the difference in pitch between the first note and the last is a(n) ________. 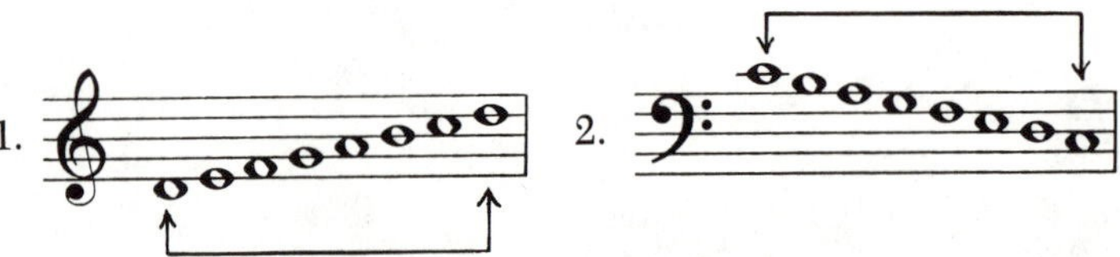 (Remember that "tone" refers to sound, while "note" refers to symbol.)

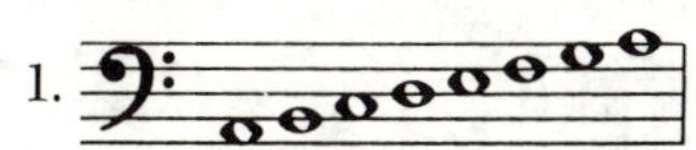

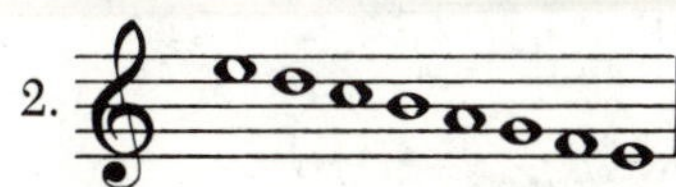

2. The basic seven-tone scales with which this chapter is concerned are notated by using *adjacent* lines and spaces of the staff, in ascending or descending order of pitch.

Complete these examples to form scales, using all lines and spaces between the given notes. Do not use accidentals.

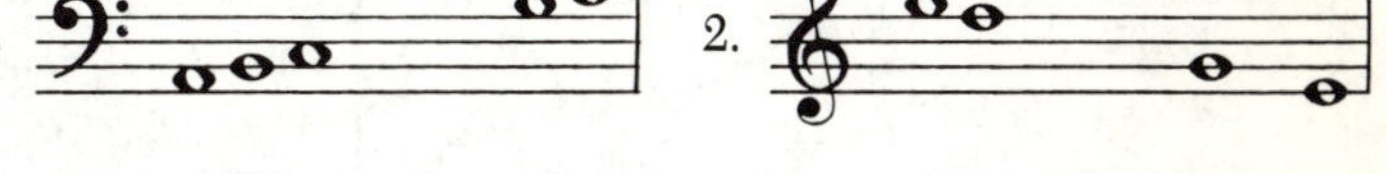

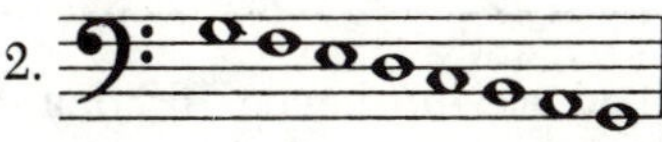

3. Complete these examples to form scales, using all lines and spaces between the given notes. Do not use accidentals.

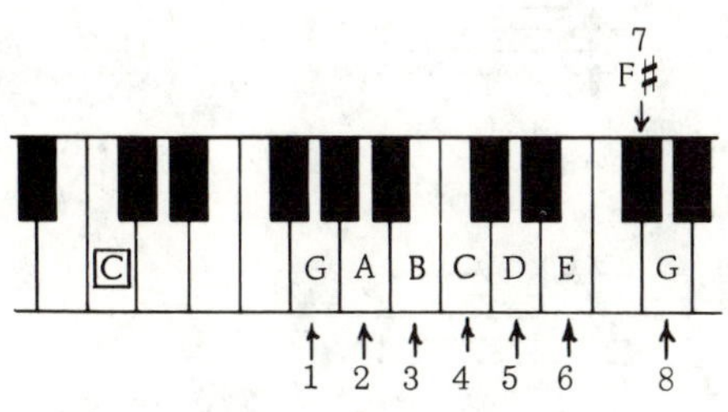

4. This ascending scale is transferred to the keyboard below, as the arrows indicate. Write the pitch names on the white keys or above the arrows of black keys.

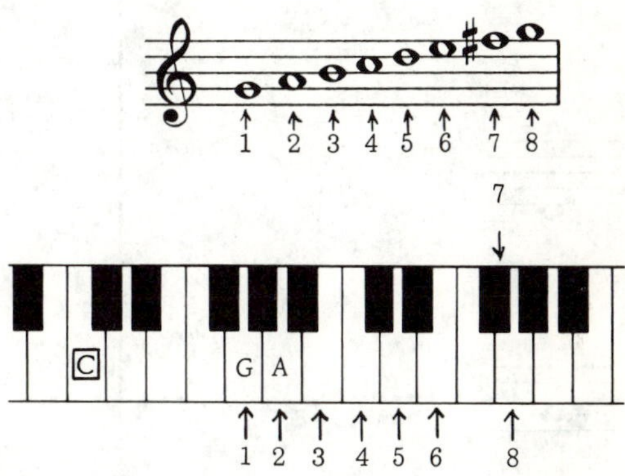

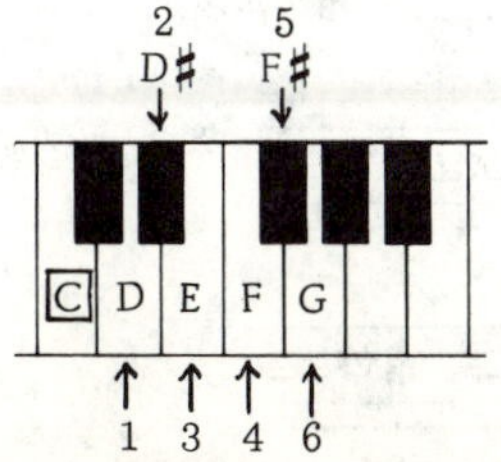

5. Complete the transfer of these notes to the keyboard diagram, inserting pitch names, numbers, and arrows. For clarity, place black-key arrows above the keyboard and white-key arrows below.

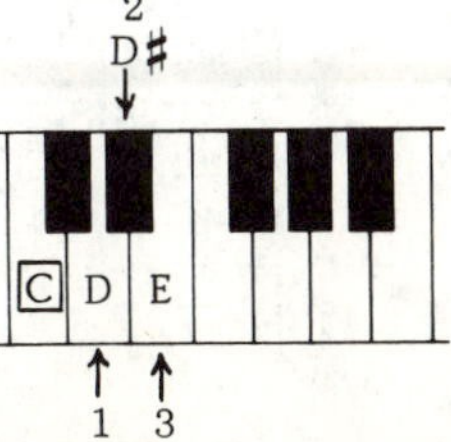

6. In the series of tones below, notice that each tone is followed by an *adjacent* tone on the keyboard.

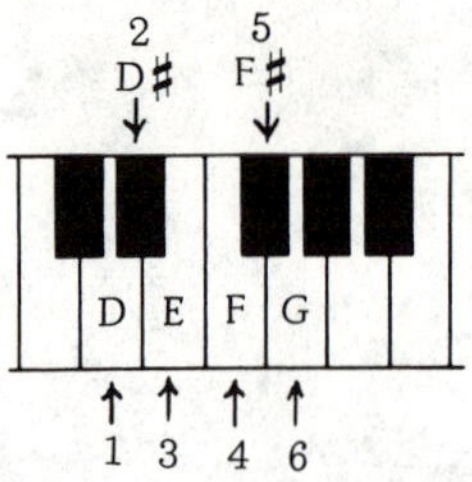

2 D♯ 5 F♯

D E F G

1 3 4 6

The distance from any key on the keyboard to an adjacent key (such as D to D♯) is a *half step.*

Is E up to F a half step? _____

yes

7. The pitch distance from any key on the keyboard to an _______________ key is a half step.

adjacent

8. Using whole notes, transfer each keyboard example below to the adjacent staff. Place checks by those which are half steps.

1. 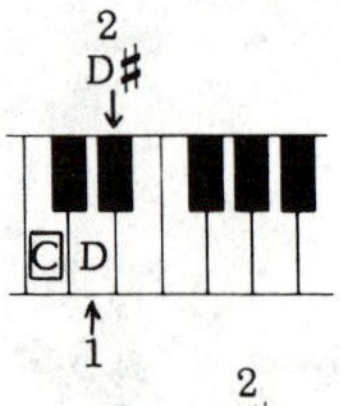 2 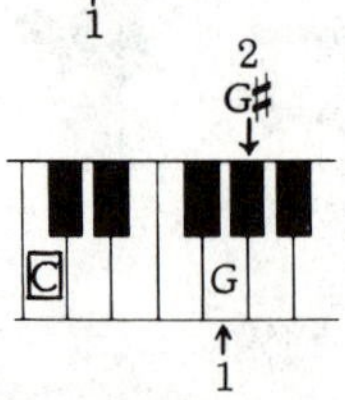 D♯ — C D — 1 _____

2. 2 G♯ — C G — 1 _____

3. 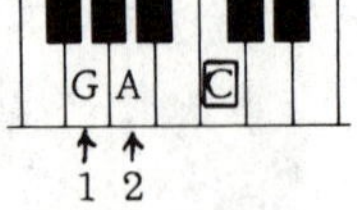 G A C — 1 2 _____

1.  _√_

2.  _√_

3. _____

9. The pitch distance from any key on the keyboard to an adjacent key is a __________ __________.

Place a check by any of the following which are half steps.

1. 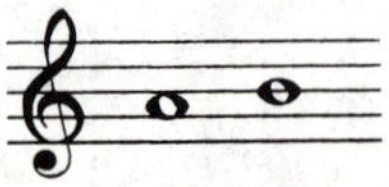 _____ 3. _____

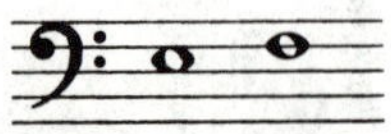

2.  _____ 4. _____

half step

1. _____ 3. _√_

2. _√_ 4. _____

10. Two successive half steps form one *whole step.*

= = whole step

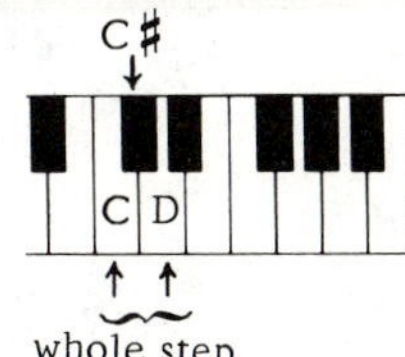

On the keyboard, C up to D is a __________ __________.

whole step

---

11. Just as the distance spanned by every *two* adjacent keys on the keyboard is a half step, the distance spanned by every *three* adjacent keys is a whole step.

How many adjacent keys are spanned by a whole step? _____

Two successive half steps form a __________ __________.

three

whole step

---

12. Complete the following with either "half step" or "whole step."

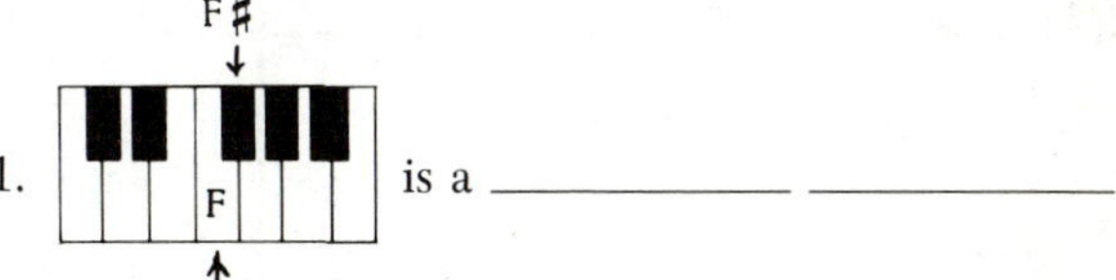

1. is a __________ __________.

2. is a __________ __________.

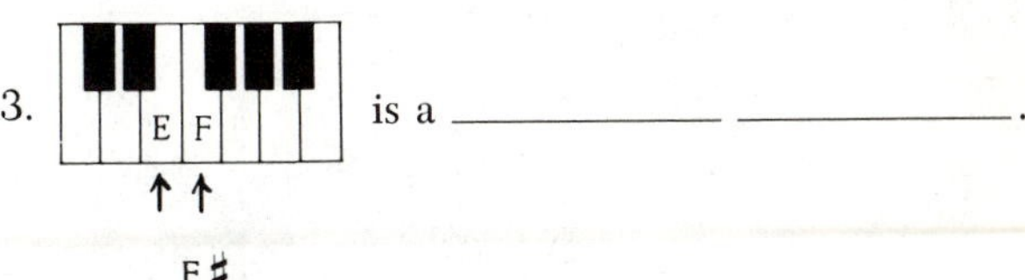

3. is a __________ __________.

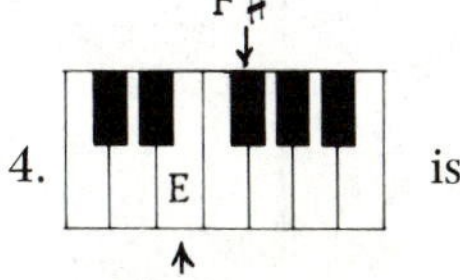

4. is a __________ __________.

1. half step
2. whole step
3. half step
4. whole step

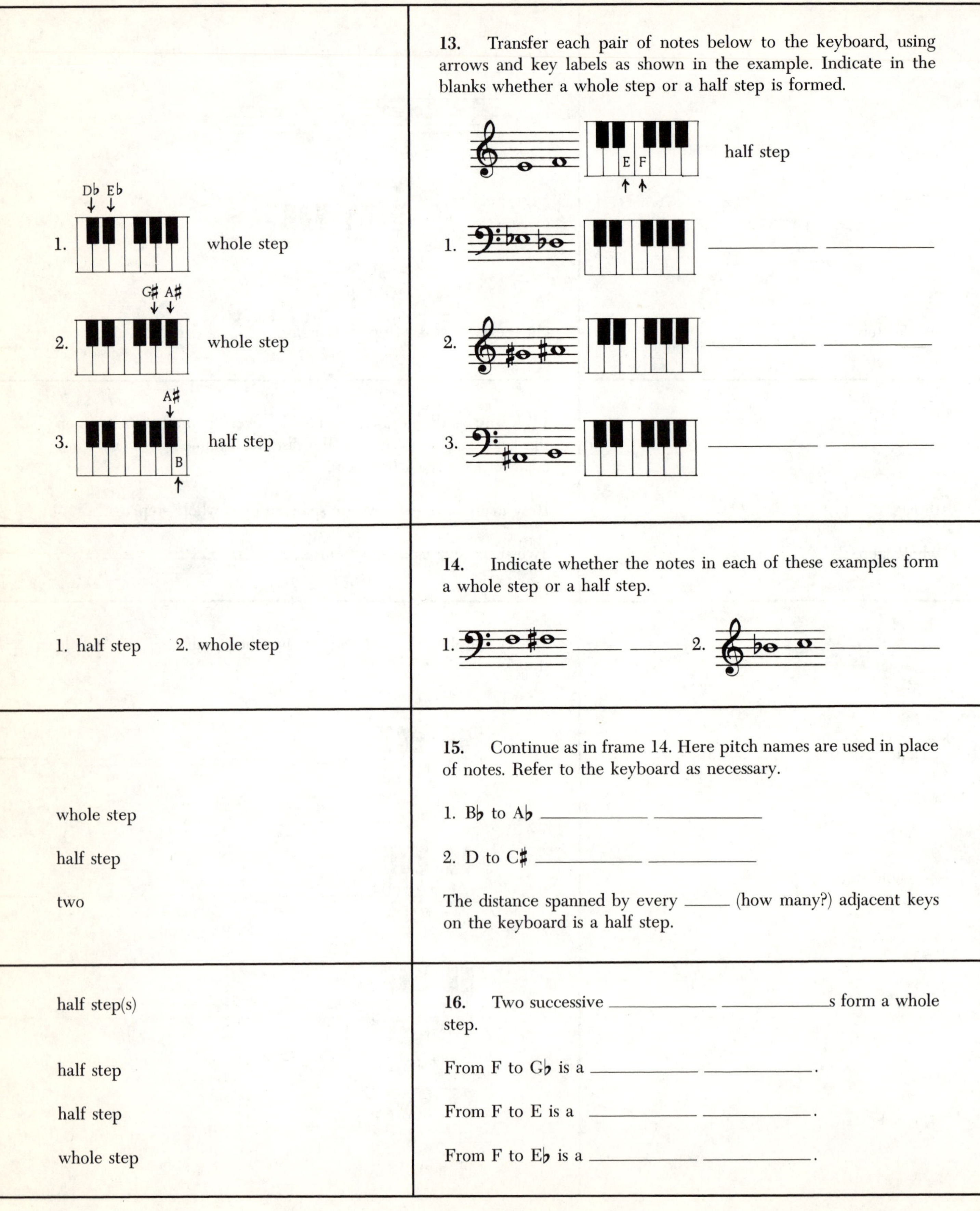

13. Transfer each pair of notes below to the keyboard, using arrows and key labels as shown in the example. Indicate in the blanks whether a whole step or a half step is formed.

1. D♭ E♭ — whole step
2. G♯ A♯ — whole step
3. A♯ B — half step

1. ____________ ____________

2. ____________ ____________

3. ____________ ____________

---

1. half step 2. whole step

14. Indicate whether the notes in each of these examples form a whole step or a half step.

1. _____ _____ 2. _____ _____

---

whole step

half step

two

15. Continue as in frame 14. Here pitch names are used in place of notes. Refer to the keyboard as necessary.

1. B♭ to A♭ ____________ ____________

2. D to C♯ ____________ ____________

The distance spanned by every _____ (how many?) adjacent keys on the keyboard is a half step.

---

half step(s)

half step

half step

whole step

16. Two successive ____________ ____________s form a whole step.

From F to G♭ is a ____________ ____________.

From F to E is a ____________ ____________.

From F to E♭ is a ____________ ____________.

Answers	Frames
	17. There are two kinds of half steps, named according to their notation and musical behavior: 1. A *chromatic* half step is notated using the same basic letter name (C to C♯, F to F♯, B♭ to B♮). 2. A *diatonic* half step is notated using adjacent letter names (C to D♭, F to G♭, B♭ to C♭). Which of these half steps are chromatic? _____ _____ _____ 1. E to E♭ 2. E to D♯ 3. G to G♯ 4. G to A♭ 5. A♭ to A♮
1 3 5	
the same	**18.** A chromatic half step is notated with ____________ (the same/a different) letter name(s). Name the pitch which is one chromatic half step *above* each given pitch. (Do not alter any given pitch.) 1. D to _____ 2. F to _____ 3. A to _____
1. D♯ 2. F♯ 3. A♯	
chromatic	**19.** A half step notated with the same letter name is called ____________. Name the pitch that is one chromatic half step *below* each given pitch. 1. E to _____ 2. G to _____ 3. B to _____
1. E♭ 2. G♭ 3. B♭	
a different diatonic	**20.** A *diatonic* half step is notated with ______________ (the same/a different) letter name(s). The two kinds of half steps are chromatic and ____________.
1 3 5	**21.** Which half steps below are *diatonic*? _____ _____ _____ 1. F to G♭ 2. F to F♯ 3. C to B 4. C to C♭ 5. E♭ to D
	22. Name the pitch that is one diatonic half step *above* each given pitch. 1. E to _____ 3. D to _____ 2. A to _____ 4. G♯ to _____
1. F 3. E♭ 2. B♭ 4. A	

1. C♯ 3. F♯

2. E 4. A

23. Name the pitch that is one diatonic half step *below* each given pitch.

1. D to _____ 3. G to _____

2. F to _____ 4. B♭ to _____

diatonic

chromatic

24. A __________ half step is notated with different letter names.

A __________ half step is notated with the same letter name.

1.

2.

3.

25. Following the given example, supply both kinds of half steps *above* each given pitch. Continue to refer to the keyboard as necessary.

CHROMATIC DIATONIC

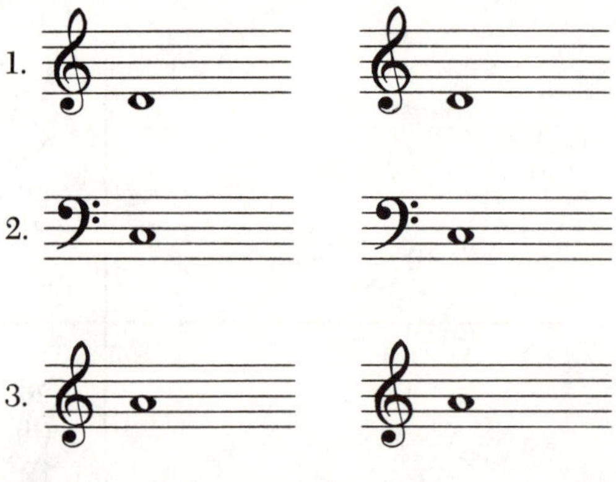

1.

2.

3.

1.

2.

3.

26. Supply both kinds of half steps *below* each given pitch.

CHROMATIC DIATONIC

1.

2.

3.

diatonic

27. Adjacent tones in the basic seven-tone scales are notated with whole steps and *diatonic* half steps. Chromatic half steps are not used in the notation of these scales.

The half steps in the scale below occur where indicated. Both half steps are ____________ (diatonic/chromatic).

half step
half step

two

28. Since chromatic half steps are not used in these scales, all half steps in the remainder of this chapter will be diatonic. Therefore, in succeeding frames the term "half step" will always mean *diatonic* half step.

The distance spanned by every _____ (how many?) adjacent keys on the keyboard is a half step.

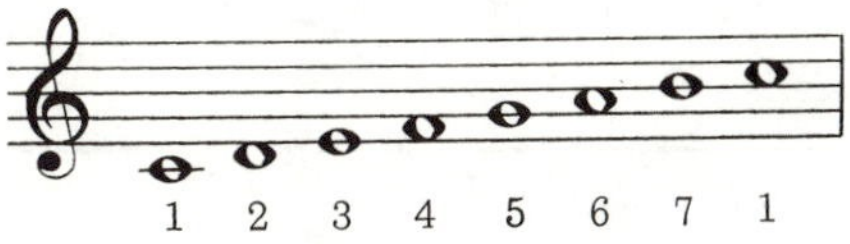

1 2 3 4 5 6 7 1

29. Each tone of a scale is called a *scale degree.*

Complete the numbering of the scale degrees in the scale below. Notice that the first scale degree receives the same number when it occurs an octave higher.

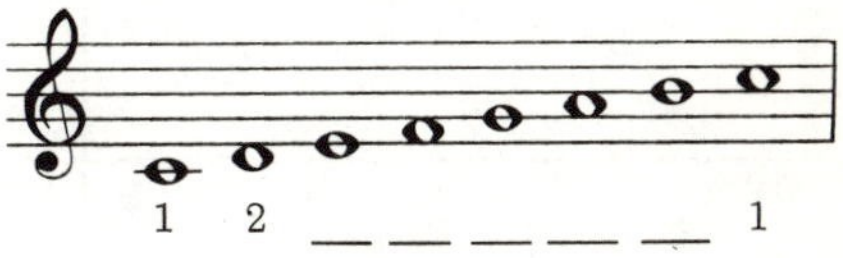

1 2 __ __ __ __ __ 1

degree

scale

30. Each tone of a scale is called a scale ____________.

The distances *between* scale degrees are called *scale steps.*[*]

In the scale below, the distance from scale degree 1 to scale degree 2 is a whole step. In other words, ____________ step 1 to 2 is a whole step.

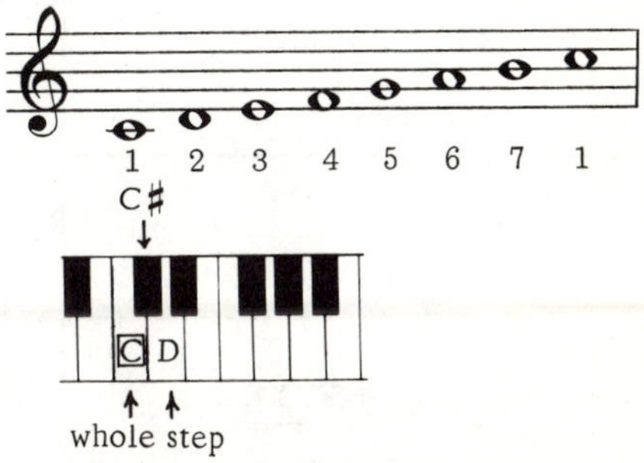

1 2 3 4 5 6 7 1

C♯

C D

whole step

[*] "Scale degrees" are sometimes called "scale steps." In this book, however, the term "scale step" is reserved for the distances between "scale degrees."

whole step

half step

whole step

whole step

whole step

half step

31. In the scale below, scale step 1 to 2 is a whole step.

What is scale step 2 to 3? ______ ______.

3 to 4? ______ ______.

4 to 5? ______ ______.

5 to 6? ______ ______.

6 to 7? ______ ______.

7 to 1? ______ ______.

half step   half step

1 2 3 4 5 6 7 1

---

half steps

whole steps

steps

32. The scale below has ________ ________ at 3 to 4 and 7 to 1. All the rest of the scale steps are ________ ________.

half step   half step

1 2 3 4 5 6 7 1

The distances between scale degrees are called scale ________.

---

3 to 4

7 to 1   WS's

33. For convenience we will use the abbreviations HS for half step and WS for whole step in the remainder of this chapter.

The scale below has HS's (half steps) at ____ to ____ and ____ to ____. All the remaining scale steps are ________'s.

HS   HS

1 2 3 4 5 6 7 1

---

1 2 3 4 5 6 7 1

HS   HS

34. Complete this scale, providing HS's at 3 to 4 and 7 to 1 and WS's for all the remaining scale steps.

1 2 3 4 5 6 7 1

HS   HS

major

35. A scale having HS's at 3 to 4 and 7 to 1 and WS's at all other scale step locations is a *major* scale.

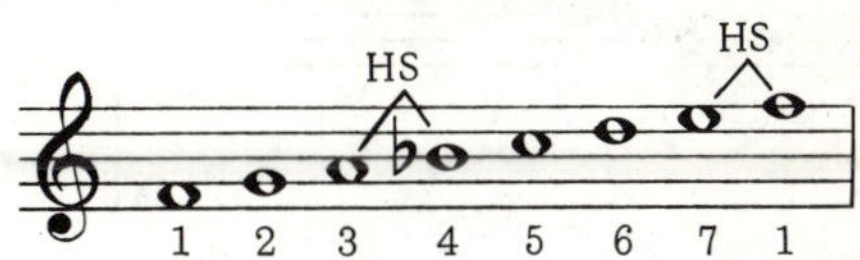

A ____________ scale has HS's at 3 to 4 and 7 to 1 and WS's at all other scale step locations.

3 to 4

36. The major scale has HS's at _____ to _____ and 7 to 1.

Draw HS brackets where appropriate on the two scales below, following the example given.

1. 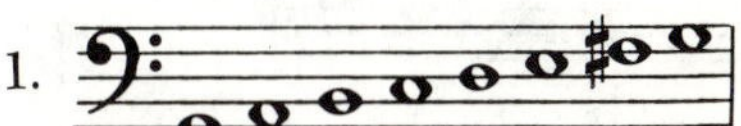

2. 

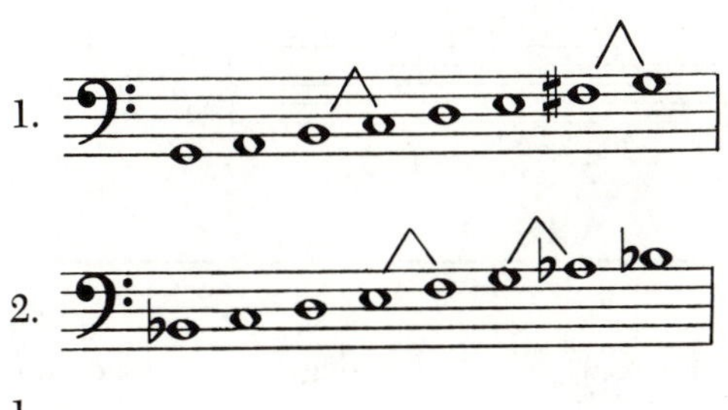

1

Which one is a major scale? _____

3 to 4

7 to 1

37. In the major scale the HS's are found at _____ to _____ and _____ to _____.

Draw HS brackets on the scales below.

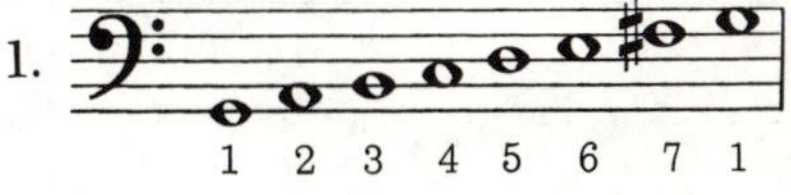

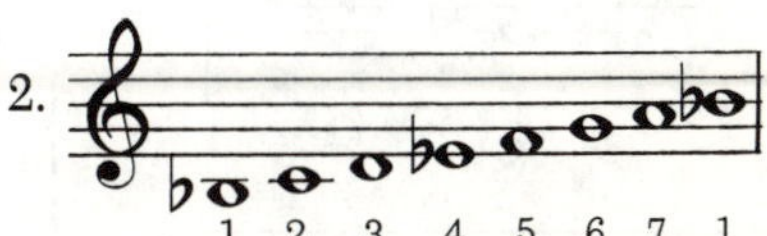

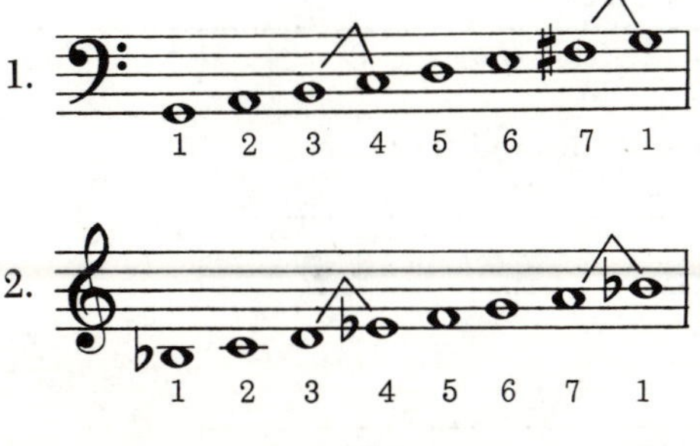

yes

Are the above scales both major scales? _____

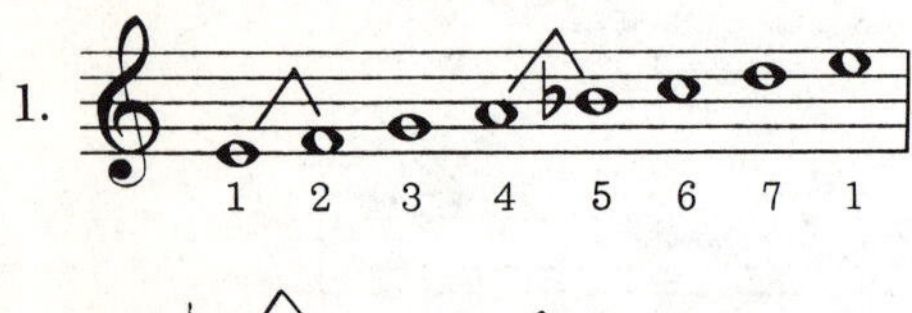

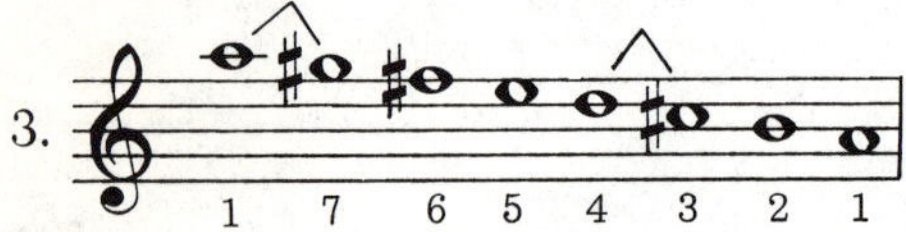

3

38. Draw HS brackets on the scales below.

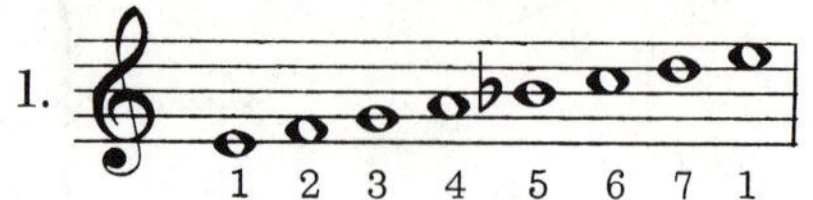

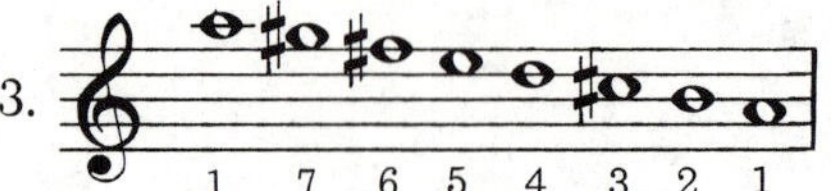

Which one is a major scale? _____

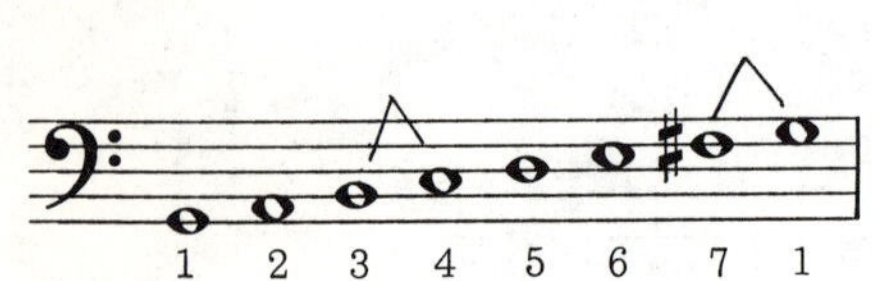

39. Construct the ascending major scale whose first degree is G. Include scale degree numbers and HS brackets.

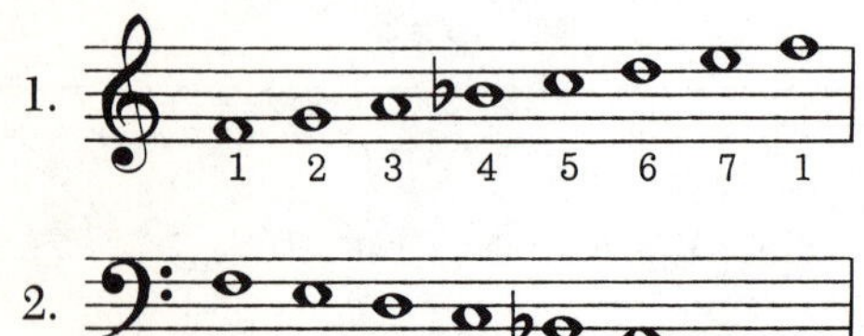

40. Construct the major scale whose first degree is F, ascending and descending. Observe the clefs.

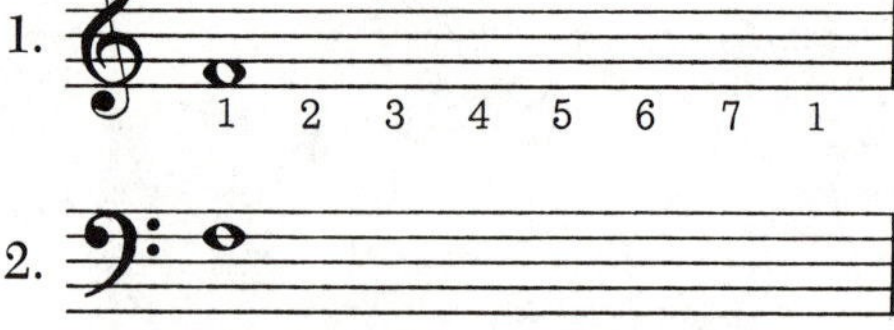

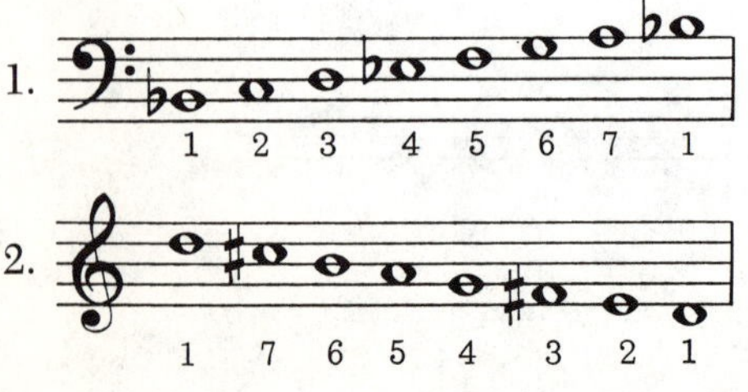

41. Construct the major scales indicated below.

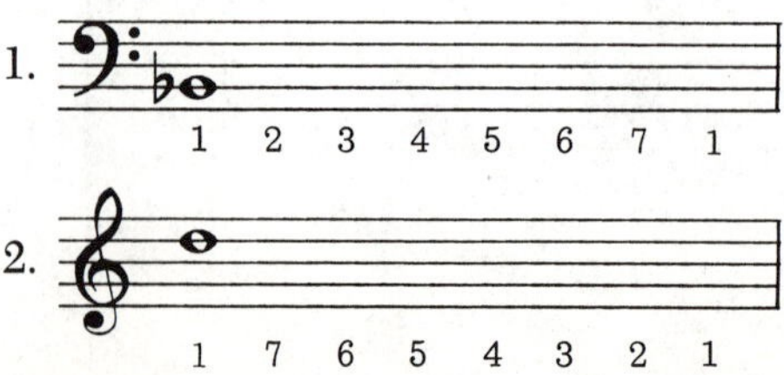

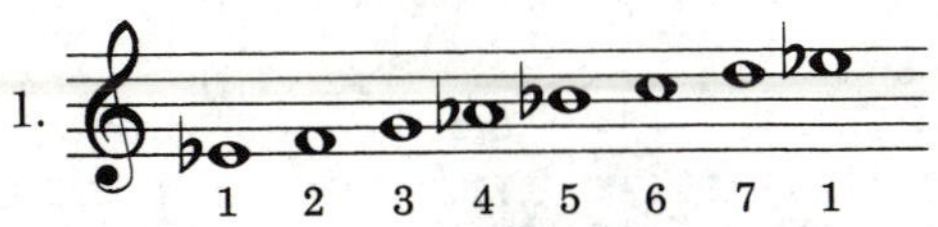

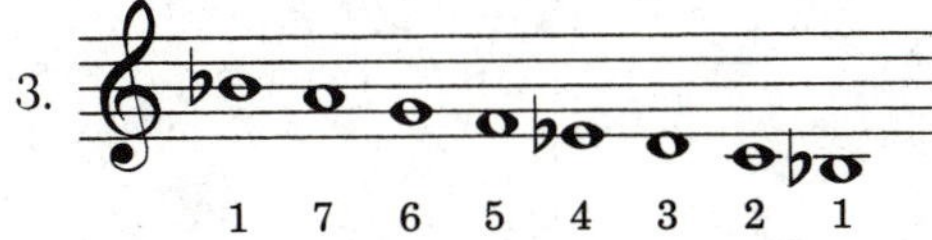

42. Construct the major scales indicated below.

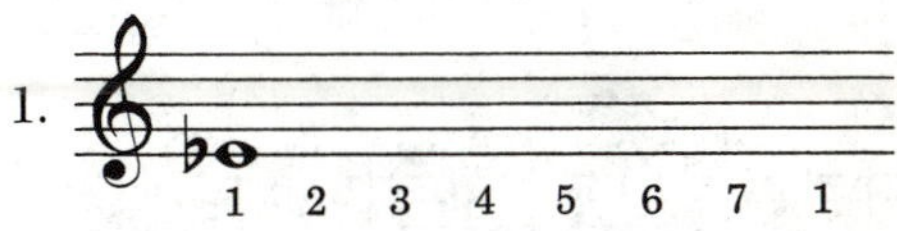

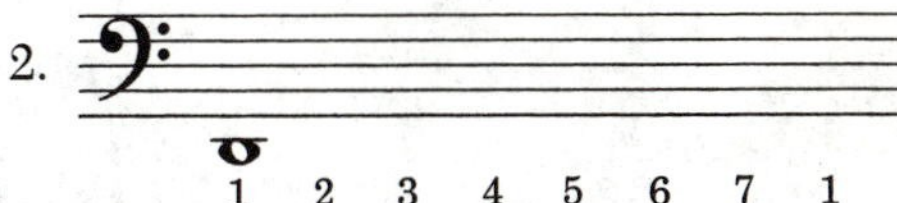

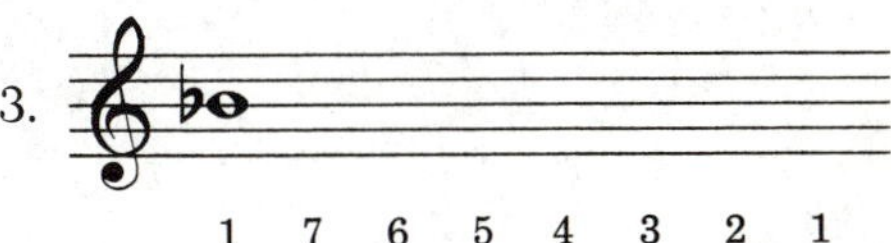

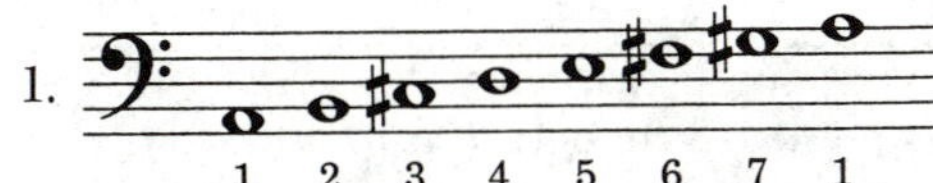

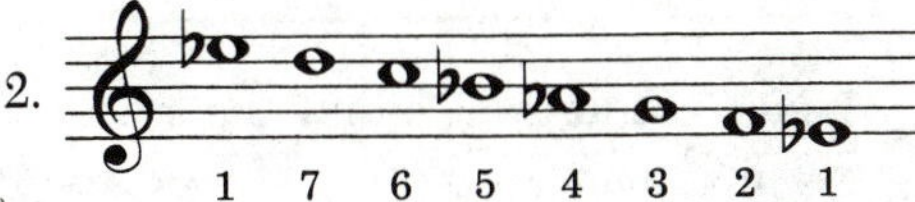

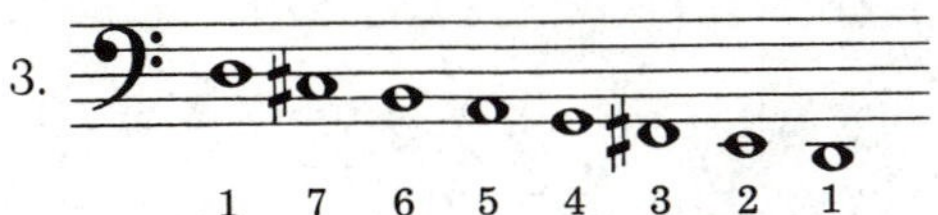

43. Continue as in frame 42.

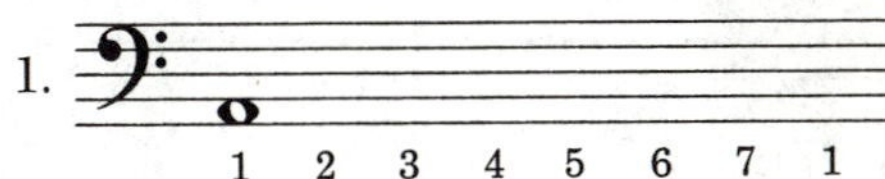

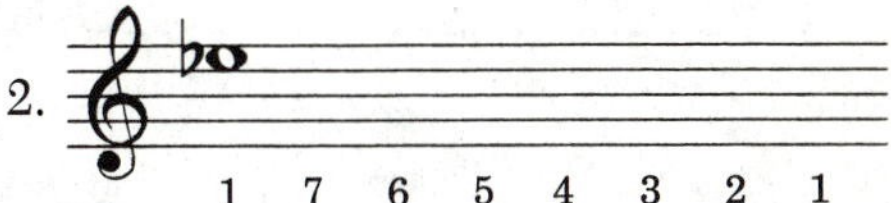

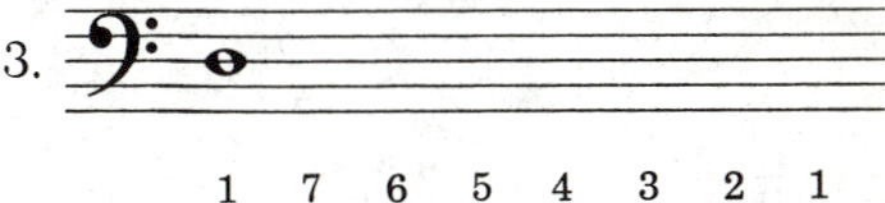

44. Now play at the keyboard all of the scales, half steps, and whole steps appearing in frames 1–43.

LISTENING FRAMES

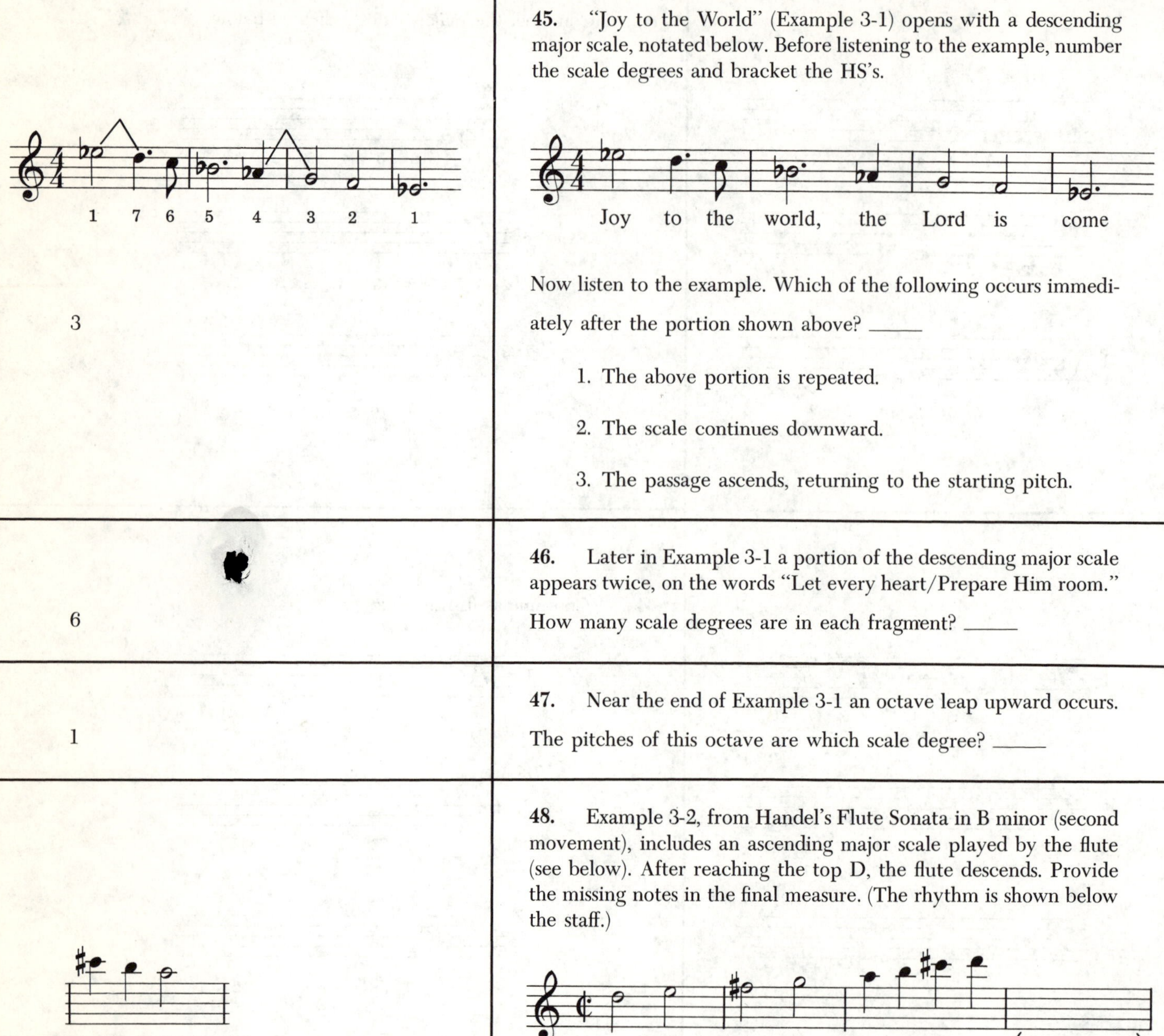

1 7 6 5 4 3 2 1

45. "Joy to the World" (Example 3-1) opens with a descending major scale, notated below. Before listening to the example, number the scale degrees and bracket the HS's.

Joy to the world, the Lord is come

3

Now listen to the example. Which of the following occurs immediately after the portion shown above? _____

1. The above portion is repeated.
2. The scale continues downward.
3. The passage ascends, returning to the starting pitch.

6

46. Later in Example 3-1 a portion of the descending major scale appears twice, on the words "Let every heart/Prepare Him room." How many scale degrees are in each fragment? _____

1

47. Near the end of Example 3-1 an octave leap upward occurs. The pitches of this octave are which scale degree? _____

48. Example 3-2, from Handel's Flute Sonata in B minor (second movement), includes an ascending major scale played by the flute (see below). After reaching the top D, the flute descends. Provide the missing notes in the final measure. (The rhythm is shown below the staff.)

MINOR SCALES

The *minor* scale is usually heard in one of three closely related forms: the *pure* minor scale, the *melodic* minor scale, and the *harmonic* minor scale. All three forms are identical in their first five ascending scale degrees; it is in scale degrees 6 and 7 that the differences are heard. Accordingly, we shall begin our minor scale study with the first five scale degrees, which are common to all forms of minor scales.

major	**49.** The __________ scale has HS's at 3 to 4 and 7 to 1.
2 to 3	Shown below are the first five notes of the *minor* scale. All the scale steps of these first five notes are WS's, with the exception of the HS at _____ to _____. 1 2 3 4 5
1. 1 2 3 4 5 2. 1 2 3 4 5	**50.** Draw HS brackets at the appropriate locations on the examples below. 1. major 1 2 3 4 5 2. minor 1 2 3 4 5
3	The first five scale degrees of the major and minor scales are the same, except for scale degree _____.
3 to 4	**51.** In the first five scale degrees of the major scale, the HS is found at scale step _____ to _____.
2 to 3	Scale degrees 1 to 5 of the minor scale contain a HS at scale step _____ to _____.
2 to 3 1 2 3 4 5	**52.** Write the first five notes of the minor scale which begins on D. Where is the HS located? _____ to _____. Place a HS bracket at the appropriate location. 1 2 3 4 5

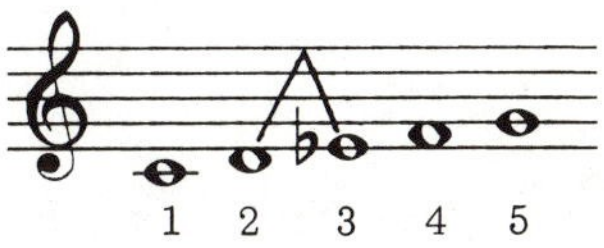

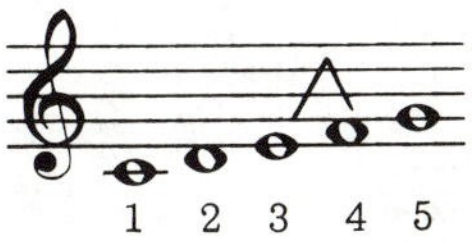

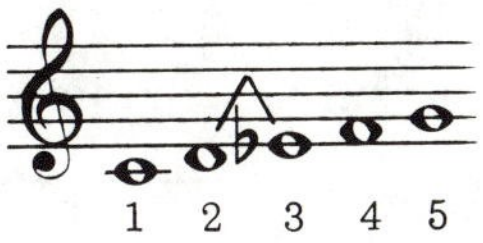

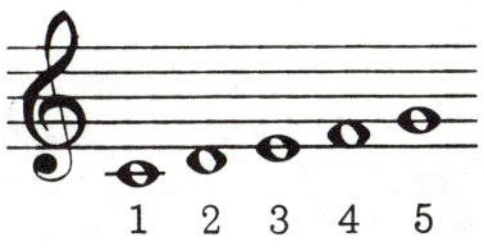

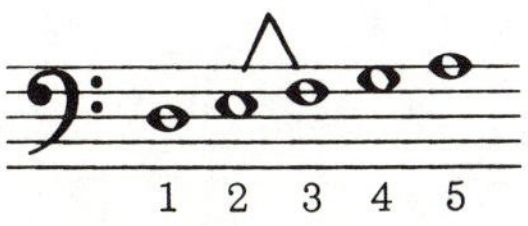

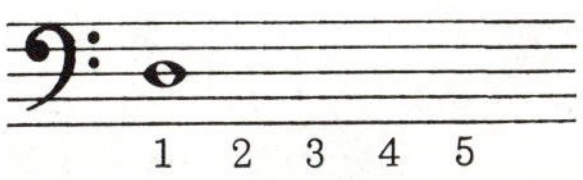

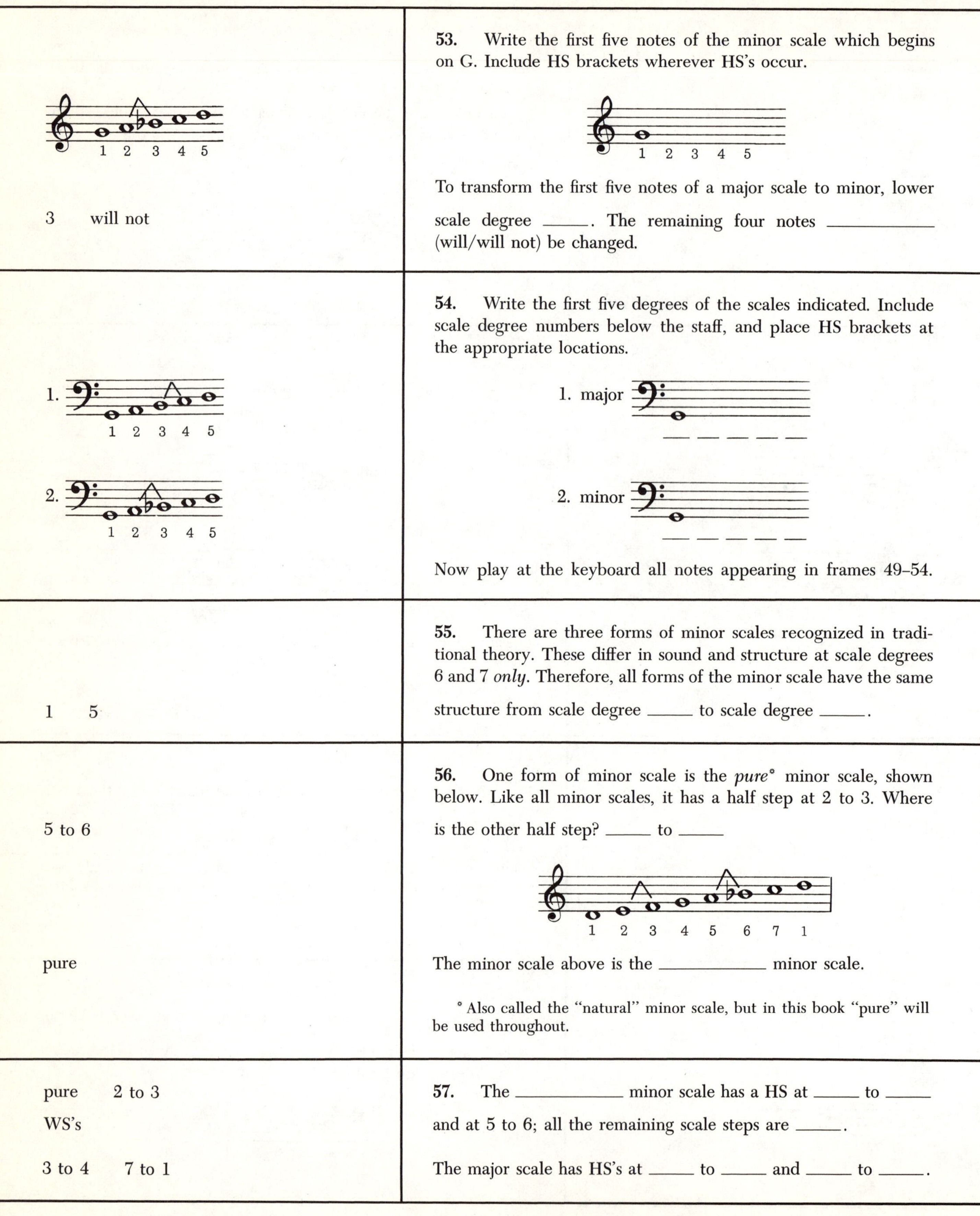

1 2 3 4 5

3 will not

53. Write the first five notes of the minor scale which begins on G. Include HS brackets wherever HS's occur.

1 2 3 4 5

To transform the first five notes of a major scale to minor, lower scale degree ____. The remaining four notes __________ (will/will not) be changed.

1\. 1 2 3 4 5

2\. 1 2 3 4 5

54. Write the first five degrees of the scales indicated. Include scale degree numbers below the staff, and place HS brackets at the appropriate locations.

1\. major

2\. minor

Now play at the keyboard all notes appearing in frames 49–54.

---

1 5

55. There are three forms of minor scales recognized in traditional theory. These differ in sound and structure at scale degrees 6 and 7 *only*. Therefore, all forms of the minor scale have the same structure from scale degree ____ to scale degree ____.

---

5 to 6

pure

56. One form of minor scale is the *pure** minor scale, shown below. Like all minor scales, it has a half step at 2 to 3. Where is the other half step? ____ to ____

1 2 3 4 5 6 7 1

The minor scale above is the __________ minor scale.

* Also called the "natural" minor scale, but in this book "pure" will be used throughout.

---

pure 2 to 3

WS's

3 to 4 7 to 1

57. The __________ minor scale has a HS at ____ to ____ and at 5 to 6; all the remaining scale steps are ____.

The major scale has HS's at ____ to ____ and ____ to ____.

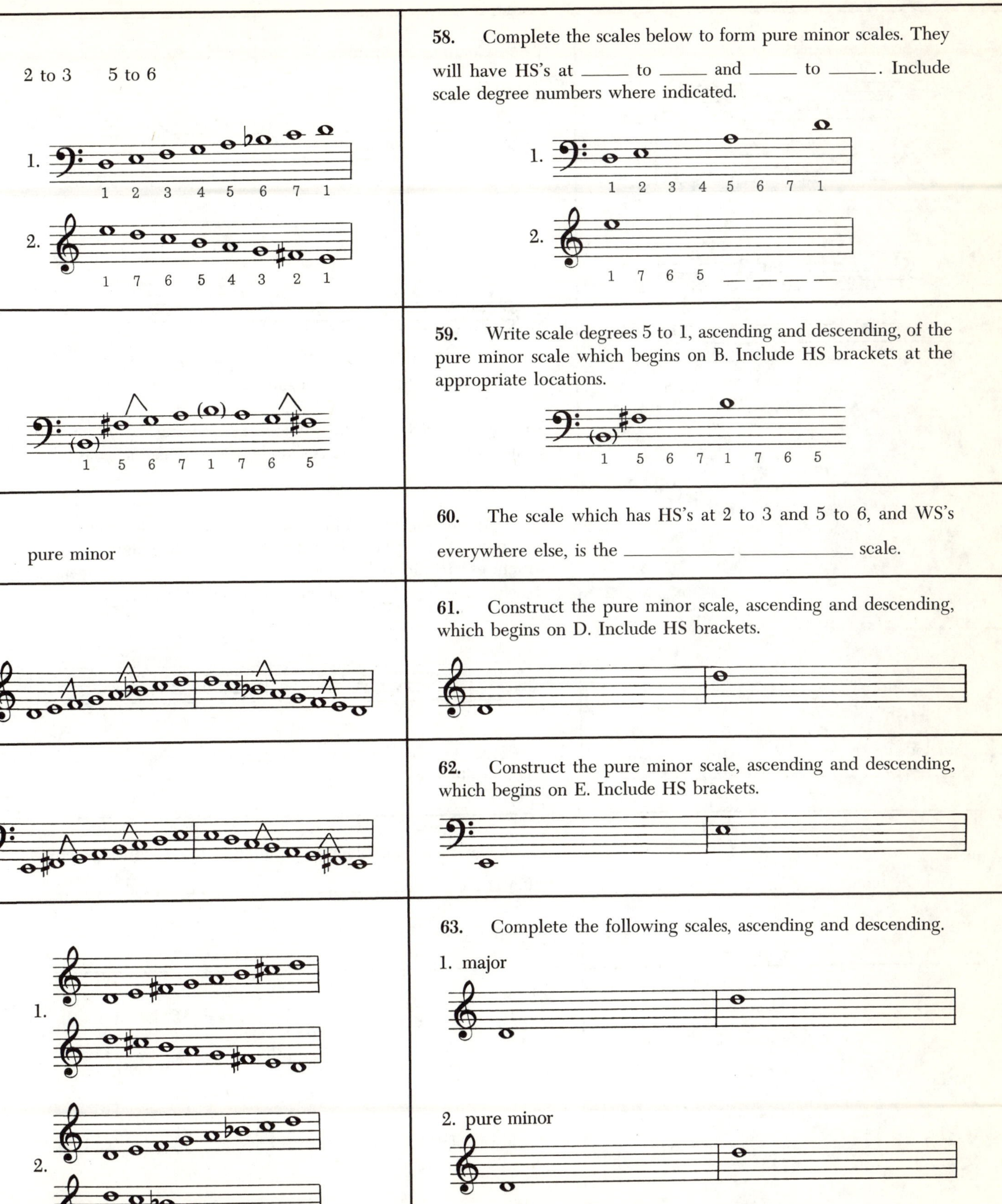

2 to 3   5 to 6

1. 1 2 3 4 5 6 7 1

2. 1 7 6 5 4 3 2 1

58. Complete the scales below to form pure minor scales. They will have HS's at _____ to _____ and _____ to _____. Include scale degree numbers where indicated.

1. 1 2 3 4 5 6 7 1

2. 1 7 6 5 __ __ __ __

1 5 6 7 1 7 6 5

59. Write scale degrees 5 to 1, ascending and descending, of the pure minor scale which begins on B. Include HS brackets at the appropriate locations.

1 5 6 7 1 7 6 5

pure minor

60. The scale which has HS's at 2 to 3 and 5 to 6, and WS's everywhere else, is the __________ __________ scale.

61. Construct the pure minor scale, ascending and descending, which begins on D. Include HS brackets.

62. Construct the pure minor scale, ascending and descending, which begins on E. Include HS brackets.

1.

2.

63. Complete the following scales, ascending and descending.

1. major

2. pure minor

1.

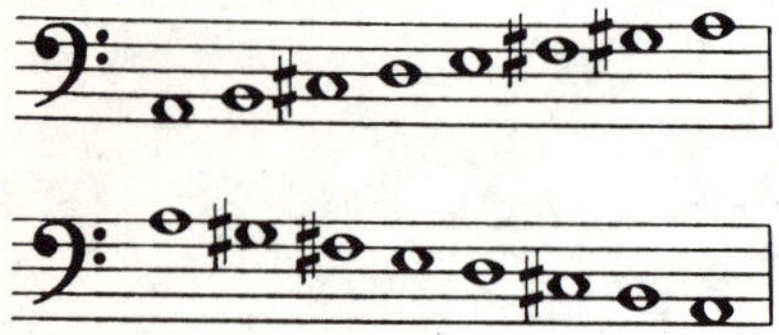

2.

64. Continue as in frame 63.

1. major

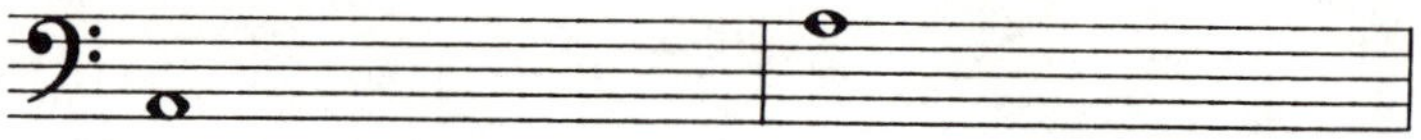

2. pure minor

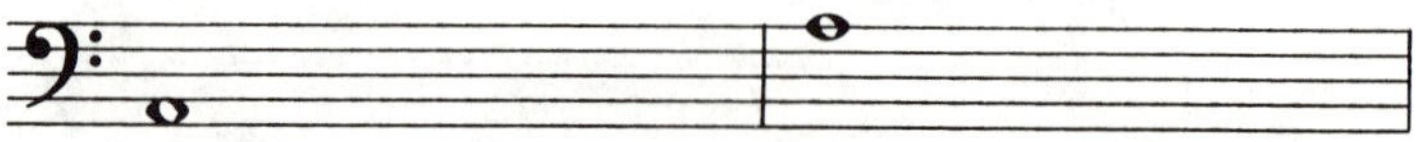

Now at the keyboard play all scales appearing in frames 55–64, listening closely to their similarities and differences.

You will find it extremely helpful to refer to the keyboard frequently while working through the remainder of this chapter.

---

melodic

65. Another form of minor scale is the *melodic* minor scale, shown below. It is the only scale whose ascending and descending structures are different: scale degrees 6 and 7 in the ascending structure are *higher* than in the descending structure.

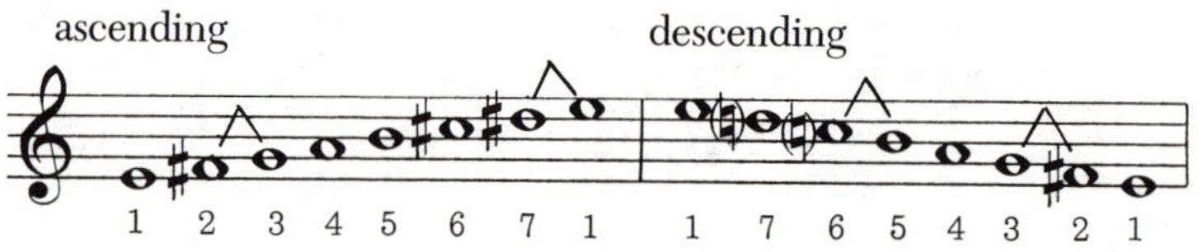

ascending descending

1 2 3 4 5 6 7 1 1 7 6 5 4 3 2 1

The ascending and descending structures of the __________ minor scale differ.

---

melodic minor

2 to 3

66. The minor scale whose ascending and descending structures differ is the __________ __________ scale.

All minor scales have a HS at _____ to _____.

---

2 to 3 7 to 1

3

67.

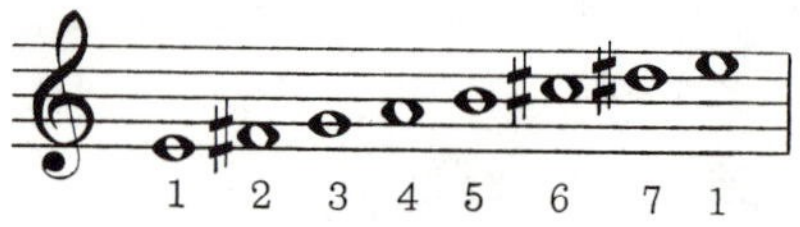

1 2 3 4 5 6 7 1

Shown above is the ascending structure of the melodic minor scale.

It consists of WS's, except for HS's at _____ to _____ and _____ to _____.

It is identical to the major scale except for scale degree _____.

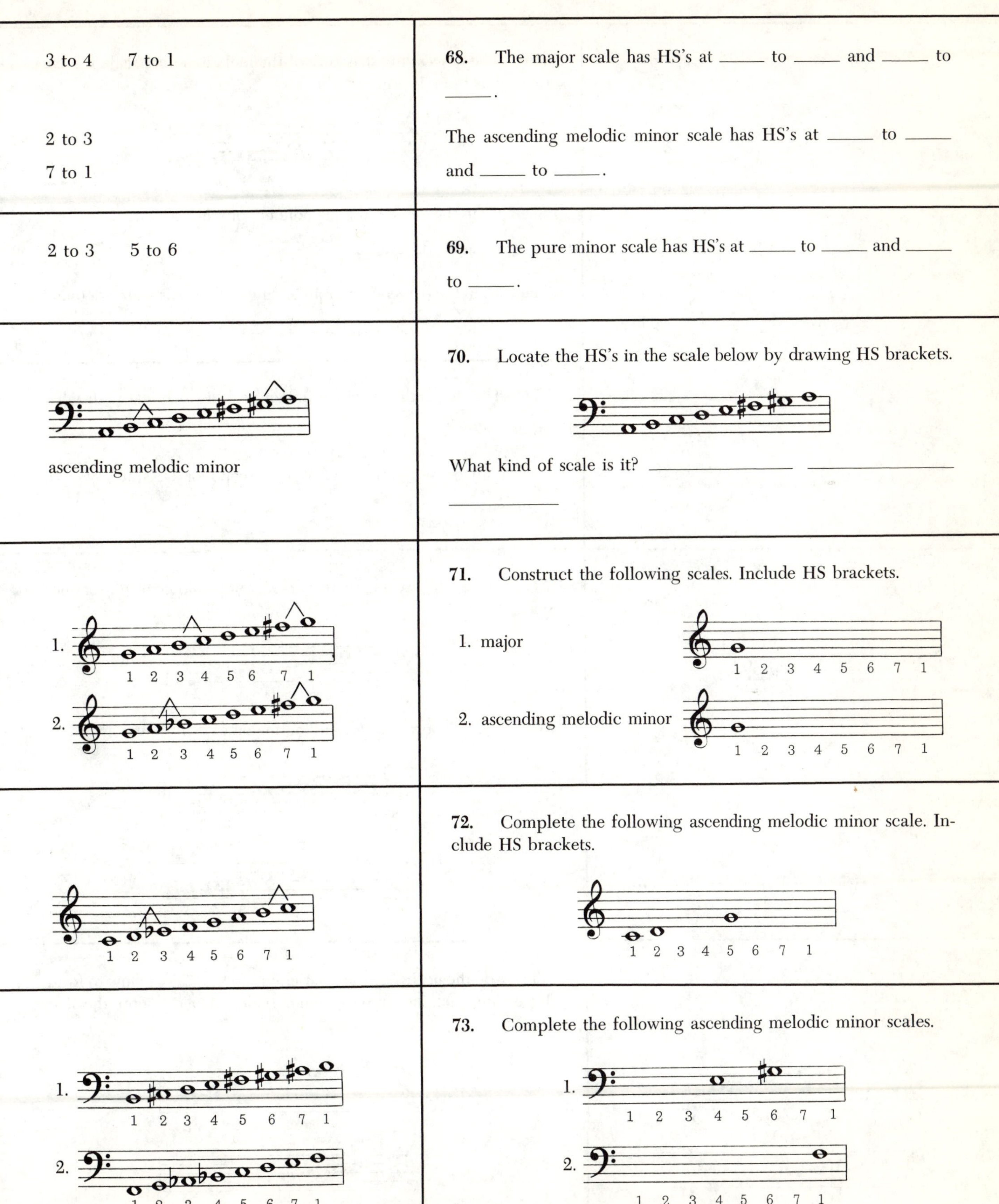

3 to 4 7 to 1

68. The major scale has HS's at ____ to ____ and ____ to ____.

2 to 3
7 to 1

The ascending melodic minor scale has HS's at ____ to ____ and ____ to ____.

2 to 3 5 to 6

69. The pure minor scale has HS's at ____ to ____ and ____ to ____.

ascending melodic minor

70. Locate the HS's in the scale below by drawing HS brackets.

What kind of scale is it? ________ ________ ________

1. 1 2 3 4 5 6 7 1
2. 1 2 3 4 5 6 7 1

71. Construct the following scales. Include HS brackets.

1. major 1 2 3 4 5 6 7 1
2. ascending melodic minor 1 2 3 4 5 6 7 1

1 2 3 4 5 6 7 1

72. Complete the following ascending melodic minor scale. Include HS brackets.

1 2 3 4 5 6 7 1

1. 1 2 3 4 5 6 7 1
2. 1 2 3 4 5 6 7 1

73. Complete the following ascending melodic minor scales.

1. 1 2 3 4 5 6 7 1
2. 1 2 3 4 5 6 7 1

74. The *descending* structure of the melodic minor scale is identical with the pure minor scale.

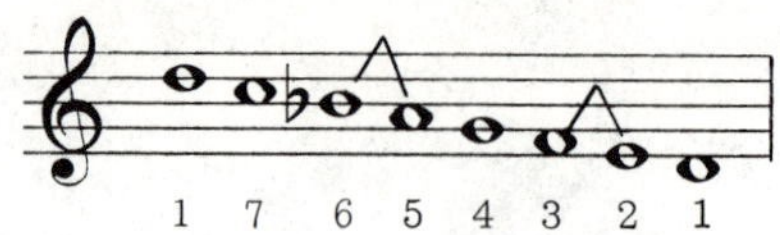

The HS's in the descending melodic minor scale are found at _____ to _____ and _____ to _____.

6 to 5 (or 5 to 6)   3 to 2 (or 2 to 3)

The HS's in the descending or ascending pure minor scale are found at _____ to _____ and _____ to _____.

2 to 3   5 to 6

---

75. The descending melodic minor scale is identical with what other scale? ____________ ____________

pure minor

They both consist entirely of WS's, except for HS's at _____ to _____ and _____ to _____.

2 to 3 (or 3 to 2)
5 to 6 (or 6 to 5)

---

76. Place HS brackets on this descending melodic or pure minor scale.

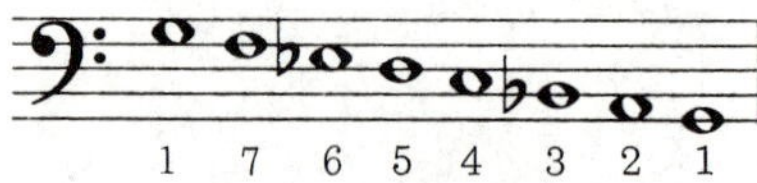

Which scale below is a descending melodic or pure minor? _____

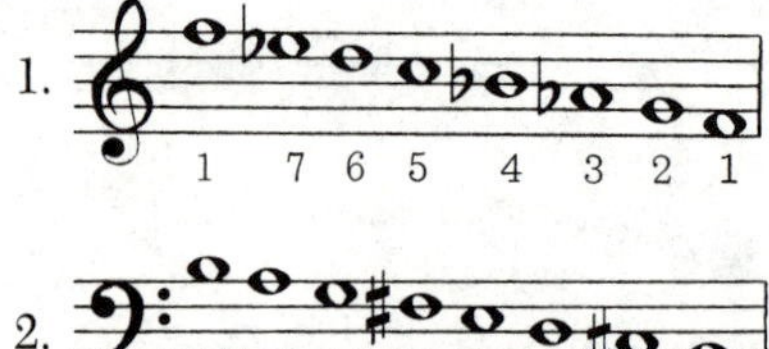

2

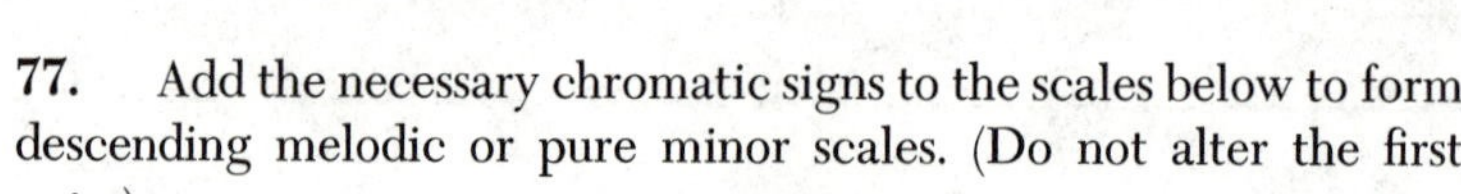

77. Add the necessary chromatic signs to the scales below to form descending melodic or pure minor scales. (Do not alter the first note.)

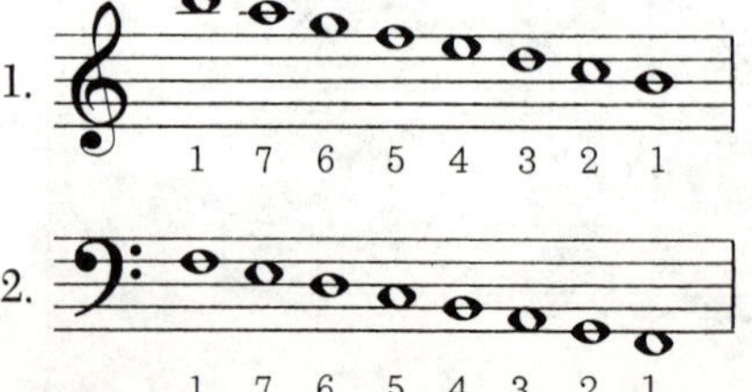

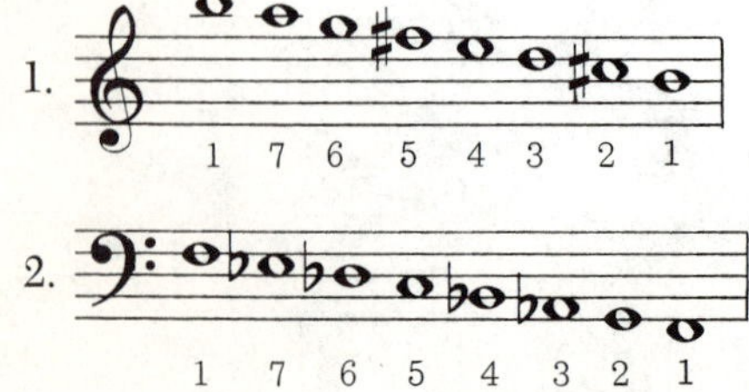

2 to 3

7 to 1

6 to 5 (or 5 to 6)

3 to 2 (or 2 to 3)

78. The ascending melodic minor scale has HS's at _____ to _____ and _____ to _____.

The descending melodic minor scale has HS's at _____ to _____ and _____ to _____.

Naturals and other chromatic signs in parentheses (♮) are sometimes placed before notes involving unusual or unexpected chromatic alterations to prevent misreading. Sometimes called "courtesy accidentals," their use is optional.

1 2 3 4 5 6 7 1 1 7 6 5 4 3 2 1

79. Construct the melodic minor scale, ascending and descending, which begins on D. Include scale degree numbers and HS brackets.

1 1

1 2 3 4 5 6 7 1

80. Complete the following melodic minor scale, ascending and descending. Include HS brackets.

1 2 3 4 5 6 7 1

81. Complete the following melodic minor scale, ascending and descending.

82. Add the necessary accidentals to the scale below to form a melodic minor scale. (Do not alter the first scale degree.)

1. pure minor

2. major

3. pure minor

4. melodic minor

83. Indicate whether the scales below are major, pure minor, or melodic minor.

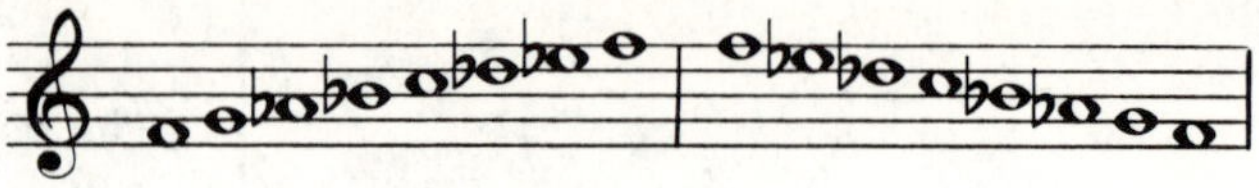

1. ____________________

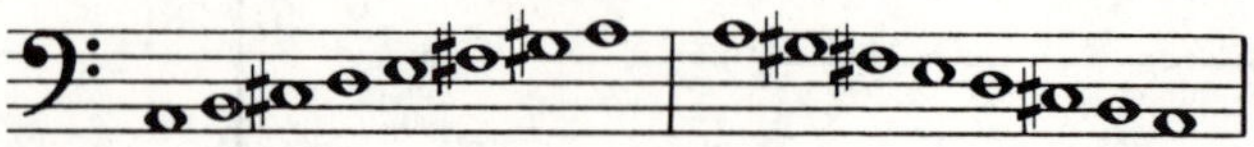

2. ____________________

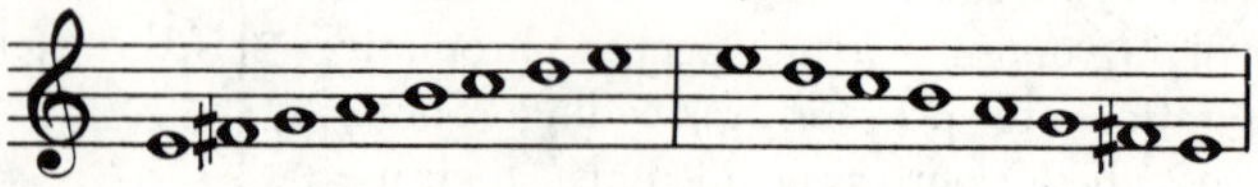

3. ____________________

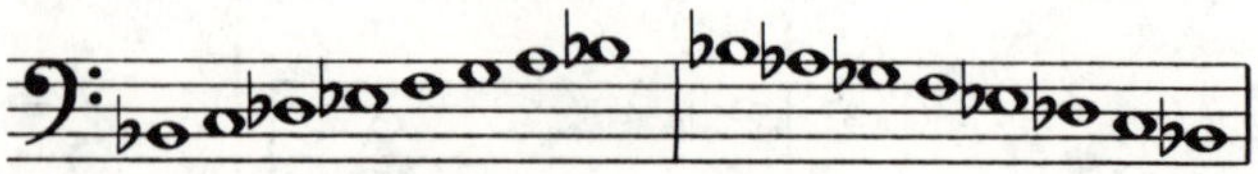

4. ____________________

---

pure melodic
(either order)
2 to 3

84. The two forms of minor scales covered thus far are the ____________ minor and the ____________ minor scales.

All minor scales have a HS at _____ to _____.

---

6 7

descending

85. The scale degrees which differ in the ascending and descending structures of the melodic minor scale are _____ and _____.

The ____________________ melodic minor scale is constructed exactly like the pure minor scale.

---

2 to 3

5 to 6 7 to 1

86. The third form of minor scale is the *harmonic* minor scale, shown below. Where are the HS locations? _____ to _____, _____ to _____, and _____ to _____.

1 2 3 4 5 6 7 1 1 7 6 5 4 3 2 1

Notice that the harmonic minor scale's ascending and descending structures are the same.

Answers	Frames
harmonic	**87.** The minor scale which has HS's at 2 to 3, 5 to 6, and 7 to 1 is the ________________ minor scale.
HS	The distance spanned by every two adjacent keys on the keyboard is a _____.
WS	Two successive HS's form one _____.
 1 2 3 4 5 6 7 1	**88.** Place HS brackets at the appropriate locations in this harmonic minor scale. 1 2 3 4 5 6 7 1
three	How many HS's separate scale degrees 6 and 7? ____________
HS	This is the equivalent of one WS plus one _____.
	89. Notice that the harmonic minor is the only scale of the three which contains three sizes of scale steps: HS, WS, and HS + WS. 1 2 3 4 5 6 7 1
6 to 7	What is the scale step location of the HS + WS? _____ to _____
three	**90.** How many sizes of scale steps does the harmonic minor scale contain? ____________
1 2 3 4 5 6 7 1	Complete the harmonic minor scale below. Include HS brackets. 1 2 3 4 5 6 7 1
are	**91.** The ascending and descending structures of the harmonic minor scale ____________ (are, are not) the same.
2 to 3 5 to 6 7 to 1 6 to 7	**92.** The HS's in harmonic minor scales are located at scale steps _____ to _____, _____ to _____, and _____ to _____; the HS + WS is located at _____ to _____.
WS's	All the remaining scale steps are _____.

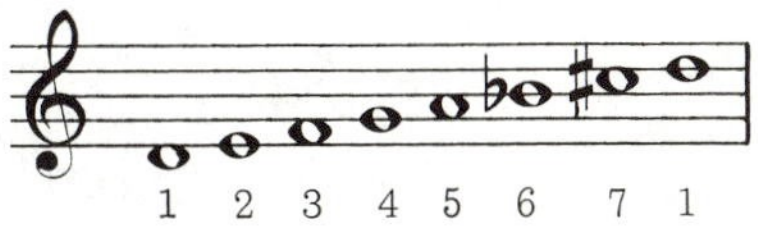

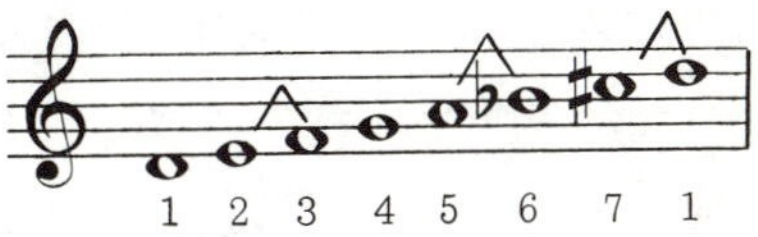

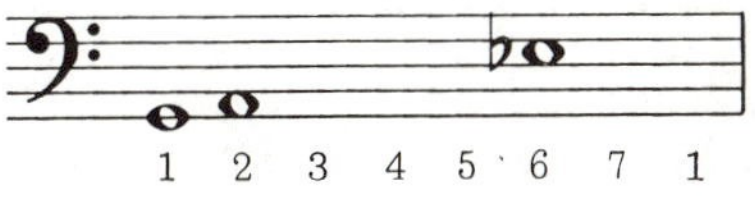

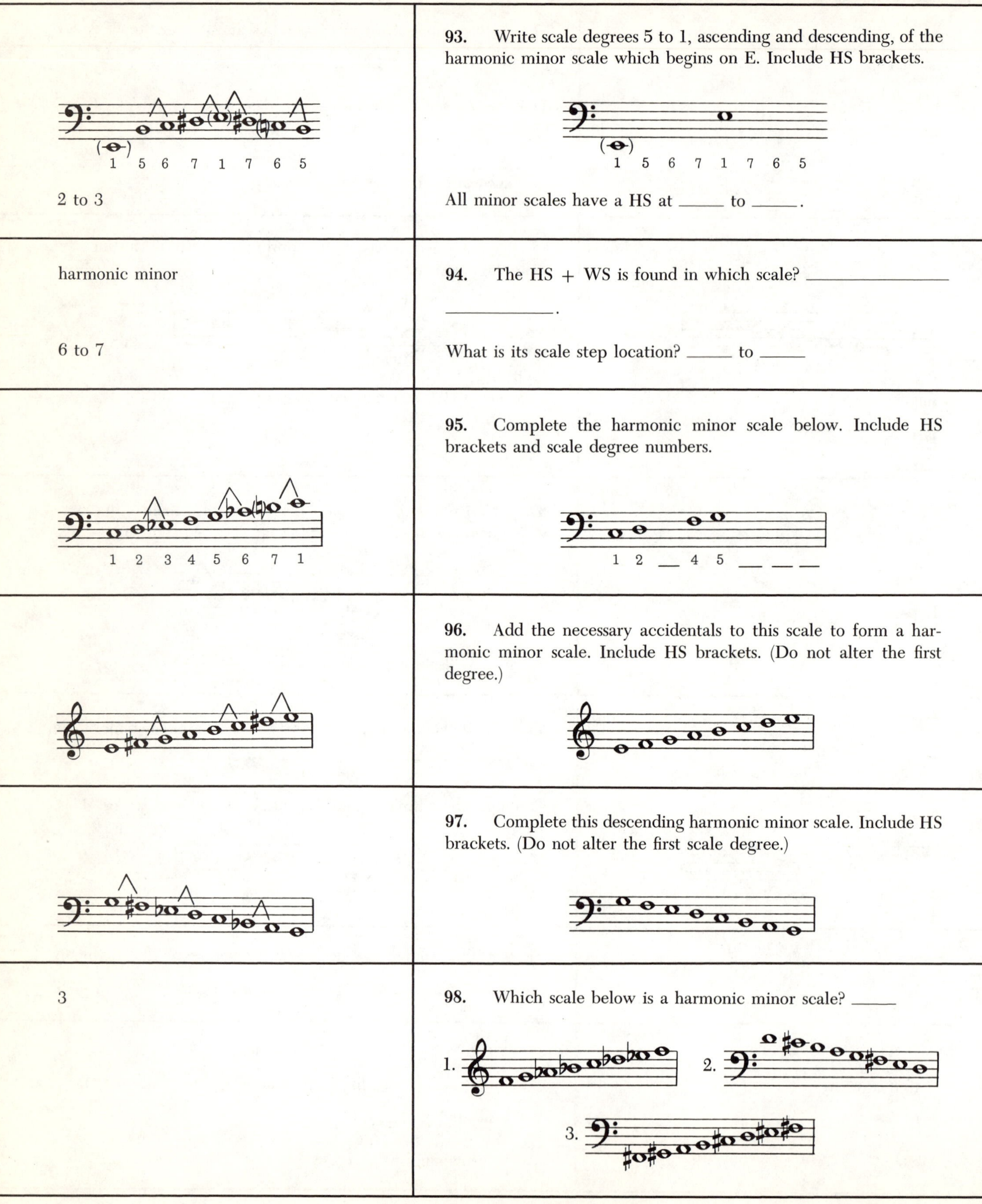

2 to 3

93. Write scale degrees 5 to 1, ascending and descending, of the harmonic minor scale which begins on E. Include HS brackets.

All minor scales have a HS at _____ to _____.

harmonic minor

6 to 7

94. The HS + WS is found in which scale? _______________ _____________.

What is its scale step location? _____ to _____

95. Complete the harmonic minor scale below. Include HS brackets and scale degree numbers.

96. Add the necessary accidentals to this scale to form a harmonic minor scale. Include HS brackets. (Do not alter the first degree.)

97. Complete this descending harmonic minor scale. Include HS brackets. (Do not alter the first scale degree.)

3

98. Which scale below is a harmonic minor scale? _____

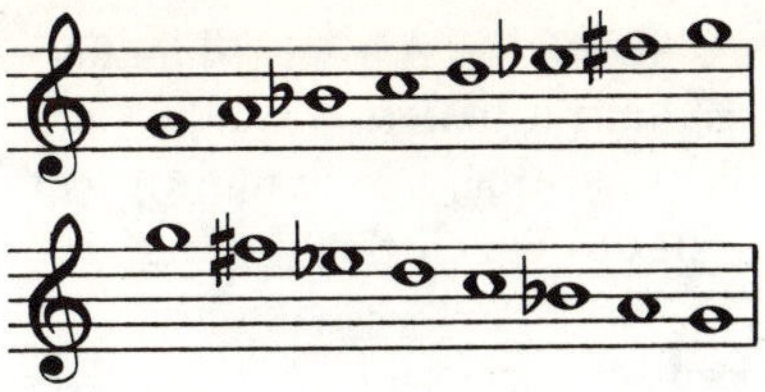

	99. Construct the harmonic minor scale, ascending and descending, which begins on G.
	100. Construct the harmonic minor scale, ascending and descending, which begins on F♯.
major pure minor melodic minor harmonic minor	**101.** The four traditional scales this section has covered are __________, __________ __________, __________ __________, and __________ __________.
1. pure minor 2. harmonic minor 3. major 4. melodic minor	**102.** Identify the following scales. 1. __________ __________ 2. __________ __________ 3. __________ 4. __________ __________
1. harmonic minor 2. major	**103.** Identify the scale form to which each of these fragments belongs. 1. 7 6 __________ __________ 2. 3 4 __________

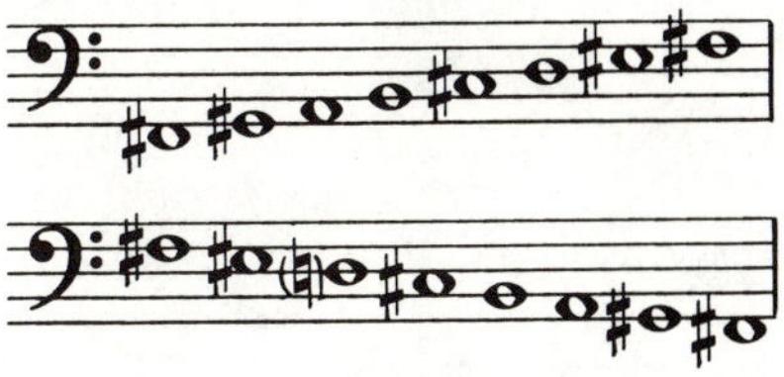

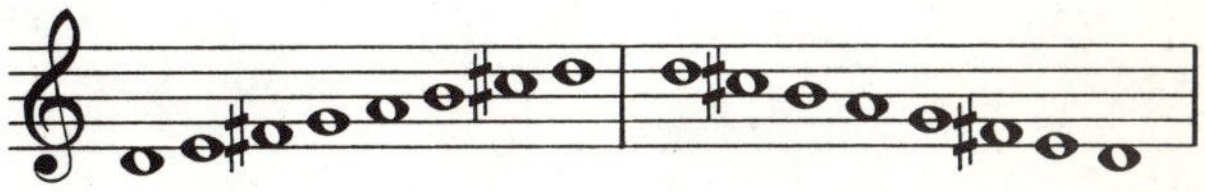

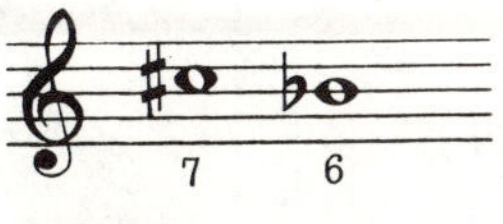

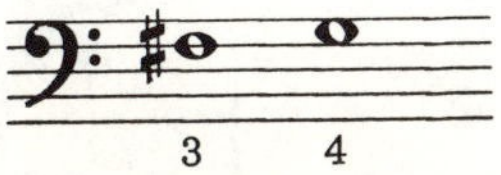

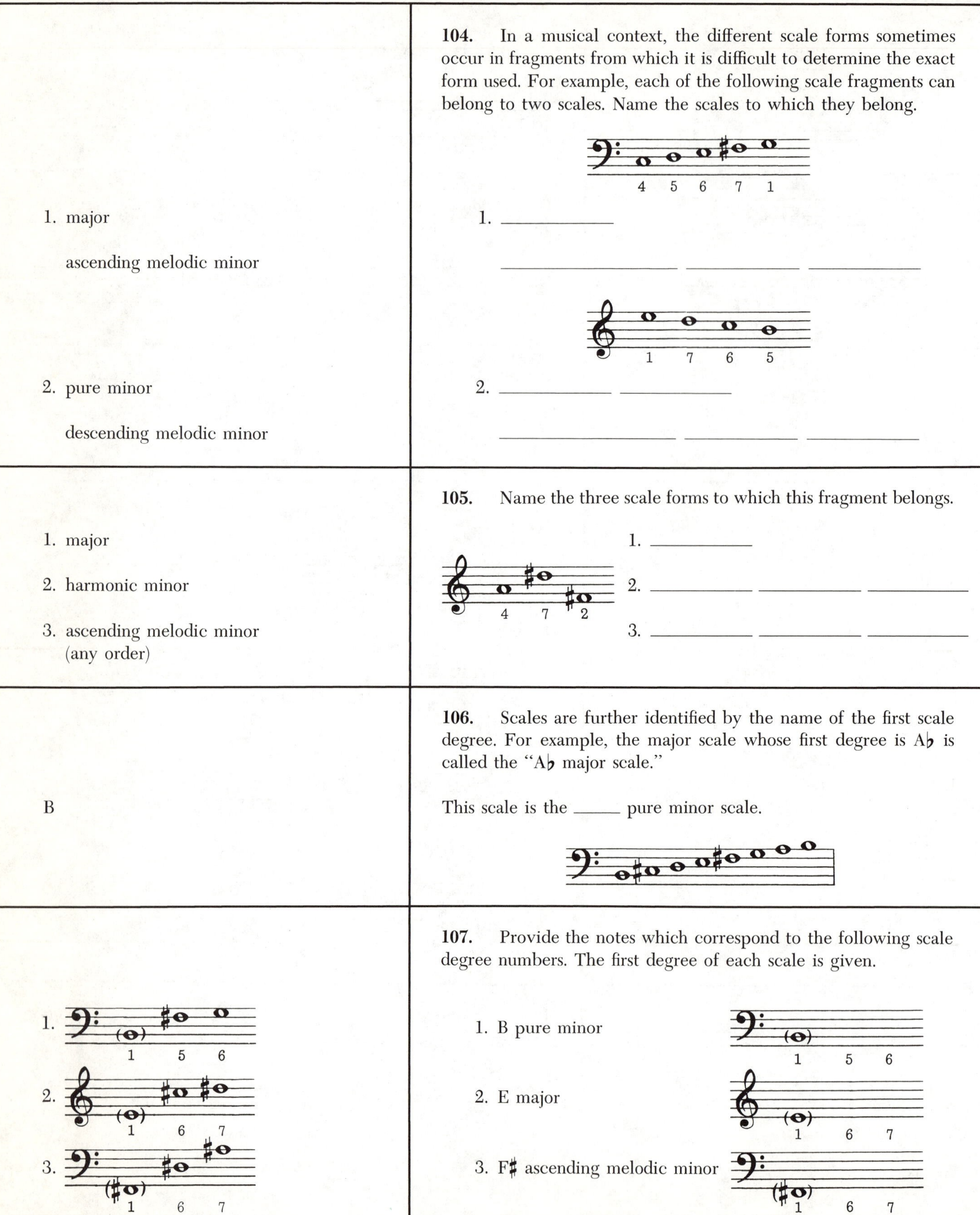

104. In a musical context, the different scale forms sometimes occur in fragments from which it is difficult to determine the exact form used. For example, each of the following scale fragments can belong to two scales. Name the scales to which they belong.

1. ____________

______________ ____________ ____________

2. ____________ ____________

______________ ____________ ____________

1. major

   ascending melodic minor

2. pure minor

   descending melodic minor

105. Name the three scale forms to which this fragment belongs.

1. ____________
2. ____________ ____________ ____________
3. ____________ ____________ ____________

1. major
2. harmonic minor
3. ascending melodic minor (any order)

106. Scales are further identified by the name of the first scale degree. For example, the major scale whose first degree is A♭ is called the "A♭ major scale."

This scale is the _____ pure minor scale.

B

107. Provide the notes which correspond to the following scale degree numbers. The first degree of each scale is given.

1. B pure minor

2. E major

3. F♯ ascending melodic minor

1\.

2\.

3\.

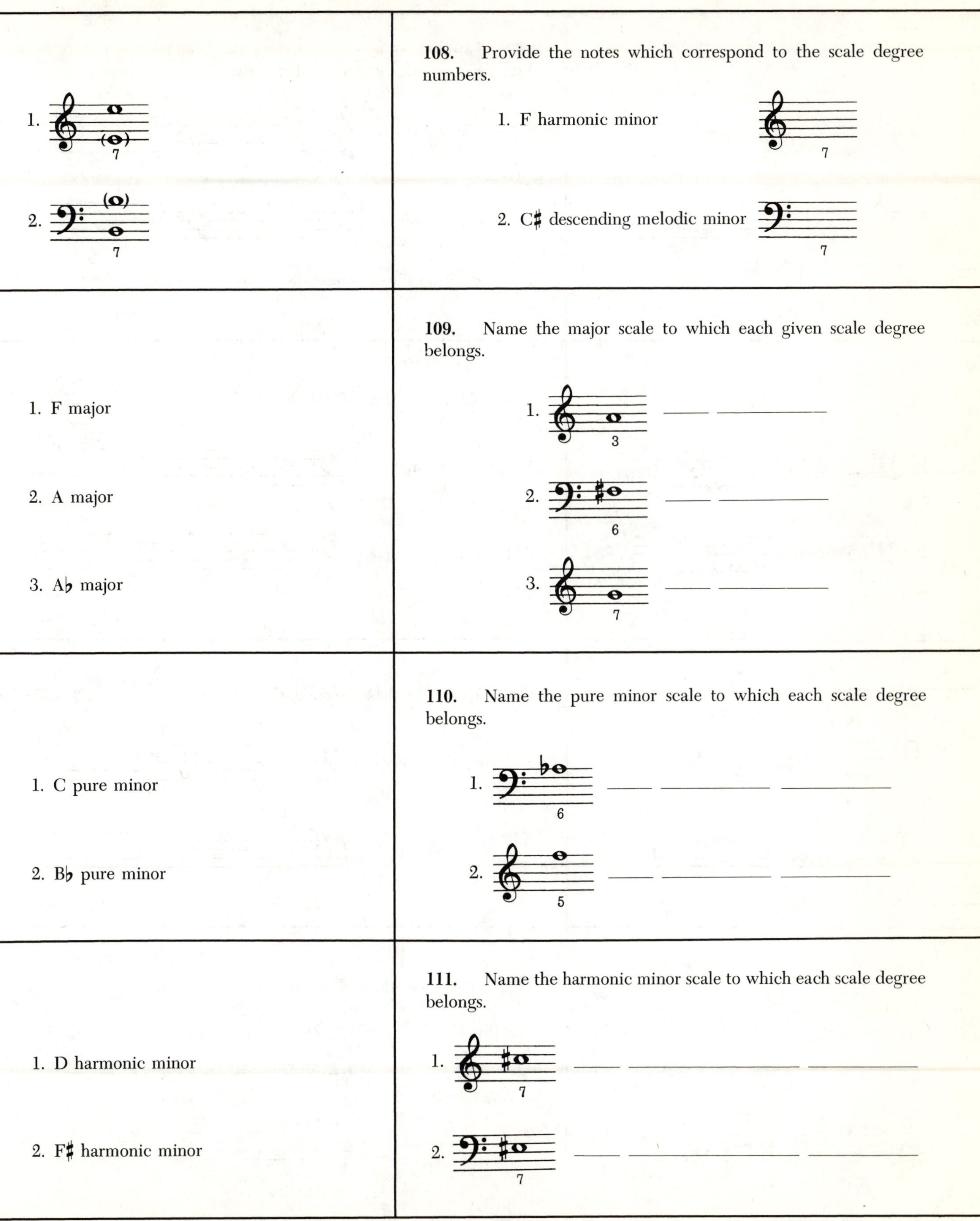

1. (treble clef staff: notes with degree 7)
2. (bass clef staff: notes with degree 7)

108. Provide the notes which correspond to the scale degree numbers.

1. F harmonic minor (7)
2. C♯ descending melodic minor (7)

1. F major
2. A major
3. A♭ major

109. Name the major scale to which each given scale degree belongs.

1. (3) ____ __________
2. (6) ____ __________
3. (7) ____ __________

1. C pure minor
2. B♭ pure minor

110. Name the pure minor scale to which each scale degree belongs.

1. (6) ____ __________ __________
2. (5) ____ __________ __________

1. D harmonic minor
2. F♯ harmonic minor

111. Name the harmonic minor scale to which each scale degree belongs.

1. (7) ____ __________ __________
2. (7) ____ __________ __________

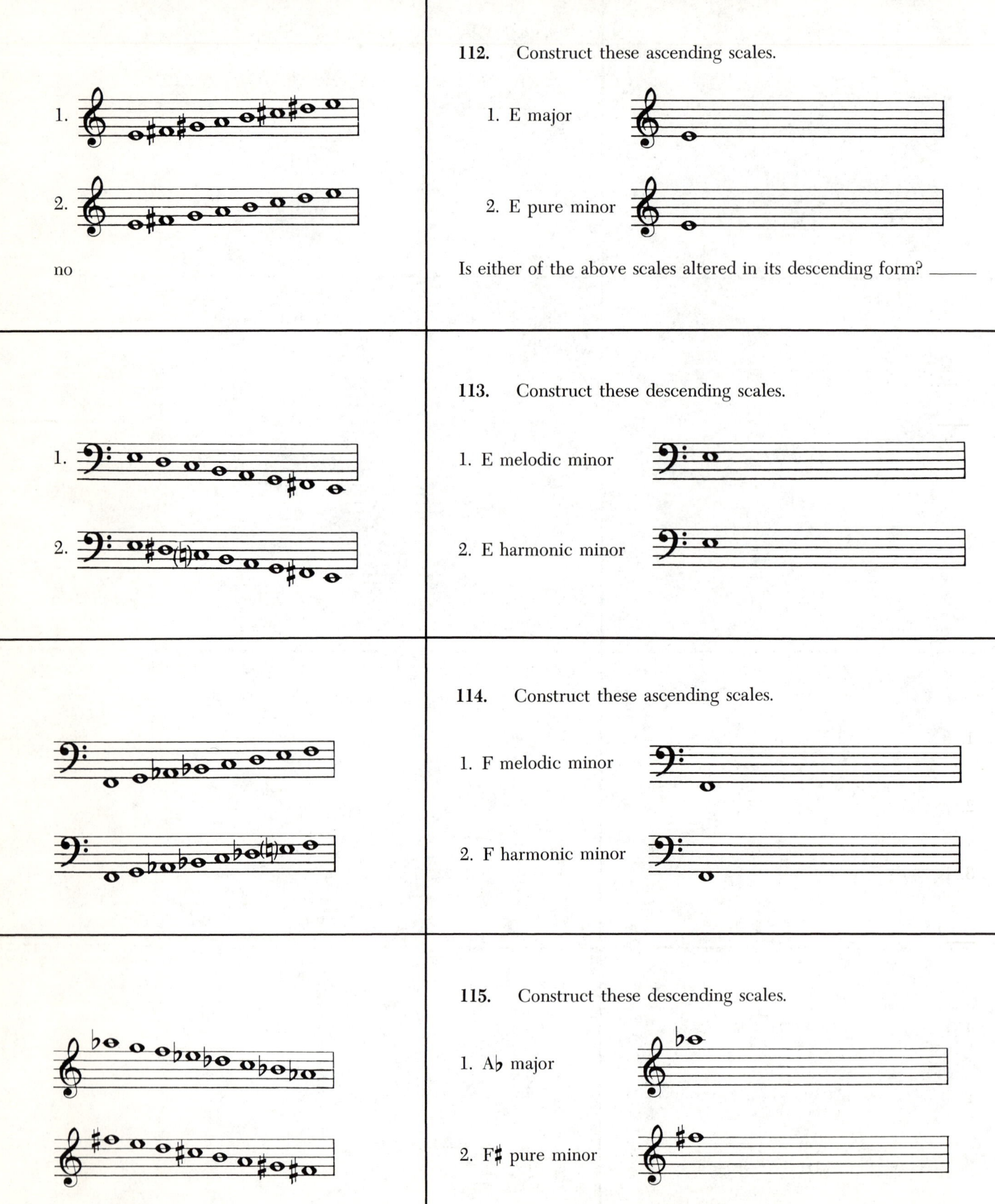
1.
2.
no
112. Construct these ascending scales.
1. E major
2. E pure minor
Is either of the above scales altered in its descending form? ______
1.
2.
113. Construct these descending scales.
1. E melodic minor
2. E harmonic minor
114. Construct these ascending scales.
1. F melodic minor
2. F harmonic minor
115. Construct these descending scales.
1. A♭ major
2. F♯ pure minor

1. F pure minor

2. A major

3. B harmonic minor

4. G melodic minor

116. Identify these scales.

1. ______ ______ ______

2. ______ ______

3. ______ ______ ______

4. ______ ______ ______

---

1. (G) A B C D E F♯ G

2. A B C D E F G♯ A

3. B A G F♯ E D C♯ B

117. Scales also may be "spelled" alphabetically, without direct reference to staff notation. For example, the A major scale (ascending) can be spelled

A B C♯ D E F♯ G♯ A

Note that the pitch names are in alphabetical order, except when returning to "A," just as they are on the staff.

Spell the following scales as indicated. Be sure to include all necessary accidentals.

1. G major (ascending) G ___ ___ ___ ___ ___ ___ ___

2. A harmonic minor (ascending) ___ ___ ___ ___ ___ ___ ___ ___

3. B pure minor (descending) ___ ___ ___ ___ ___ ___ ___ ___

---

1. C♯ D♯ E F♯ G♯ A♯ B♯ C♯

2. A♭ G F E♭ D♭ C B♭ A♭

3. A♭ B♭ C♭ D♭ E♭ F♭ G♭ A♭

118. Spell these scales.

1. C♯ melodic minor (ascending) ___ ___ ___ ___ ___ ___ ___ ___

2. A♭ major (descending) ___ ___ ___ ___ ___ ___ ___ ___

3. A♭ pure minor (ascending) ___ ___ ___ ___ ___ ___ ___ ___

119. Continue as in frame 118.

1. F melodic minor ___ ___ ___ ___ ___ ___ ___ ___
(descending)

2. F pure minor ___ ___ ___ ___ ___ ___ ___ ___
(descending)

3. B major ___ ___ ___ ___ ___ ___ ___ ___
(ascending)

1. F E♭ D♭ C B♭ A♭ G F

2. F E♭ D♭ C B♭ A♭ G F

3. B C♯ D♯ E F♯ G♯ A♯ B

120. Continue as in frame 119.

1. F♯ melodic minor ___ ___ ___ ___ ___ ___ ___ ___
(ascending)

2. F♯ melodic minor ___ ___ ___ ___ ___ ___ ___ ___
(descending)

3. B♭ harmonic minor ___ ___ ___ ___ ___ ___ ___ ___
(descending)

4. G♯ pure minor ___ ___ ___ ___ ___ ___ ___ ___
(ascending)

1. F♯ G♯ A B C♯ D♯ E♯ F♯

2. F♯ E D C♯ B A G♯ F♯

3. B♭ A G♭ F E♭ D♭ C B♭

4. G♯ A♯ B C♯ D♯ E F♯ G♯

121. Play at the keyboard, if you have not already done so, all of the scales introduced thus far in the chapter. Notice particularly their similarities and differences.

LISTENING FRAMES

Scales sometimes occur in their complete form in music (that is, all scale degrees in order of pitch) or continue beyond the single octave. More often, however, fragments of scales are employed, or the scale tones occur in a different order, or chromatic alterations are introduced for interest and variety. Thus, scales may be used unchanged for melodic material, while in a larger sense they serve as a set of tones providing the basic melodic and harmonic pitch material in a composition.

2

122. An interesting use of scales and scale fragments occurs in J. S. Bach's Partita No. 4, first movement (Example 3-3). Immediately following the opening sounds you will hear the piano play a rapidly ascending scale. Which scale form below does Bach use here? _____

1. harmonic minor
2. major
3. melodic minor

HS (A–B♭)

123. In Example 3-4 you will hear the beginning portion of Felix Mendelssohn's Symphony No. 4 ("Italian"), second movement. The orchestra plays a three-measure introduction before the melody shown below is heard. As you listen, count the beats in the first three measures; the melody below enters on the fourth beat of the third measure.

1. In the introduction, the first two pitches form a _____ (HS/WS).
2. Supply the missing notes in the fifth measure, indicated by the bracket. Note that this measure is identical to an earlier measure notated here.

pure (D pure minor; melodies usually end on the first scale degree, but sometimes begin on another scale degree.)

124. The melody in frame 123 uses the notes of which minor scale form? __________

125. Example 3-5 is from the overture to Mozart's opera *Don Giovanni,* shown below. Two of these four measures contain melodic minor scales, ascending and descending. As you study the notation, observe that chromatic signs are omitted from the fourth measure. Listen carefully to the entire excerpt before answering the following questions.

1. Which two measures contain melodic minor scales? _____ and _____ (1/2/3/4)

2. The first one is the _____ (letter name) melodic minor scale. The last one is the _____ melodic minor scale.

3. Complete measure 4 by adding the necessary chromatic signs. The first note should *not* be chromatically altered. (Refer to the answers to the above questions as necessary.)

(The other two scales are major and minor scales chromatically altered to lead gradually upward from the first melodic minor scale to the last.)

1 4

D

G

126. Mozart's Piano Concerto No. 24 (Example 3-6) employs a descending minor scalar passage several times in the first movement. Listen carefully to the whole excerpt as you answer the questions below.

1. Which minor scale form is being used? ____________

2. Does each scalar passage span more than an octave? _____

3. How many scalar passages are played in the example? _____

4. The final tone of each passage is which scale degree? _____

harmonic

yes

four

1

MODES

The major and minor scales, as we have seen, result from dividing the octave into various patterns of whole and half steps. Other patterns are also possible; some of them provided the basic pitch material in the music of our civilization until about 1600, when major and minor scales began to prevail. The earlier scale forms, known as the *Church Modes,* consist of seven basic arrangements of whole and half steps, two of which are identical in structure to the major and pure minor scales.

The Church Modes have a long and complex history, as their names—of ancient Greek origin —suggest: Aeolian, Locrian, Ionian, Dorian, Phrygian, Lydian, and Mixolydian. And they did not pass into oblivion with the predominance of the major and minor scales. On the contrary, a strong modal influence has continued in art music (particularly in sacred music), in folk music, and in blues, jazz, and other recent musical idioms. In fact, modes have never ceased to exert a profound, if sometimes subtle, effect on our entire musical heritage.

As you work through this basic presentation of modes, continue to refer frequently to a piano or other instrument in order to *hear* the modes and to become familiar with their individual qualities.

---

127. Without using chromatic signs, spell an ascending scale from each given note.

1. A: A ____ ____ ____ ____ ____ ____ A
2. B: ____ ____ ____ ____ ____ ____ ____ ____
3. C: ____ ____ ____ ____ ____ ____ ____ ____
4. D: ____ ____ ____ ____ ____ ____ ____ ____
5. E: ____ ____ ____ ____ ____ ____ ____ ____
6. F: ____ ____ ____ ____ ____ ____ ____ ____
7. G: ____ ____ ____ ____ ____ ____ ____ ____

1. (A) B C D E F G (A)
2. B C D E F G A B
3. C D E F G A B C
4. D E F G A B C D
5. E F G A B C D E
6. F G A B C D E F
7. G A B C D E F G

---

128. At the piano, play each scale in frame 127, both ascending and descending. Compare these with scales with which you are already familiar. Two of these seven scales, No. 1 and No. 3, have already been studied earlier in this chapter.

No. 1 is ____________ ____________.

No. 3 is ____________.

pure minor

major

129. The seven scales in frame 127 are known as the seven Church Modes, referred to hereafter simply as "modes." As shown below, they are spelled without chromatic signs, that is, using only the white keys of the piano. Their modal names are:

1. A B C D E F G A: Aeolian
2. B to B: Locrian
3. C to C: Ionian
4. D to D: Dorian
5. E to E: Phrygian
6. F to F: Lydian
7. G to G: Mixolydian

Which mode sounds like the major scale? ____________

Ionian

130. In all modes, the ascending and descending forms are the same.

How many modes are there? ____________

seven

131. Associate the modal names with their white-key structures for the present.

A to A is the Aeolian mode.

Complete the Aeolian mode below.

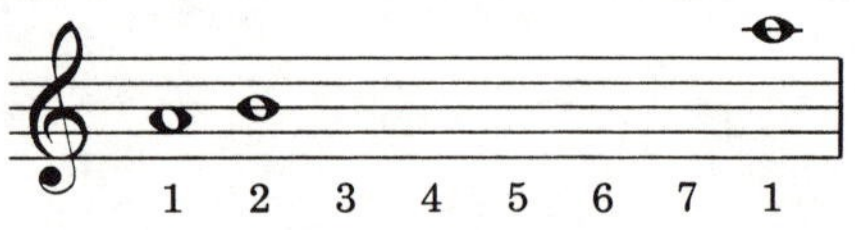

1 2 3 4 5 6 7 1

The Aeolian mode sounds the same as which scale studied previously? ____________ ____________

1 2 3 4 5 6 7 1

pure minor (Although Aeolian sounds like pure minor, and Ionian like major, there are musical and historical reasons, based on musical practice, for maintaining the separate names. For our purposes, simply remember that Aeolian and pure minor have the same scale step structure, as do Ionian and major.)

Dorian

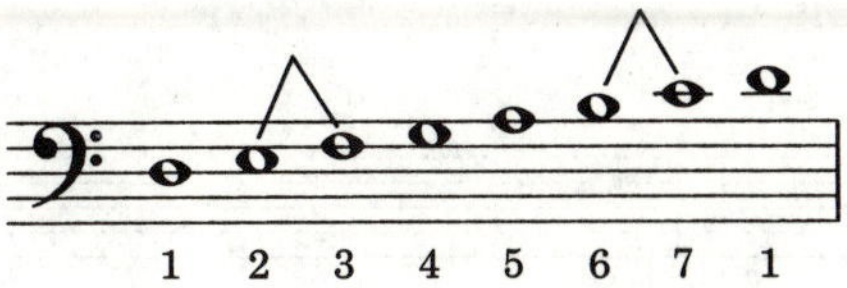

132. Which mode is D to D? ___________ (Refer to frame 129 if necessary.)

Complete the Dorian mode below; then draw HS brackets where appropriate.

1 2 3 4 5 6 7 1

1 2 3 4 5 6 7 1

2 to 3

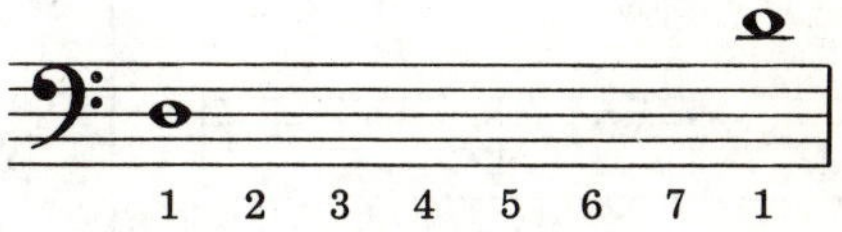

Both Aeolian and Dorian modes have HS's at scale step _____ to _____.

---

133. Identify these modes.

1. 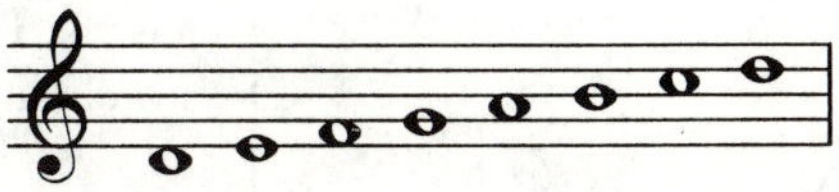 Dorian

1. ___________

2. 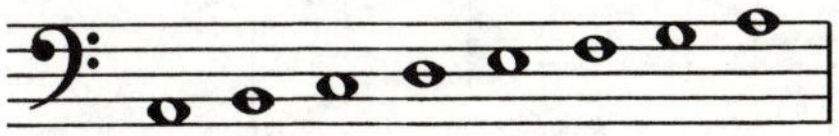 Aeolian

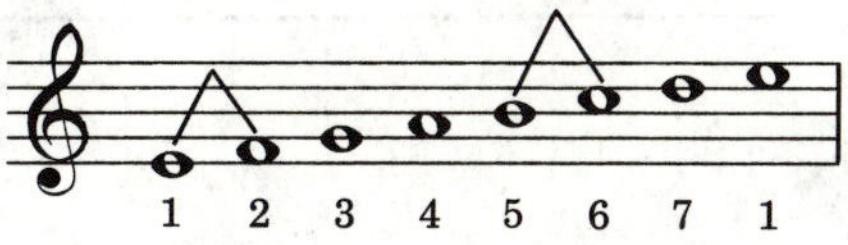

2. ___________

---

134. Draw HS brackets where appropriate over this mode.

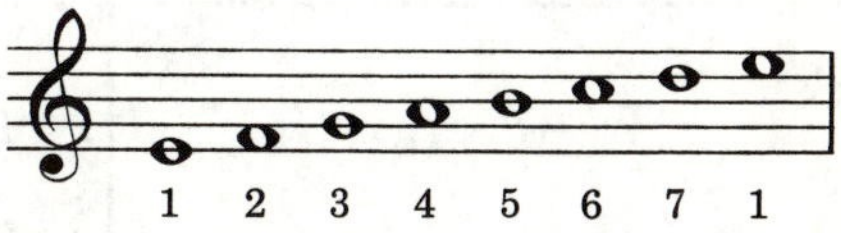

1 2 3 4 5 6 7 1

1 2 3 4 5 6 7 1

2

This is the Phrygian mode. A distinguishing feature of this mode is its HS between scale degrees 1 and _____.

---

135. Identify these modes.

1. Dorian
2. Aeolian
3. Phrygian

1. D to D ___________
2. A to A ___________
3. E to E ___________

the same

In all modes the ascending and descending forms are _______________ (the same/different).

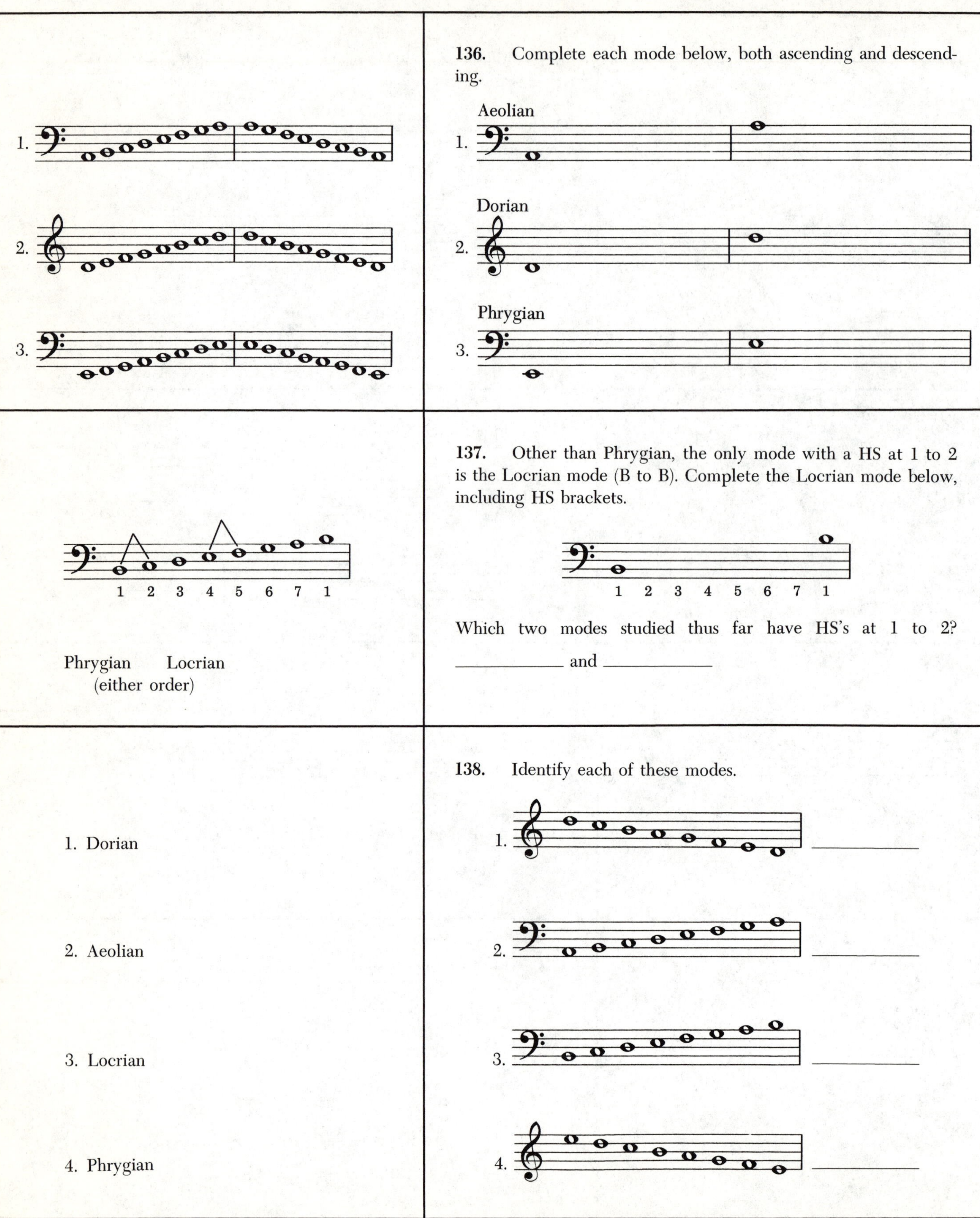

136. Complete each mode below, both ascending and descending.

Phrygian Locrian
(either order)

137. Other than Phrygian, the only mode with a HS at 1 to 2 is the Locrian mode (B to B). Complete the Locrian mode below, including HS brackets.

Which two modes studied thus far have HS's at 1 to 2?

__________ and __________

1. Dorian
2. Aeolian
3. Locrian
4. Phrygian

138. Identify each of these modes.

1. __________
2. __________
3. __________
4. __________

Answers	Frames
1. D 2. E 3. B 4. A	**139.** According to their white-key structures, these modes begin and end on which pitch? 1. Dorian ____ 2. Phrygian ____ 3. Locrian ____ 4. Aeolian ____
3	**140.** The Locrian mode rarely occurs in music, and is sometimes considered only a "theoretical" mode. However, it has very interesting expressive characteristics and therefore deserves inclusion among the modes. Which mode below is Locrian? ____ 1. 2. 3.
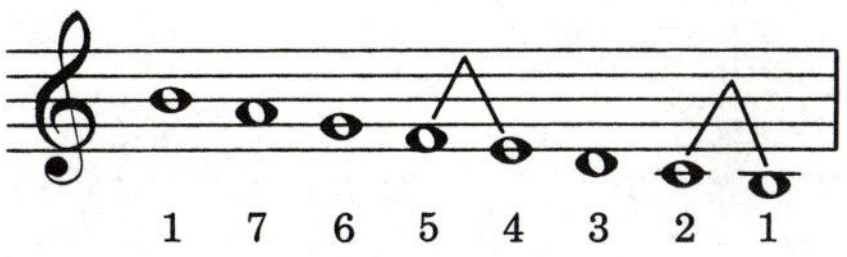 1 7 6 5 4 3 2 1 4 to 5	**141.** Complete the descending Locrian mode below, including HS brackets. 1 7 6 5 4 3 2 1 The Locrian mode is the only mode studied thus far with a HS from ____ to ____.
1. Phrygian 2. Aeolian 3. Locrian 4. Dorian	**142.** Identify these modes. 1. E to E ________ 2. A to A ________ 3. B to B ________ 4. D to D ________

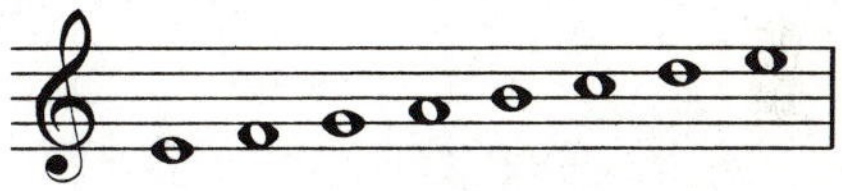

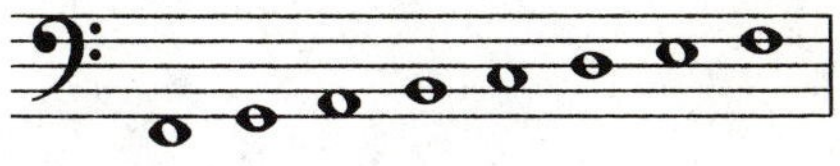

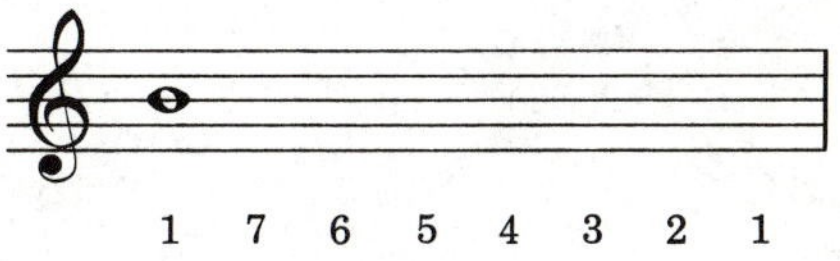

Phrygian Locrian (either order)	**143.** The two modes containing HS's at 1 to 2 are ________ and ________.
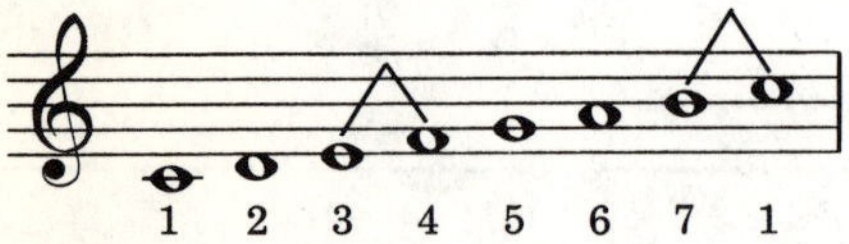 1 2 3 4 5 6 7 1 major	**144.** The mode built from C to C is called Ionian. Complete the Ionian mode below. Include HS brackets. 1 2 3 4 5 6 7 1 The Ionian mode is identical in structure to which scale already studied? ________
Ionian 3 to 4 7 to 1 (either order) 2	**145.** The ________ mode is built from C to C. Like the major scale, it has HS's at ___ to ___ and at ___ to ___. Which mode below is Ionian? ___ 1. 2. 3. 4.
1. Ionian 2. Aeolian 3. Dorian	**146.** Identify these modes. 1. C to C ________ 2. A to A ________ 3. D to D ________
1. E 2. C 3. B 4. D	**147.** According to their white-key structures, these modes begin and end on which pitch? 1. Phrygian ___ 2. Ionian ___ 3. Locrian ___ 4. Dorian ___

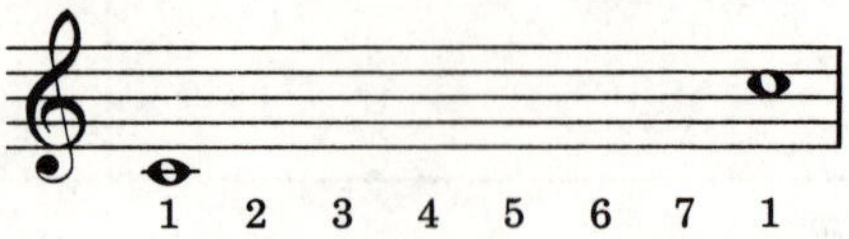

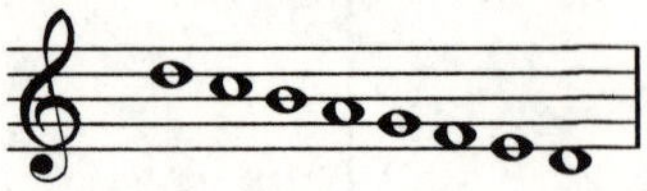

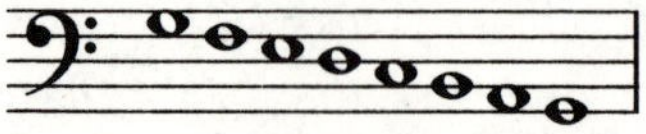

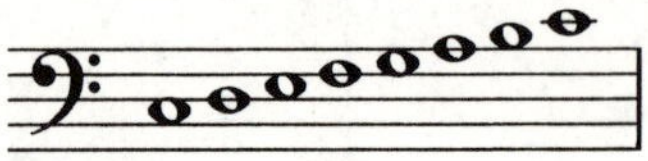

Answers	Frames
1. Ionian 2. Locrian 3. Dorian 4. Aeolian	**148.** Identify each of these modes. 1. ________ 2. ________ 3. ________ 4. ________
1. Aeolian 4. Dorian 2. Locrian 5. Phrygian 3. Ionian	**149.** Shown below in alphabetical order are the beginning pitches of each mode studied thus far. Identify each mode. 1. A ________ 4. D ________ 2. B ________ 5. E ________ 3. C ________
1. 1 2 3 4 5 6 7 1 2. 1 2 3 4 5 6 7 1	**150.** The two remaining modes are Lydian (F to F) and Mixolydian (G to G). Place HS brackets above the Lydian and Mixolydian modes below. 1. 1 2 3 4 5 6 7 1 Lydian 2. 1 2 3 4 5 6 7 1 Mixolydian
Lydian no (Both Lydian and Locrian modes have HS's at 4 to 5.) Mixolydian	**151.** Which mode in frame 150 begins on F? ________ Is Lydian the only mode with a HS at 4 to 5? ______ The mode which begins and ends on G is ________.

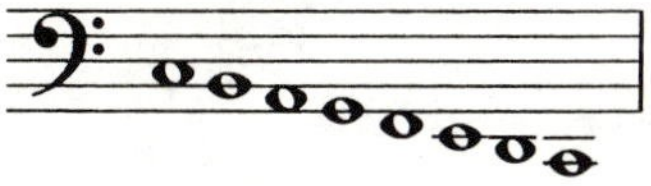

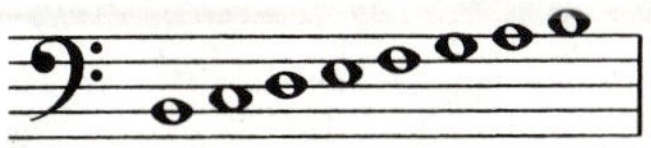

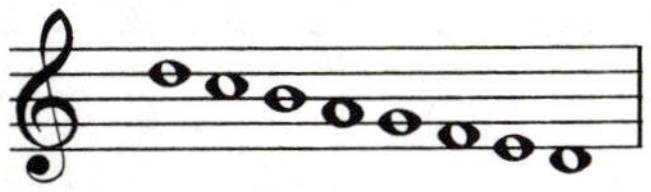

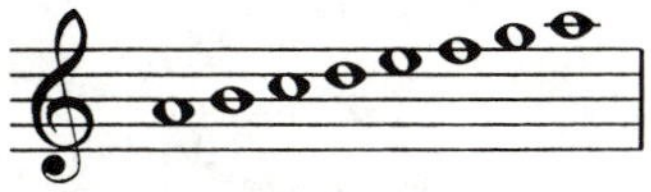

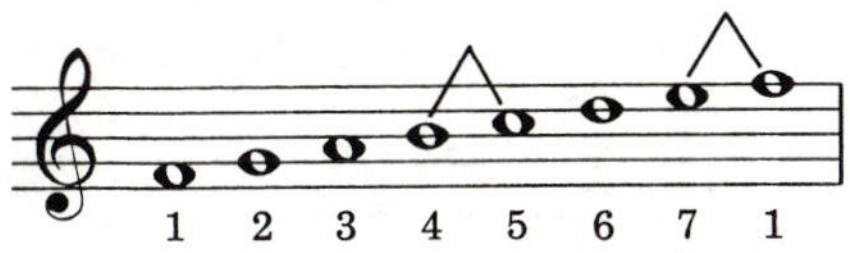

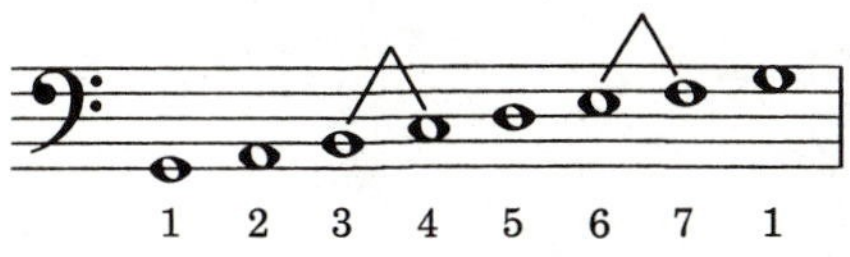

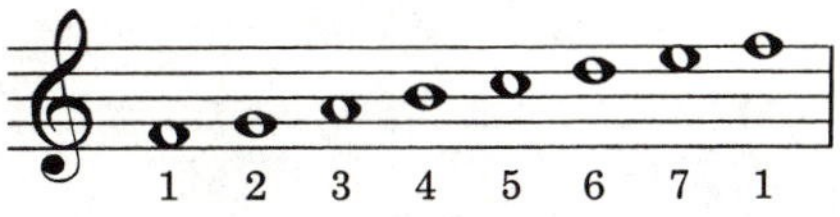

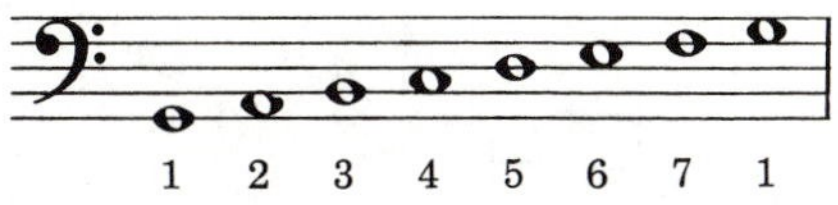

1. Mixolydian
2. Phrygian
3. Ionian
4. Lydian

152. Identify these modes.

1. G to G ____________
2. E to E ____________
3. C to C ____________
4. F to F ____________

Ionian Mixolydian
(either order)

Phrygian Locrian
(either order)

153. The two modes with HS's at 3 to 4 are ____________ and ____________.

The two modes with HS's at 1 to 2 are ____________ and ____________.

1. Phrygian 3. Lydian

2. Aeolian 4. Mixolydian

154. Identify each of these modes.

1. 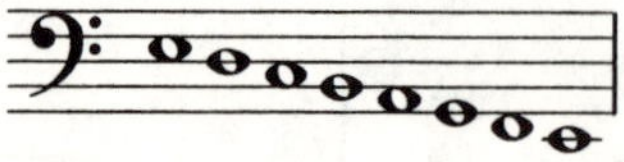 ____________ 3. ____________

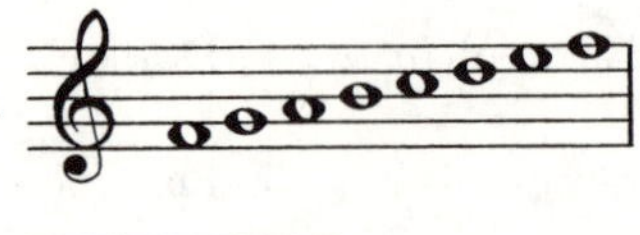

2.  ____________ 4. ____________

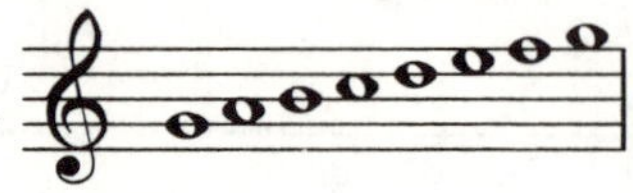

1.

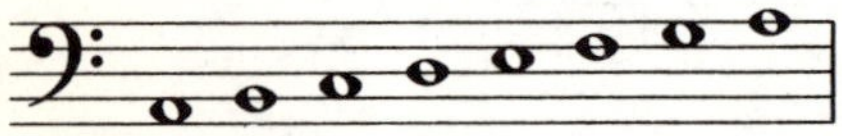

2.

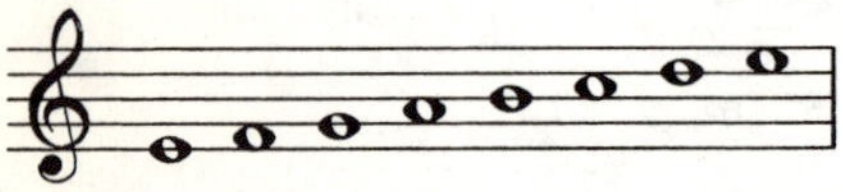

3.

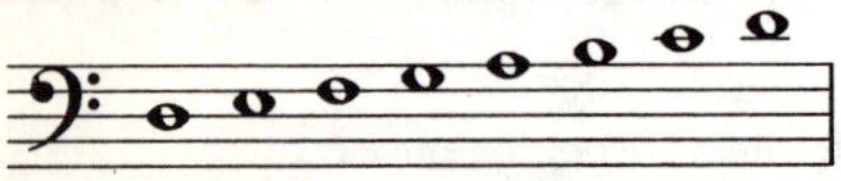

4.

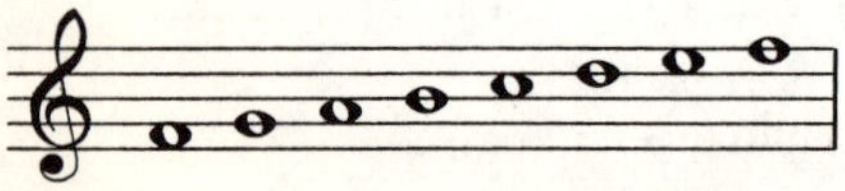

155. Without using chromatic signs, notate each mode below, ascending, in whole notes.

1. 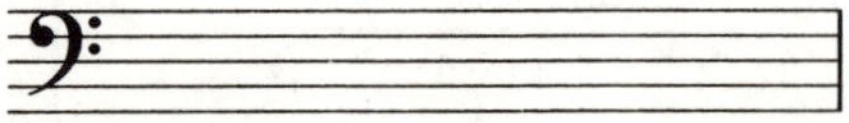 Aeolian

2. 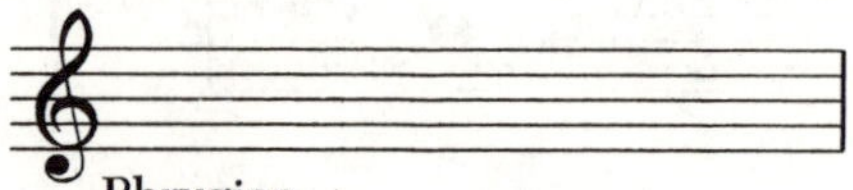 Phrygian

3. 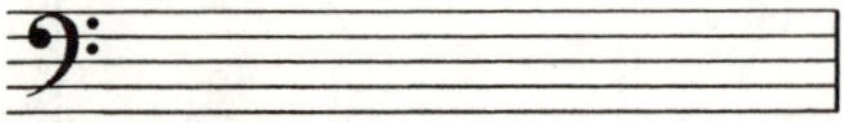 Dorian

4.  Lydian

156. As is the case with major and minor scales, modes may be constructed from any pitch by preserving the original arrangement of WS's and HS's. For example, the Aeolian mode built from A (called A Aeolian) and the Aeolian mode built from G (called G Aeolian) are both shown below.

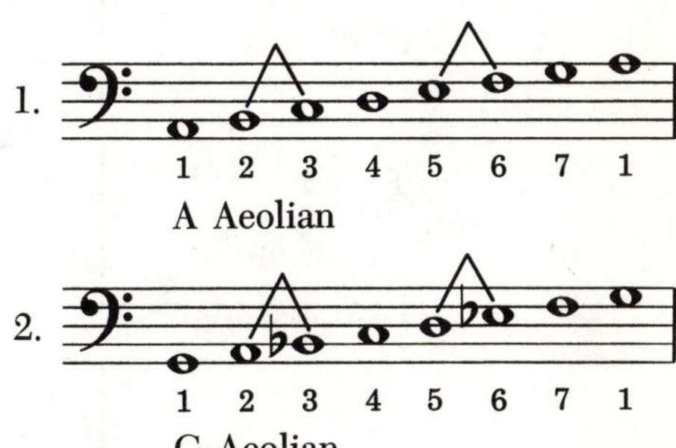

The Aeolian mode has HS's at _____ to _____ and at _____ to _____.

2 to 3 5 to 6
(either order)

157. The D Dorian mode is shown below. Observing the HS locations, write the E Dorian mode on the lower staff. Include HS brackets and all necessary chromatic signs.

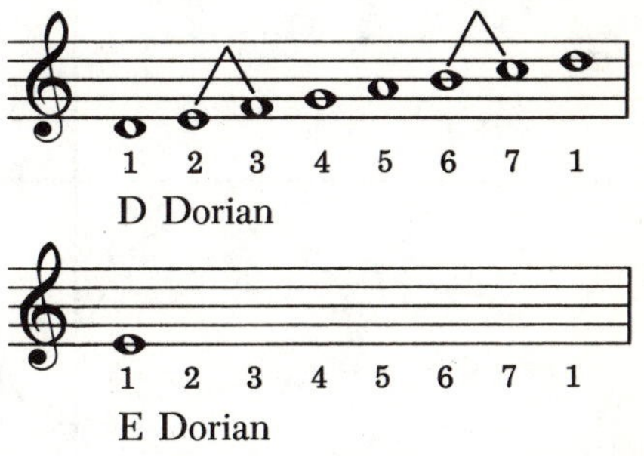

158. Following the same procedure as in frame 157, write these modes.

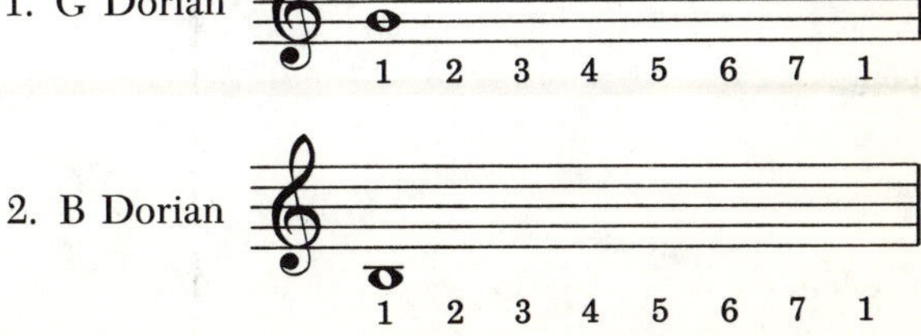

1. B C D E F♯ G A B

2. F♯ G A B C♯ D E F♯

159. Spell the Phrygian modes as indicated, including HS brackets.

E Phrygian: E F G A B C D E

1. B Phrygian: ____ ____ ____ ____ ____ ____ ____ ____

2. F♯ Phrygian: ____ ____ ____ ____ ____ ____ ____ ____

F G A B C D E F

1. C D E F♯ G A B C

2. G A B C♯ D E F♯ G

160. Without using chromatic signs, spell the F Lydian mode. Include HS brackets.

____ ____ ____ ____ ____ ____ ____ ____

Spell the following Lydian modes. (Refer to the above model if necessary.) Include HS brackets.

1. C Lydian: ____ ____ ____ ____ ____ ____ ____ ____

2. G Lydian: ____ ____ ____ ____ ____ ____ ____ ____

---

1. Aeolian
2. Locrian
3. Ionian
4. Dorian
5. Phrygian
6. Lydian
7. Mixolydian

161. Shown below in alphabetical order are the beginning pitches of each mode as they would be spelled *without* chromatic signs. Identify each mode.

1. A ____________________
2. B ____________________
3. C ____________________
4. D ____________________
5. E ____________________
6. F ____________________
7. G ____________________

1. A B C D E F G A
2. B C D E F G A B
3. C D E F G A B C
4. D E F G A B C D
5. E F G A B C D E
6. F G A B C D E F
7. G A B C D E F G

162. Each mode is spelled here according to the white-key spellings (that is, without chromatic signs). Mark the HS locations in each one.

1. Aeolian: A B C D E F G A
2. Locrian: B C D E F G A B
3. Ionian: C D E F G A B C
4. Dorian: D E F G A B C D
5. Phrygian: E F G A B C D E
6. Lydian: F G A B C D E F
7. Mixolydian: G A B C D E F G

---

1. F G A B♭ C D E F
2. F G A B♭ C D E♭ F
3. F G A♭ B♭ C D♭ E♭ F

163. Spell each of these modes, including HS brackets. Determine the HS locations from your memory of their white-key spellings. Refer to previous frames only as necessary.

1. F Ionian: __ __ __ __ __ __ __ __
2. F Mixolydian: __ __ __ __ __ __ __ __
3. F Aeolian: __ __ __ __ __ __ __ __

---

1. E F♯ G♯ A B C♯ D♯ E
2. C♯ D E F♯ G♯ A B C♯
3. E F G A B♭ C D E
4. A B C D E F♯ G A

164. Continue as in frame 163.

1. E Ionian: __ __ __ __ __ __ __ __
2. C♯ Phrygian: __ __ __ __ __ __ __ __
3. E Locrian: __ __ __ __ __ __ __ __
4. A Dorian: __ __ __ __ __ __ __ __

1. C D E♭ F G A B♭ C

2. B♭ C D E F G A B♭

3. B♭ C D E♭ F G A♭ B♭

4. G♯ A B C♯ D E F♯ G♯

165. Continue as in frame 164.

1. C Dorian: ___ ___ ___ ___ ___ ___ ___ ___

2. B♭ Lydian: ___ ___ ___ ___ ___ ___ ___ ___

3. B♭ Mixolydian: ___ ___ ___ ___ ___ ___ ___ ___

4. G♯ Locrian: ___ ___ ___ ___ ___ ___ ___ ___

---

1. G Dorian

2. B♭ Mixolydian

3. F♯ Phrygian

166. Identify each of these modes. (First find the HS locations, if necessary.)

1. 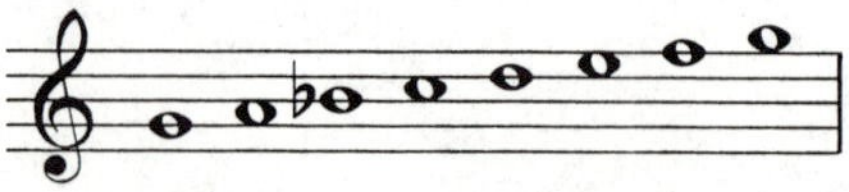 ___ ________

2. 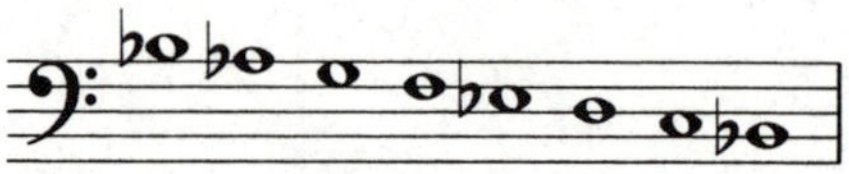 ___ ________

3. 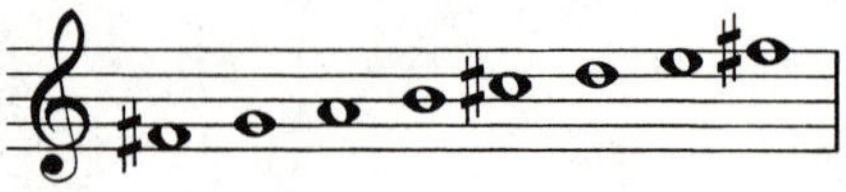 ___ ________

---

1. E♭ Lydian

2. F Ionian

3. D♯ Locrian

167. Continue as in frame 166.

1. 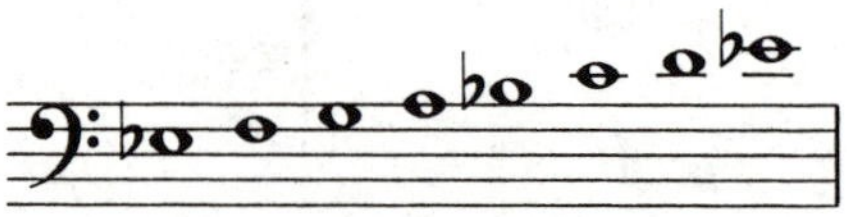 ___ ________

2. 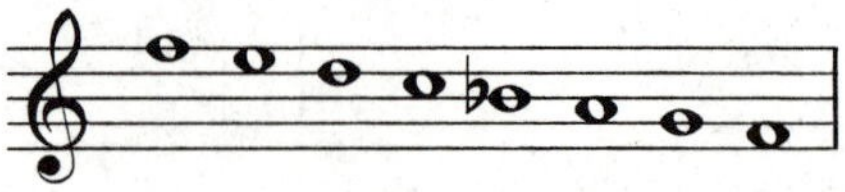 ___ ________

3.  ___ ________

Aeolian

168. Which mode is identical in structure with the pure minor scale? ________

Practice writing, spelling, and playing at the keyboard all of the scales in this chapter, starting from various notes, until you are thoroughly familiar with their individual sounds and structures.

LISTENING FRAMES

169. Example 3-7, Béla Bartók's Mikrokosmos No. 40 for piano, uses the E Mixolydian mode. As you listen to this example, you will hear it begin with a brief introduction in the lower line, after which a melody enters above.

How many different degrees of the mode are heard before the upper melody begins? ____

two

---

170. Continuing with Example 3-7, the two pitches heard in the introduction are E and B. Each pitch is heard how many times before the melody begins? ________

three

One of the two tones in the introduction becomes, an octave higher, the first pitch of the melody when it begins. This pitch is ____ (E/B).

B

Is the last tone of the melody the first modal scale degree, E? (Listen carefully to the last *upper* pitch.) ____

no (It ends on the second degree, F♯.)

---

171. The E Phrygian mode is heard in Example 3-8, part of a Russian dance from Igor Stravinsky's suite, *Petrouchka.* This melody has its origins in Russian folk music.

As you listen to the excerpt, compare it with the notation of the first four measures below. The first measure is notated correctly, but one of the others has incorrect pitches.

Which measure is incorrect? ____ (2/3/4)

4

Re-notate the measure correctly on the staff below. Notice that this measure is the same as a previous measure.

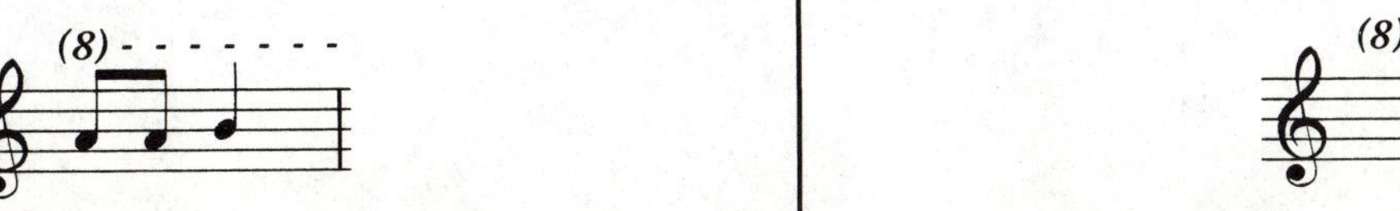

172. The first four measures of the Stravinsky excerpt heard in frame 171 (Example 3-8) are shown below. Listen to the example again.

one

Measure five is the same as which previous measure? _____

1

The final pitch in the *entire* excerpt is which degree of the mode? _____

---

173. The third movement of Peter Ilich Tchaikovsky's Serenade for Strings (Example 3-9) has a lengthy introduction employing the Dorian mode. The first three measures are notated below. Listen to the beginning of the example; then supply the two pitches in the fourth measure. (The rhythm is given below the staff.)

E

This melody uses the _____ Dorian mode.

---

174. As you hear all of Example 3-9, observe that the four-measure melodic pattern shown in frame 173 is repeated several times, but the ending is changed each time. How many times does this melodic pattern occur in the excerpt? _____

four

2

175. Examples 3-9 and 3-10 give us a somewhat rare opportunity to hear the musical effect of the same basic melodic material adapted to different scale forms.

The last nine measures of the Tchaikovsky movement begun in frame 173 are heard in Example 3-10. This portion uses the same basic melodic material, but employs a different scale. As you listen, carefully observe the location of HS's and WS's. The scale being used is which of those below? _____

1. Phrygian
2. Major
3. Locrian
4. Pure minor

SELF-QUIZ III

1. The major scale has HS's at _____ to _____ and at _____ to _____.

2. Add the necessary chromatic signs to form the indicated scales.

   1. B♭ major

   2. B major

3. The three forms of the minor scale are ___________, ___________, and ___________.

4. All three forms of the minor scale have the same structure from scale degree _____ to scale degree _____.

5. Which minor scale has differing ascending and descending forms? _______________

6. Which minor scale form has three sizes of scale steps? _______________

7. The pure minor scale is identical in structure with which mode? _______________

8. Add the necessary chromatic signs to form these scales.

1. F major

2. F pure minor

3. F melodic minor (ascending)

(descending)

4. F harmonic minor

9. Identify these major or minor scales.

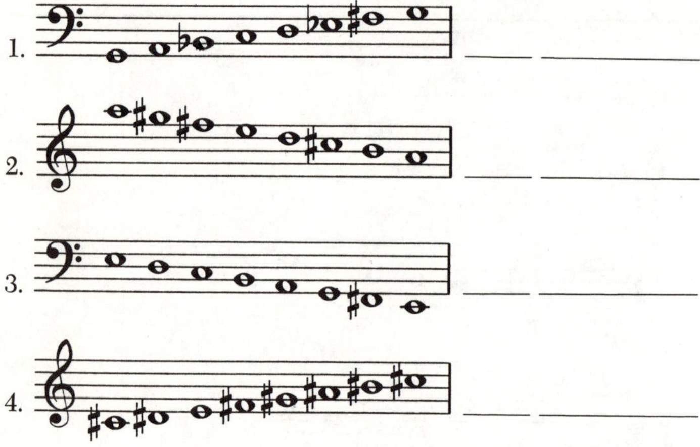

10. Spell these scales.

1. D major (ascending) ____ ____ ____ ____ ____ ____ ____ ____

2. F♯ harmonic minor (descending) ____ ____ ____ ____ ____ ____ ____ ____

3. E♭ pure minor (descending) ____ ____ ____ ____ ____ ____ ____ ____

4. A♭ harmonic minor (ascending) ____ ____ ____ ____ ____ ____ ____ ____

5. E♭ melodic minor (descending) ____ ____ ____ ____ ____ ____ ____ ____

11. In alphabetical order below are the beginning pitches of each mode as spelled *without* chromatic signs. Identify each mode.

1. A ____________________ 5. E ____________________

2. B ____________________ 6. F ____________________

3. C ____________________ 7. G ____________________

4. D ____________________

12. The two modes containing HS's at 1 to 2 are ____________________ and ____________________.

13. Which mode is identical in structure to the major scale? ____________________

14. Spell each of these modes (ascending).

1. ___ ___ ___ ___ ___ ___ ___ ___ (D Lydian)

2. ___ ___ ___ ___ ___ ___ ___ ___ (B Dorian)

15. Spell each of these modes (descending).

1. ___ ___ ___ ___ ___ ___ ___ ___ (G♯ Phrygian)

2. ___ ___ ___ ___ ___ ___ ___ ___ (G♯ Locrian)

16. Identify each of these modes.

1. ___ ____________

2. ___ ____________

3. ___ ____________

17. Add the necessary chromatic signs to complete these modes.

1. C♯ Dorian (descending)

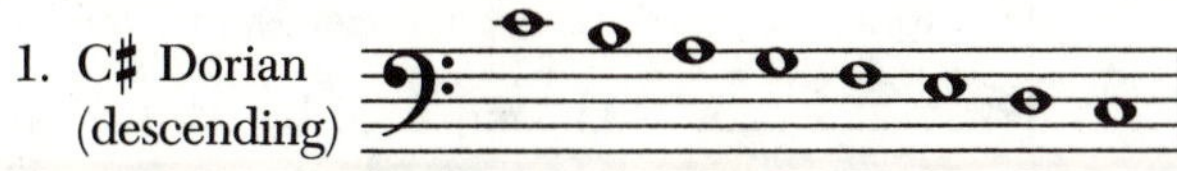

2. G Phrygian (ascending)

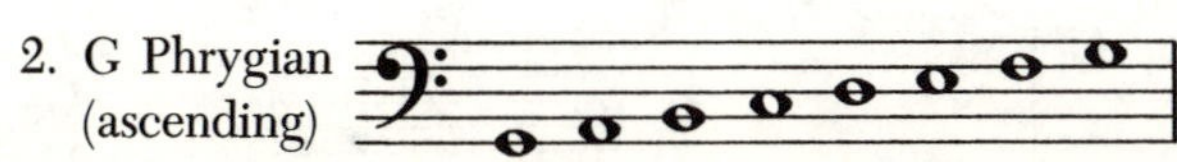

CHAPTER ▪ IV ▪ INTERVALS

The difference in pitch between two tones, whether sounded together or separately, is called an *interval.* An understanding of the measurement of intervals is basic to the study of how music is organized into melodies and harmonies. Each interval in music has a unique sound, flavor, and dramatic quality. The musical effect of any interval depends to a large degree on the musical factors surrounding its occurrence, such as rhythm, melody, harmony, and instrumentation.

This chapter, like earlier ones, should be worked near a keyboard or other instrument, so that you can become familiar with the intervals discussed and learn to associate their sounds with their appearance in notation. The listening frames will then give you an opportunity to hear how these intervals behave in a larger musical context.

PERFECT, AUGMENTED, AND DIMINISHED INTERVALS

	1. An *interval* is the difference in pitch between two tones. This difference is measured first by counting the number of lines and spaces encompassed by the two tones. These two tones encompass *four* lines and spaces: C, D, E, and F. Therefore, this interval is a *4th.*
interval spaces 5th	**2.** An ___________ is the difference in pitch between two tones. That difference is measured by the number of lines and ___________ encompassed by the two tones. Interval 1 (below) is a 4th; what is interval 2? _____ 1. 2.

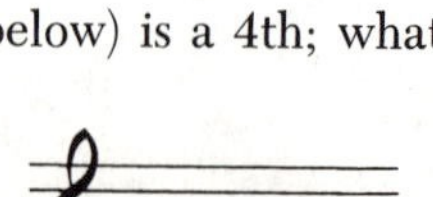

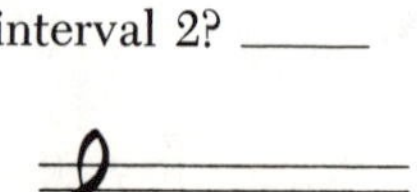

7. Continue as in frame 6.

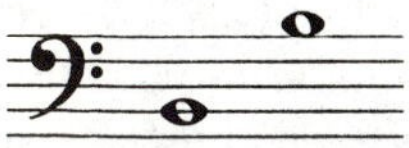

1. __________

2. __________

3. __________

octaves

8. 1sts are called __________; 8ths are called __________.

9. Which two of the intervals below are incorrectly named?

____ ____

1. 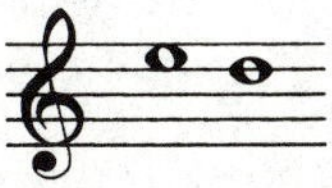 2nd
2. 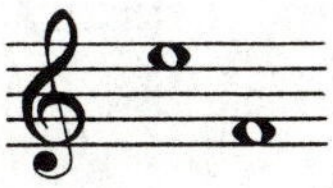 octave
3. 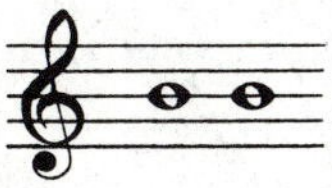 prime
4. 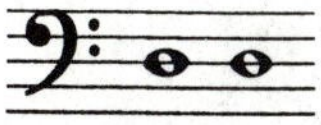 prime
5.  5th
6.  6th

10. Construct each indicated interval *above* the given notes.

2.

1. 4th 
2. octave 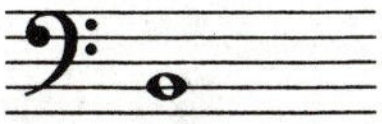
3. 5th

11. Construct each interval *below* the given notes.

2.

1. 5th 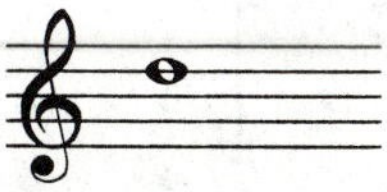
2. octave 
3. 4th

pitch	**3.** An interval is the difference tones.
5 5th	**4.** Which one of the intervals be Its correct name is ____. 1. 2nd 2. 3rd 3. 4th
prime	**5.** 1sts and 8ths are designated *primes,*° and 8ths are called *octav* prime prime What is this interval called? ° 1sts are also called "unisons," b as "primes."
1. 3rd 2. octave 3. prime	**6.** Name the intervals below b and spaces encompassed, following that 1sts are called primes and 8t 1. 2. 3.

1. 2nd

2. 6th

3. 3rd

primes

2 6

1.

3.

1.

3.

12. Observe that both intervals below are 4ths, but interval 2 is larger by one half step than interval 1.

1. 2.

Therefore, the name "4th" reveals only the general, or *numerical*, size of the interval. Another name is needed to describe the interval more exactly.

Both intervals below are _____.

Answer: 4ths

---

13. 5th is the numerical name of the above intervals. What is the numerical name of the intervals below? _____

Answer: 3rd

---

14. _____________ is the numerical name of the above intervals.

To describe more precisely the size of an interval, a *qualitative* name is added to the numerical name. Thus, the full description of every interval will consist of two names: a _______________ name and a _______________ name.

Answers: Octave; numerical qualitative (either order)

---

15. 5th is the _______________ name of the above interval.

Give the numerical names of the intervals below.

1. _____ 3. _____

2. _____ 4. _____

Answers: numerical; 1. octave 3. 4th; 2. 5th 4. prime

qualitative	**16.** The two names which fully describe an interval are the numerical name and the ____________ name.
two	**17.** Numerical intervals are classified into two groups, according to their characteristic musical behavior. One group consists of primes, 4ths, 5ths, and octaves. The remaining four intervals form the other group, which will be discussed later. Numerical intervals are classified into how many groups? ____
1. prime 3. octave 2. 4th 4. 5th	**18.** The interval group under present consideration consists of primes, 4ths, 5ths, and octaves. Give the numerical names of the intervals below. 1. ____ 3. ____ 2. ____ 4. ____
primes 4ths 5ths octaves (any order)	**19.** The qualitative name of each interval in this first group may be *perfect, augmented,* or *diminished.* The intervals whose qualitative names are perfect, augmented, or diminished* are ________, ____, ____, and ________. * The qualitative interval terms "augmented" and "diminished" may also apply to the remaining group of intervals (2nds, 3rds, 6ths, and 7ths), but this will be discussed later.
perfect augmented diminished (any order)	**20.** Primes, 4ths, 5ths, and octaves may be ________, ________, or ________. The term "perfect" is used by tradition and for historical and acoustical reasons. "Perfect" does not mean that these intervals are necessarily superior to the others.
perfect 4th	**21.** In naming intervals, put the qualitative name before the numerical name. For example, perfect 5th, augmented 4th, diminished octave, and so forth. 4th perfect Arrange these two names in the proper order: ________ ____

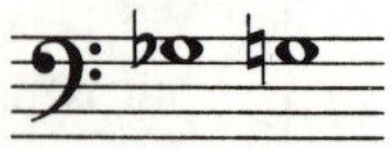

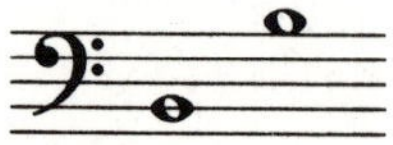

22. A prime, 4th, 5th, or octave is perfect if the upper note exists in the major scale built from the lower note.

perfect 4th C major scale

They are also perfect in minor scales, but for simplicity we shall use only major scales in connection with this procedure.

The terms "perfect," "augmented," and "diminished" apply to the following numerical intervals: __________, _____, _____, and __________.

primes 4ths 5ths octaves
(any order)

---

23. Shown below are major scales built from the lower notes of perfect intervals. Notice that the upper note also occurs in each scale. Give the qualitative and numerical names of each interval, following the given example.

1. perfect 4th

2. perfect octave (Since perfect octaves always use the same pitch name for both notes, you may find it easier to omit the scale construction with them.)

---

24. Using the necessary chromatic signs, construct a major scale* from the lower note of each given interval. Which one is a perfect interval? _____

* See Chapter III, frames 35–44 for a review of major scales.

1

1.

2.

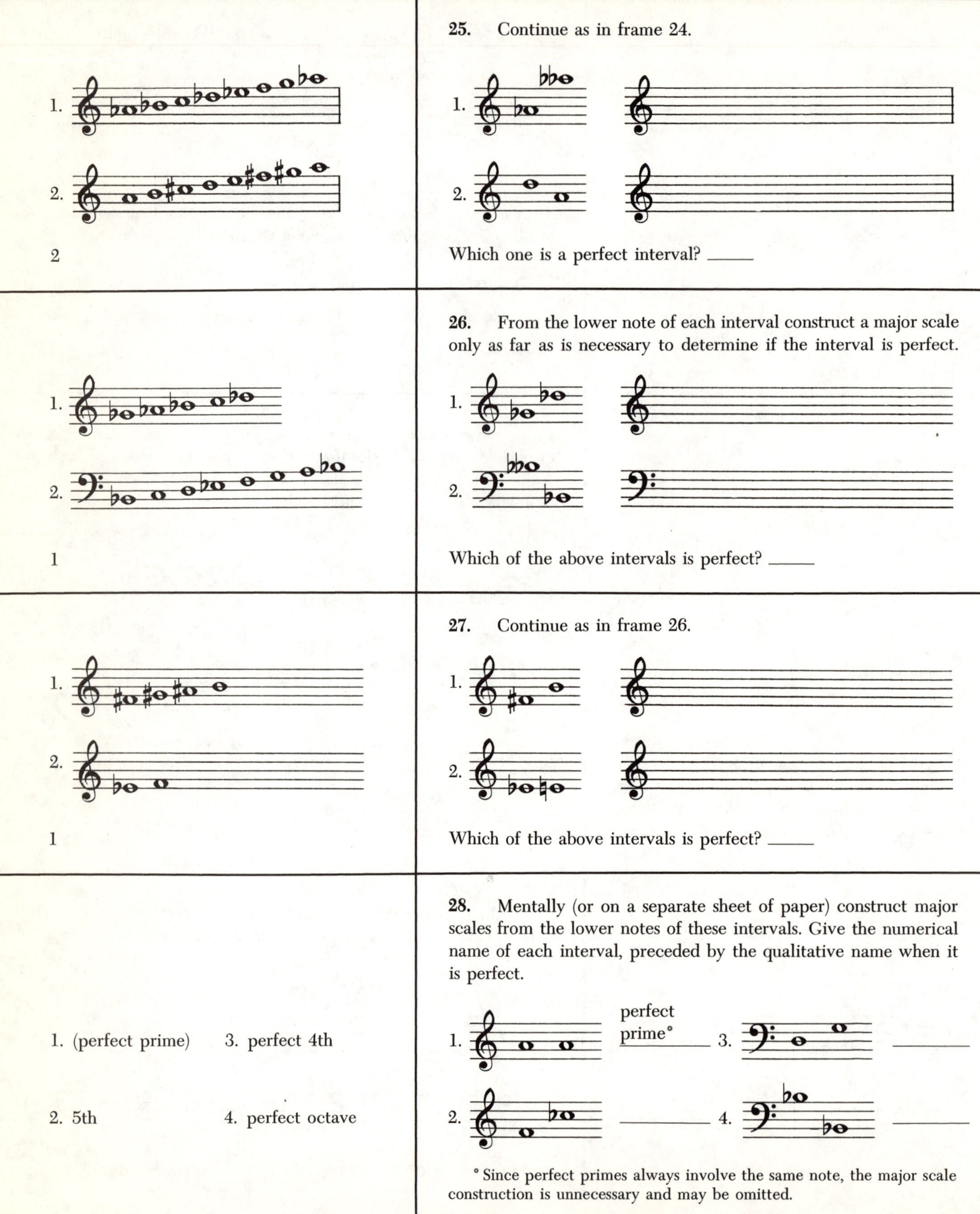

2

25. Continue as in frame 24.

1.

2.

Which one is a perfect interval? _____

1

26. From the lower note of each interval construct a major scale only as far as is necessary to determine if the interval is perfect.

1.

2.

Which of the above intervals is perfect? _____

1

27. Continue as in frame 26.

1.

2.

Which of the above intervals is perfect? _____

1. (perfect prime) 3. perfect 4th

2. 5th 4. perfect octave

28. Mentally (or on a separate sheet of paper) construct major scales from the lower notes of these intervals. Give the numerical name of each interval, preceded by the qualitative name when it is perfect.

1. perfect prime* 3. _____

2. _____ 4. _____

* Since perfect primes always involve the same note, the major scale construction is unnecessary and may be omitted.

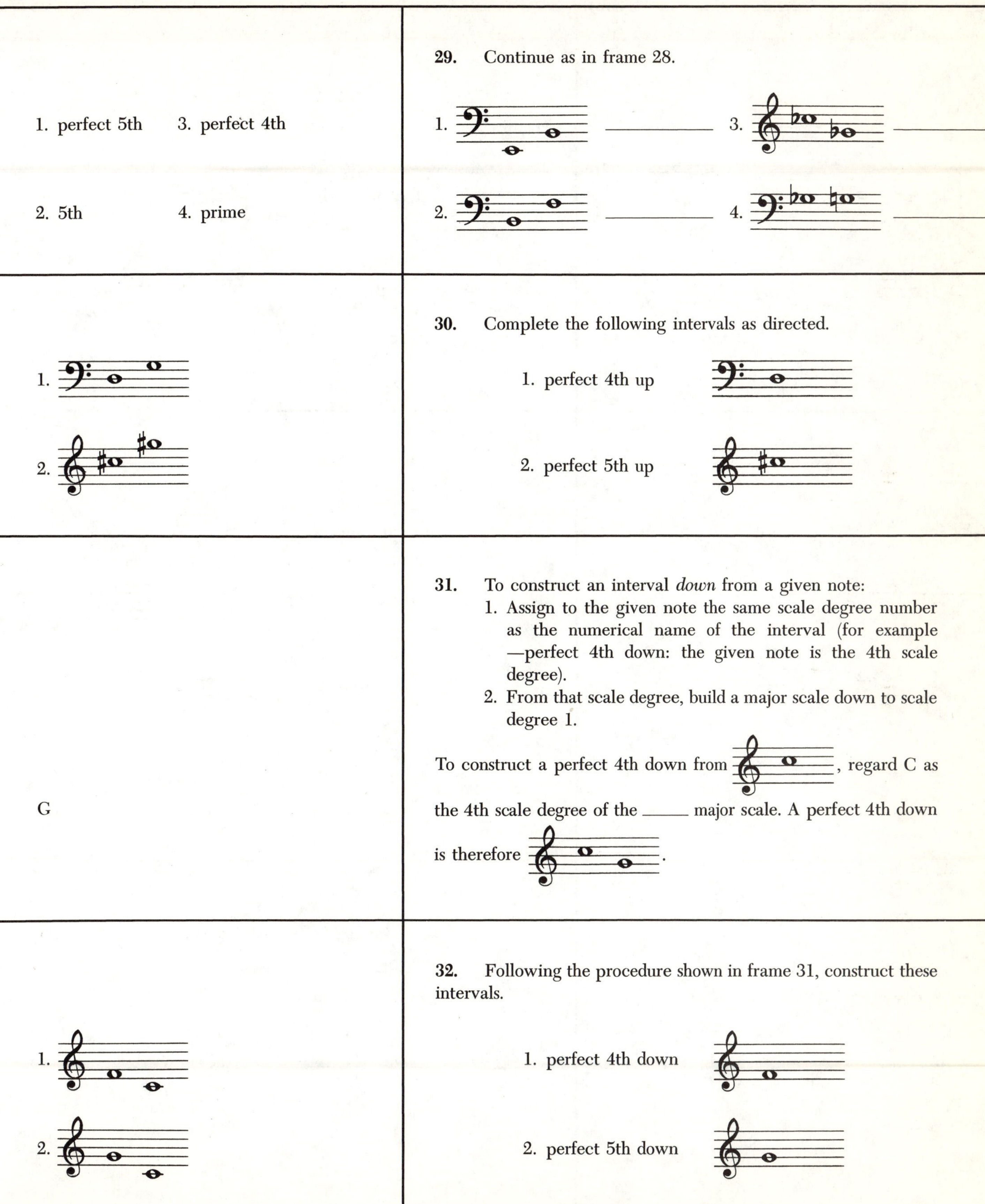

1. perfect 5th 3. perfect 4th

2. 5th 4. prime

29. Continue as in frame 28.

1. ________ 3. ________

2. ________ 4. ________

1.

2.

30. Complete the following intervals as directed.

1. perfect 4th up

2. perfect 5th up

G

31. To construct an interval *down* from a given note:

1. Assign to the given note the same scale degree number as the numerical name of the interval (for example—perfect 4th down: the given note is the 4th scale degree).
2. From that scale degree, build a major scale down to scale degree 1.

To construct a perfect 4th down from [C], regard C as the 4th scale degree of the ______ major scale. A perfect 4th down is therefore [C–G].

1.

2.

32. Following the procedure shown in frame 31, construct these intervals.

1. perfect 4th down

2. perfect 5th down

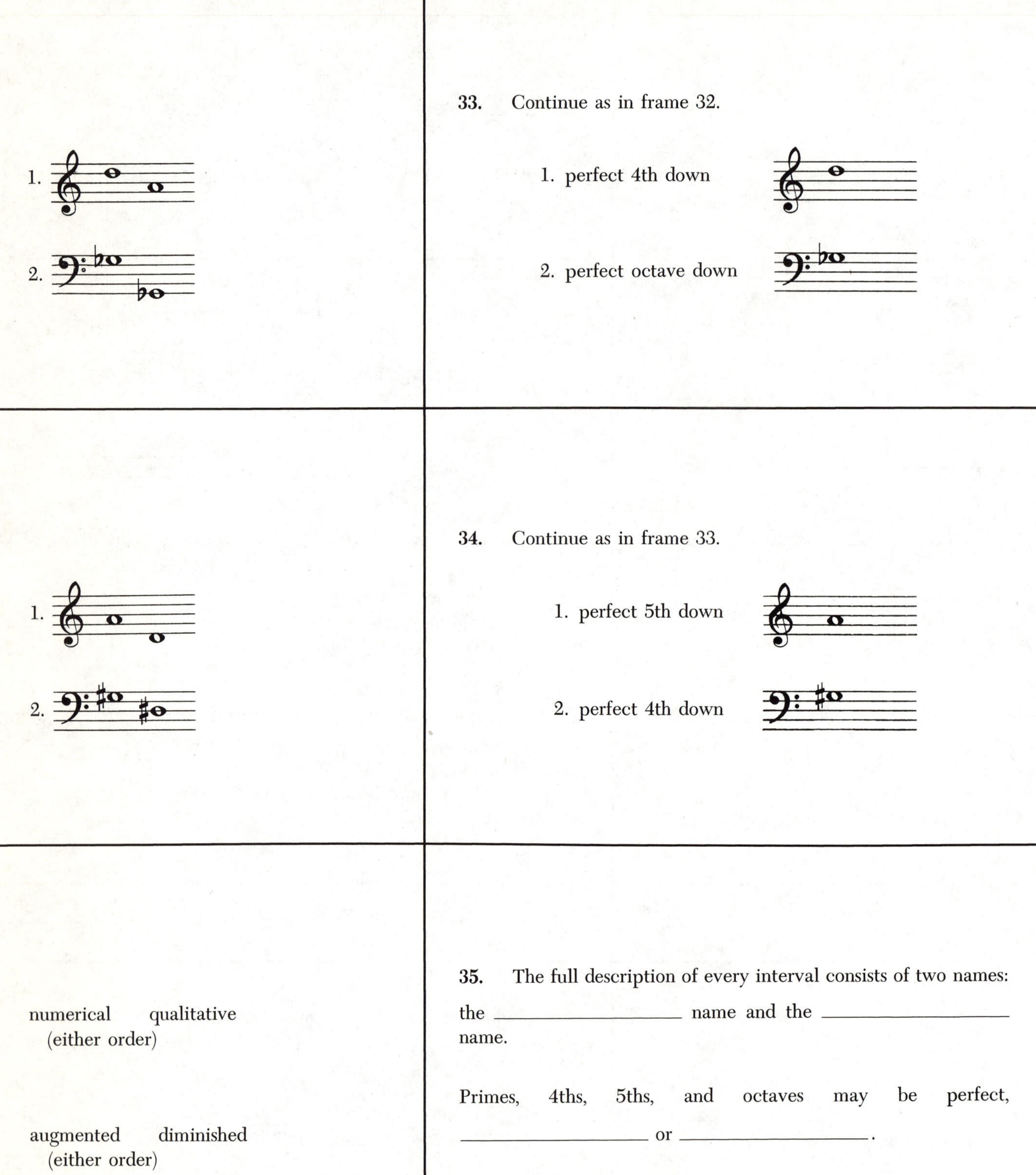

1.

2.

33. Continue as in frame 32.

1. perfect 4th down

2. perfect octave down

1.

2.

34. Continue as in frame 33.

1. perfect 5th down

2. perfect 4th down

numerical qualitative
(either order)

augmented diminished
(either order)

35. The full description of every interval consists of two names: the __________________ name and the __________________ name.

Primes, 4ths, 5ths, and octaves may be perfect, __________________ or __________________.

36. An *augmented* interval is one half step larger than the perfect interval of the same numerical size.

Each perfect interval below is made one half step larger by either lowering the bottom note or raising the upper note chromatically.*

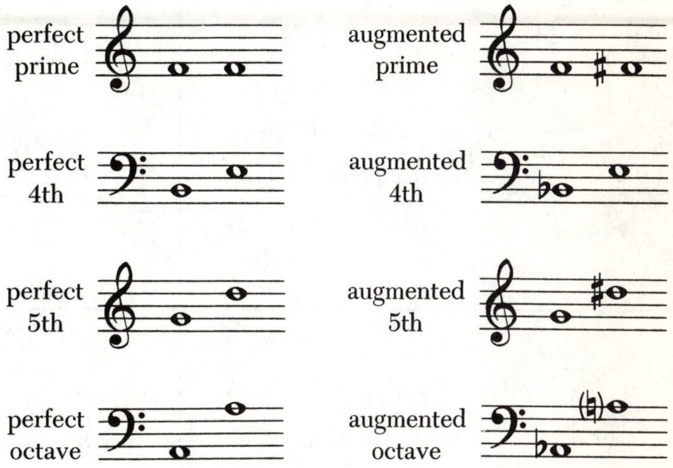

perfect prime — augmented prime

perfect 4th — augmented 4th

perfect 5th — augmented 5th

perfect octave — augmented octave

larger

An augmented interval is one half step __________ (larger/smaller) than the perfect interval of the same numerical size.

* "Chromatically" means, in this context, that the note is to be altered one chromatic half step (for example, F–F♯, C–C♭, A♯–A♮, and so forth). For a review of chromatic and diatonic half steps, see Chapter III, frames 17–26.

2

37. Which of these intervals is augmented? _____

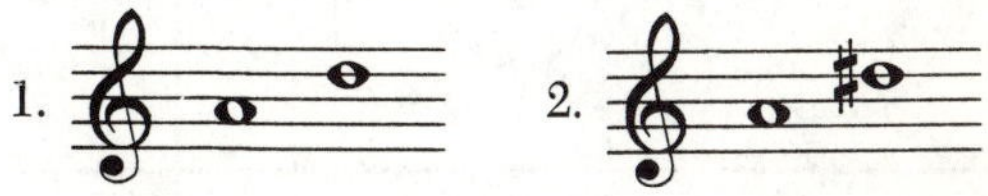

1. 2.

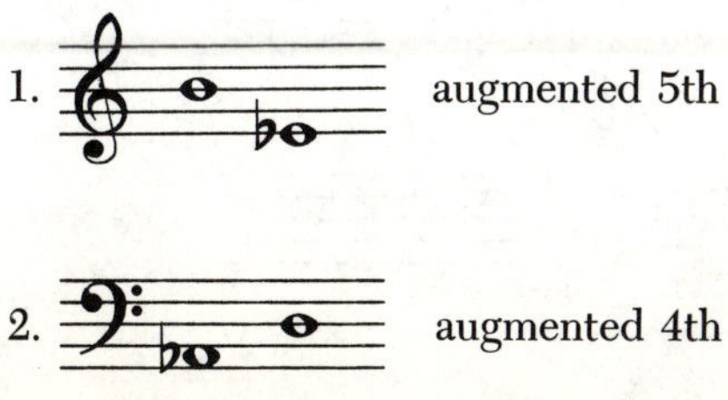

38. Augmented intervals are identified by comparison with perfect intervals of the same numerical size, rather than by reference to a scale.

Change the perfect intervals below to augmented by chromatically lowering the bottom note one half step. Include the names of the augmented intervals thus formed.

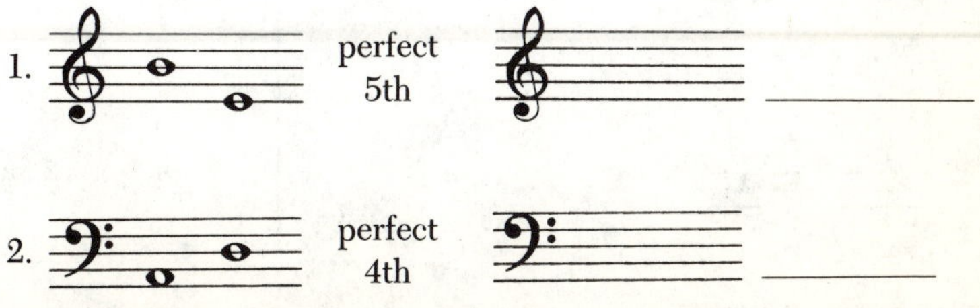

1. augmented 5th

2. augmented 4th

1. perfect 5th __________

2. perfect 4th __________

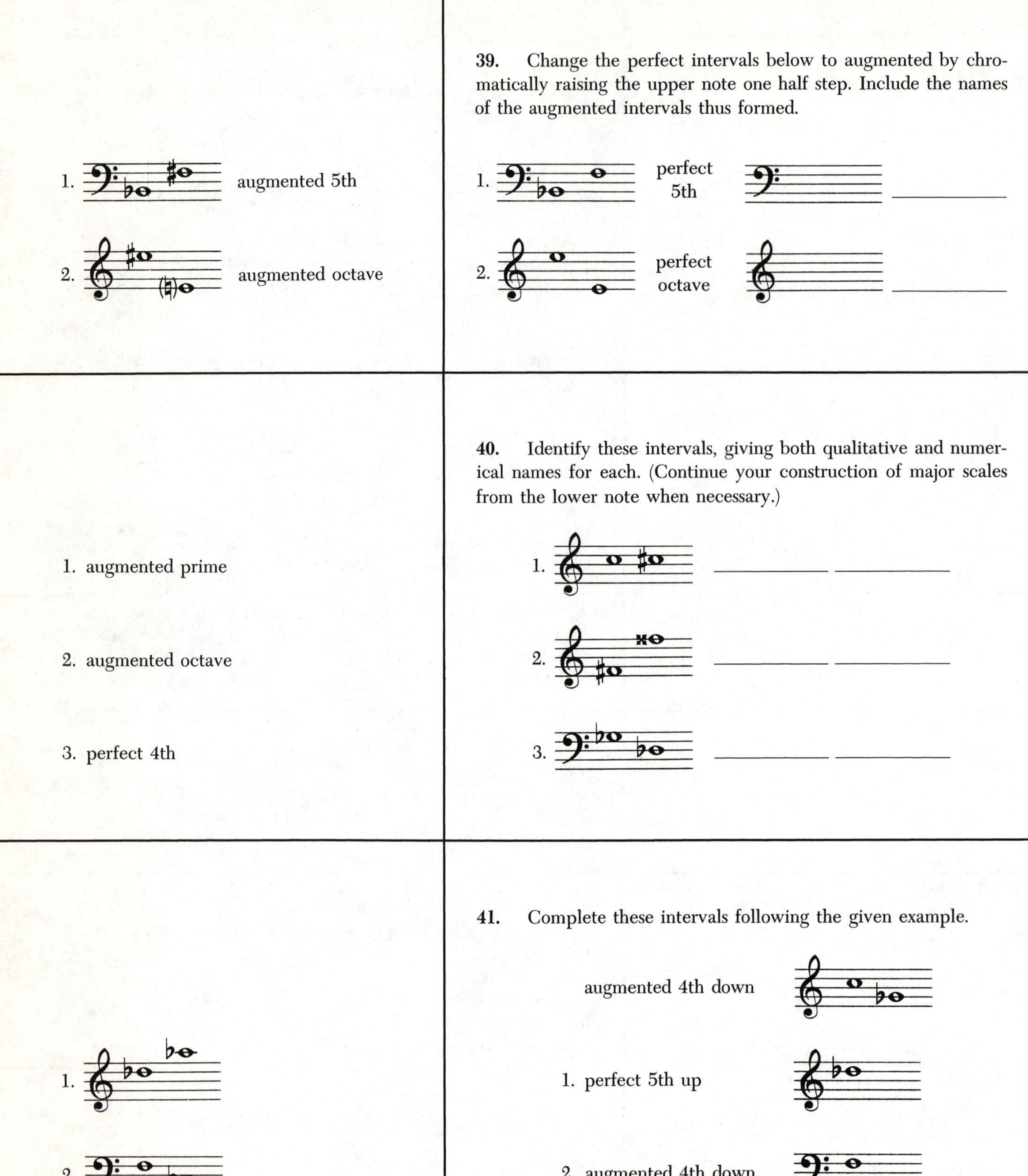

1. augmented 5th
2. augmented octave

39. Change the perfect intervals below to augmented by chromatically raising the upper note one half step. Include the names of the augmented intervals thus formed.

1. perfect 5th ______
2. perfect octave ______

1. augmented prime
2. augmented octave
3. perfect 4th

40. Identify these intervals, giving both qualitative and numerical names for each. (Continue your construction of major scales from the lower note when necessary.)

1. ______ ______
2. ______ ______
3. ______ ______

41. Complete these intervals following the given example.

augmented 4th down

1. perfect 5th up
2. augmented 4th down

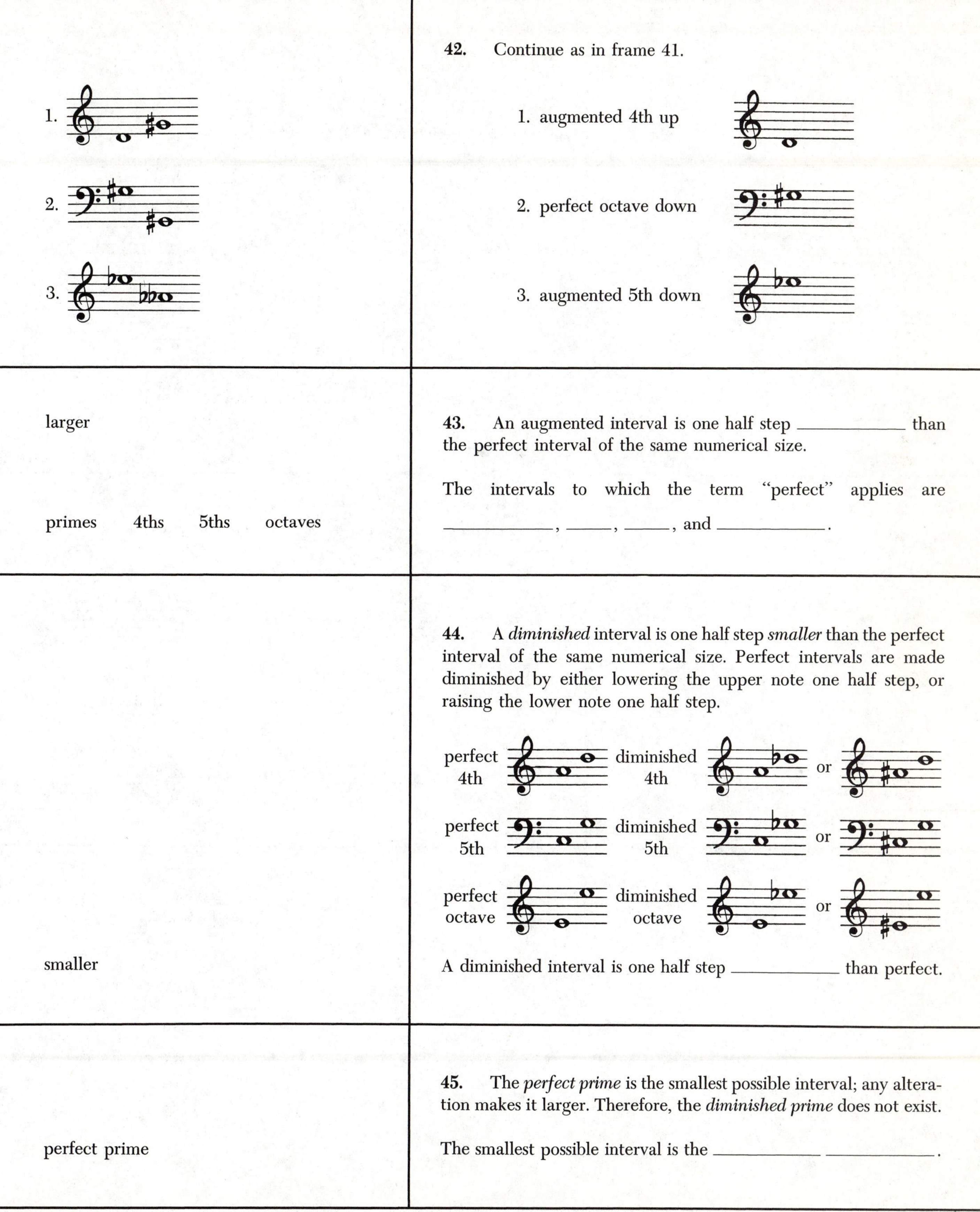

42. Continue as in frame 41.

1. augmented 4th up
2. perfect octave down
3. augmented 5th down

larger

43. An augmented interval is one half step __________ than the perfect interval of the same numerical size.

primes 4ths 5ths octaves

The intervals to which the term "perfect" applies are __________, _____, _____, and __________.

smaller

44. A *diminished* interval is one half step *smaller* than the perfect interval of the same numerical size. Perfect intervals are made diminished by either lowering the upper note one half step, or raising the lower note one half step.

A diminished interval is one half step __________ than perfect.

perfect prime

45. The *perfect prime* is the smallest possible interval; any alteration makes it larger. Therefore, the *diminished prime* does not exist.

The smallest possible interval is the __________ __________.

smaller

1. 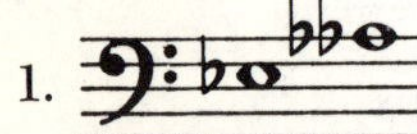

2. 

3. 

46. "Augmented" means larger.

"Diminished" means ___________.

Diminish these intervals by chromatically lowering the upper note one half step. Here we may begin using the abbreviations "P" for perfect, "A" for augmented, and "d" for diminished.

1. P 4th d 4th

2. P 5th d 5th
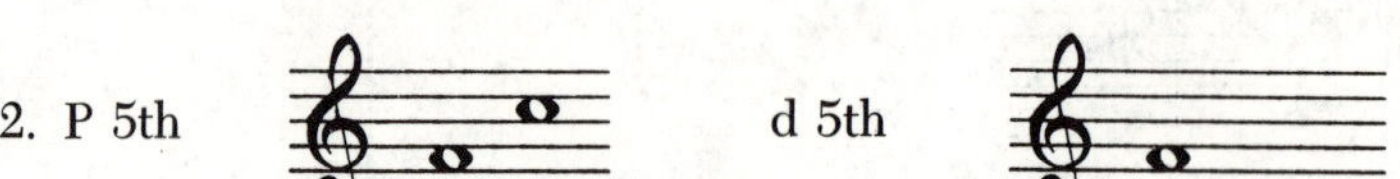

3. P octave d octave
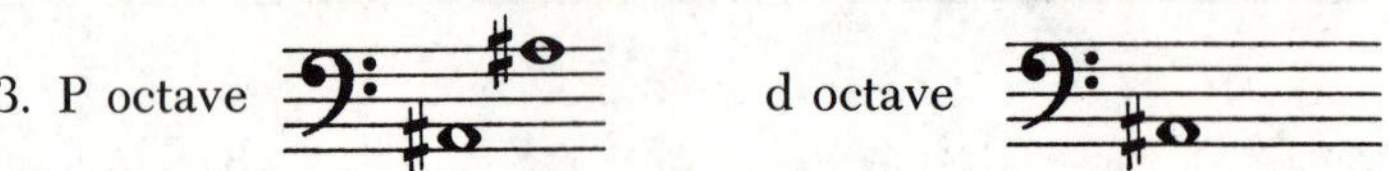

1. 

2. 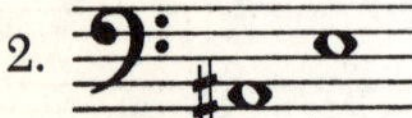

3. 

47. Diminish these intervals by chromatically raising the lower note one half step.

1. P 4th d 4th
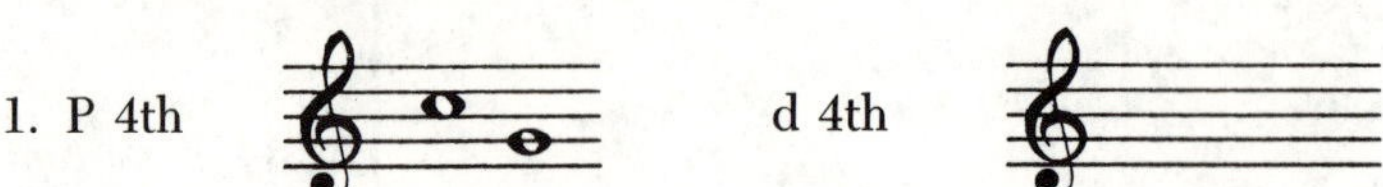

2. P 5th d 5th

3. P octave d octave
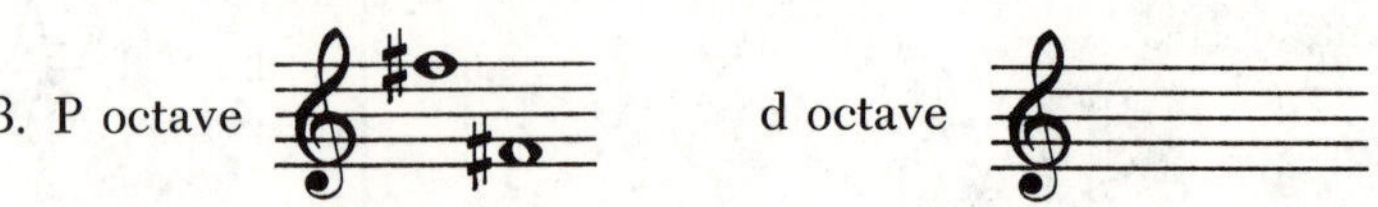

1. P 5th

2. d 5th

3. d octave

48. Supply qualitative and numerical names for each of these intervals, using the abbreviations previously defined.

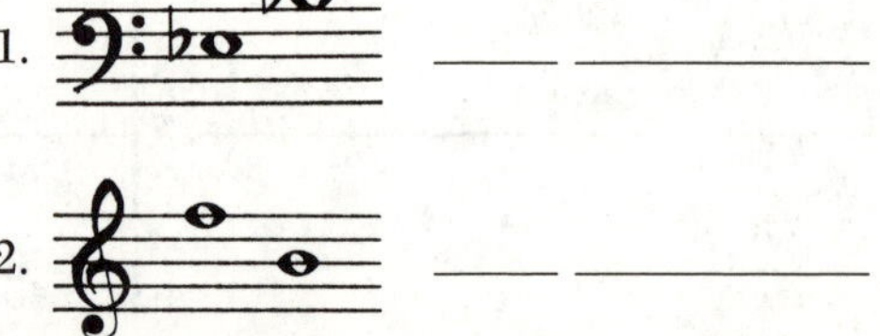

1. ____ __________

2. ____ __________

3. ____ __________

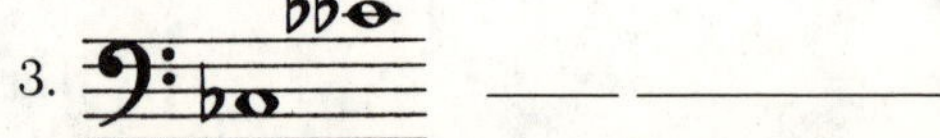

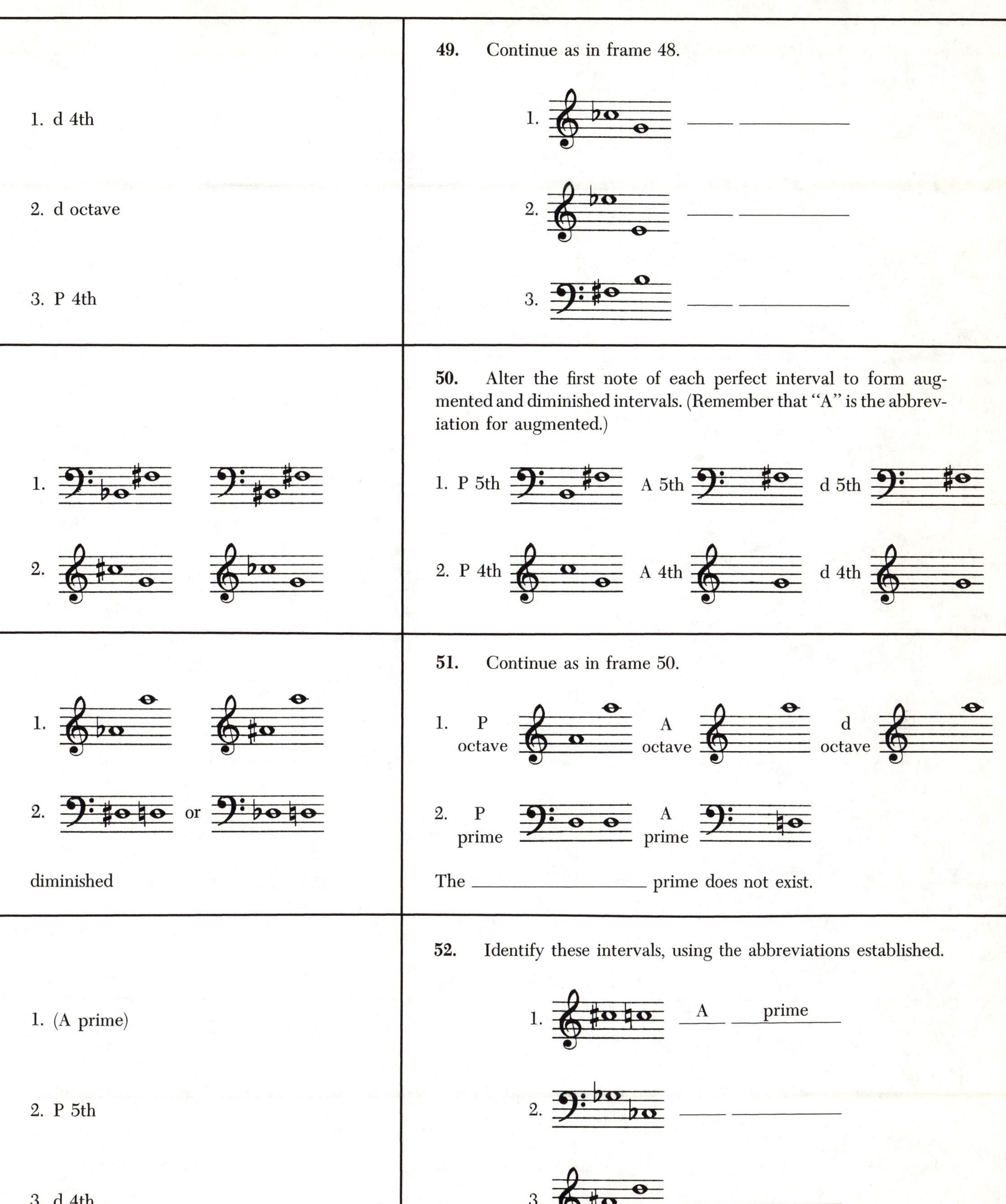
1. d 4th
2. d octave
3. P 4th
49. Continue as in frame 48.
1. ___ ______
2. ___ ______
3. ___ ______
1.
2.
50. Alter the first note of each perfect interval to form augmented and diminished intervals. (Remember that "A" is the abbreviation for augmented.)
1. P 5th
A 5th
d 5th
2. P 4th
A 4th
d 4th
1.
2.
or
diminished
51. Continue as in frame 50.
1. P octave
A octave
d octave
2. P prime
A prime
The ______ prime does not exist.
1. (A prime)
2. P 5th
3. d 4th
52. Identify these intervals, using the abbreviations established.
1. A prime
2. ___ ______
3. ___ ______

1. A octave 2. A prime	**53.** Continue as in frame 52. 1. ____ __________ 2. ____ __________
1. P 5th 2. d octave 3. A 4th	**54.** Continue as in frame 53. 1. ____ __________ 2. ____ __________ 3. ____ __________
perfect diminished augmented (any order) prime	**55.** Primes, 4ths, 5ths, and octaves are either __________, __________, or __________. The diminished __________ does not exist.
difference	**56.** Now play at the keyboard all intervals and scales appearing in frames 1–55. Observe in particular the difference in sound between the intervals studied thus far. An interval is the __________ in pitch between two tones.

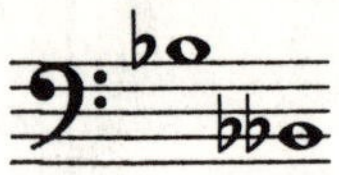

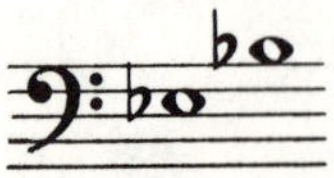

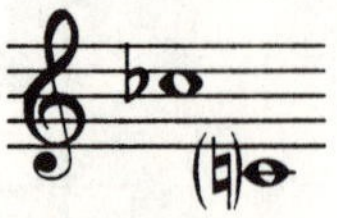

LISTENING FRAMES

57. Example 1-1, the beginning of Bach's Fugue No. 1 in C from *The Well-Tempered Clavier*, Vol. I, contains three perfect intervals near the beginning. The notation below continues through the first two perfect intervals. After identifying both given intervals, listen to the example, add the missing eighth note at the end, and identify the third interval where indicated.

1. Interval No. 1 is a _____ _____.

2. Interval No. 2 is a _____ _____.

3. Interval No. 3 is a _____ _____ (P 4th/P 5th).

1. P 4th

2. P 5th

3. P 4th

58. Example 4-1, the beginning of Franz Joseph Haydn's Symphony No. 104 ("London"), contains two perfect intervals. Part of the example is notated below. After identifying the bracketed interval in the second measure, listen to the excerpt and supply the missing half note in the *first* measure. Then identify the bracketed interval in the first measure. (If you have difficulty identifying the missing pitch, sing both half notes aloud and compare them.)

___ ___ ___ ___

* The *fermata* sign (𝄐) means that the note or rest above or below the sign is to be sustained longer than the notated rhythmic value.

P 5th P 4th

59. Example 4-2 is the beginning of Arcangelo Corelli's Trio Sonata, Op. 4, No. 8, for two violins, cello, and keyboard. A portion of the first two measures, played by the first violin, is notated below.

From the third to the fourth pitch is a perfect interval. After hearing the example, supply the missing whole note in the second measure, and identify the interval below the staff.

___ ___

The beat unit in this example is _____.

P 4th

𝅗𝅥

MAJOR-MINOR INTERVALS

The group of intervals studied thus far (primes, 4ths, 5ths, and octaves) form what we may call the "perfect" interval group. The second interval group consists of 2nds, 3rds, 6ths, and 7ths, which are sometimes called the "major-minor" intervals. Frequent reference to the keyboard will continue to be helpful in building the important listening association with these intervals. Observe, for example, that each of the two interval groups has a unique sound quality; other aural distinctions will become clearer as you proceed through the chapter.

Answers	Frames
numerical 1. 2nd 3. 6th 2. 3rd 4. 7th	**60.** 3rd is the ______________ name of the above interval. Give the numerical names of the intervals below. 1. ____ 3. ____ 2. ____ 4. ____
qualitative two	**61.** The two names which fully describe an interval are the numerical name and the ______________ name. Numerical intervals are classified into how many groups? ____
1. 6th 3. 7th 2. 2nd 4. 3rd	**62.** The interval group now under consideration consists of 2nds, 3rds, 6ths, and 7ths. Give the numerical names of these intervals. 1. ____ 3. ____ 2. ____ 4. ____
2nds 3rds 6ths 7ths (any order)	**63.** The qualitative name of each interval in this second group may be either *major* or *minor*. (They may occasionally be augmented or diminished; this will be discussed later in this chapter.) The intervals whose qualitative names are either major or minor are ____, ____, ____, and ____.

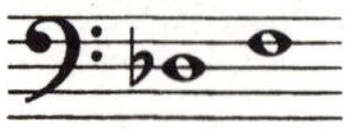

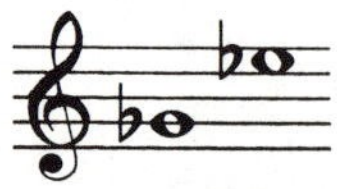

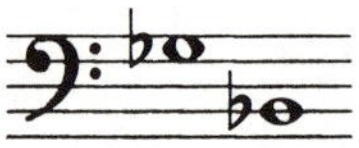

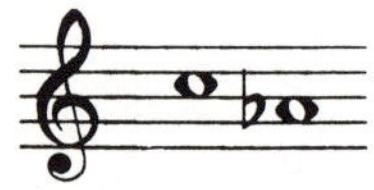

1. 6th 2. 5th 3. 7th 2	**64.** Give the numerical names of these intervals. 1. ______ 2. ______ 3. ______ Which one cannot be major or minor? ____
major minor (either order)	**65.** 2nds, 3rds, 6ths, and 7ths may be either __________ or __________.
2nds 3rds 6ths 7ths (any order)	**66.** *Major* intervals are like perfect intervals in that the *upper* note exists in the major scale built from the *lower* note. major 3rd C major scale (This does not mean that a minor interval exists in the minor scale built from the lower note. The structure of minor intervals is dealt with later.) The terms "major" and "minor" apply to the following intervals: ____, ____, ____, and ____.
1. major 3rd 2. major 2nd	**67.** Shown below are major scales built from the lower notes of major intervals. Notice that the upper note also occurs in each scale. Give the qualitative and numerical names of each interval, following the given example. major 6th 1. __________ 2. __________

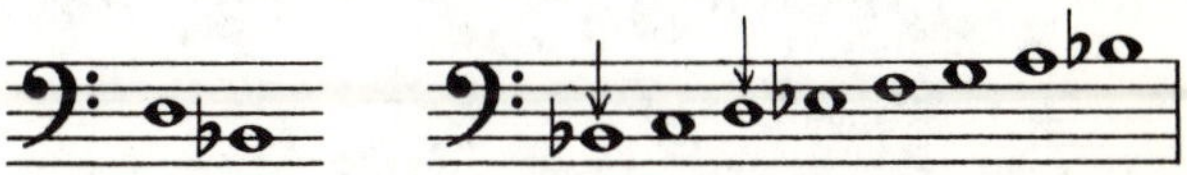

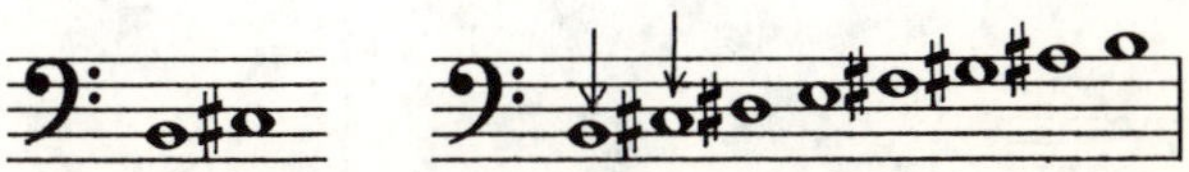

1

1.

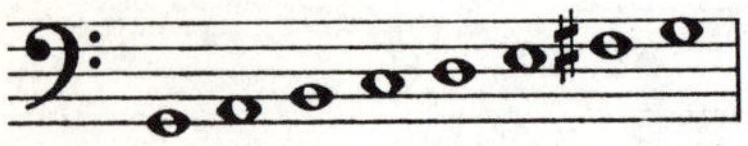

2.

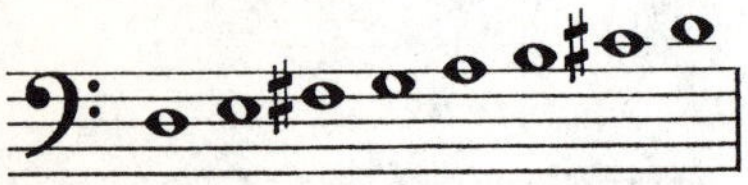

68. Using the necessary chromatic signs, construct a major scale from the lower note of each given interval. Which one is a major interval? _____

1.

2.

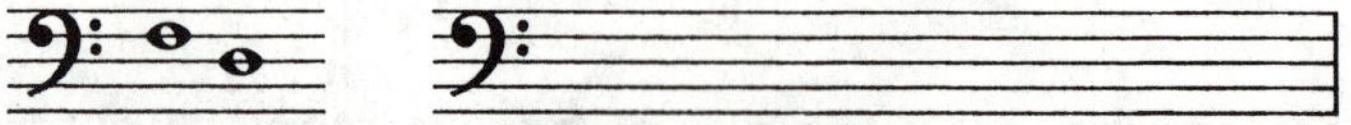

1. (major 7th) 3. major 2nd

2. 3rd 4. major 6th

69. Mentally (or on a separate piece of paper) construct major scales from the lower notes of these intervals. Give the numerical name of each, preceded by the qualitative name when it is major.

1.  major 7th 3. __________

2.  __________ 4. __________

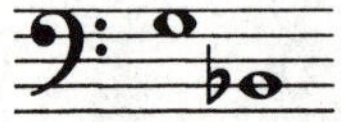

1. 6th 3. major 2nd

2. major 7th 4. 3rd

70. Continue as in frame 69.

1.  __________ 3. __________

2.  __________ 4. __________

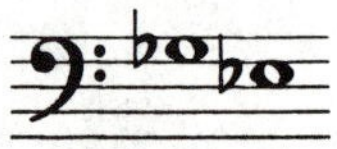

1.

2.

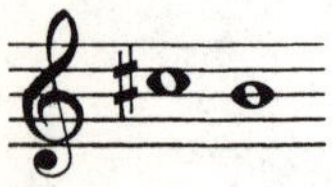

71. Complete the following intervals as directed.

1. major 2nd up

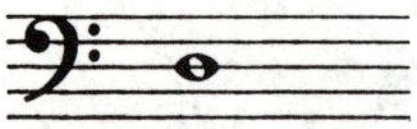

2. major 2nd down

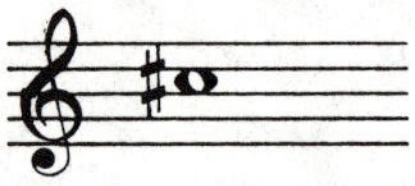

1.

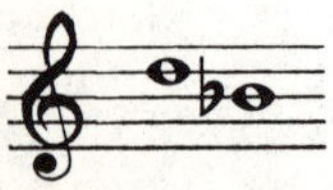

2.

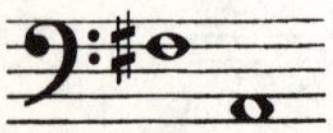

72. Continue as in frame 71.

1. major 3rd down

2. major 6th down

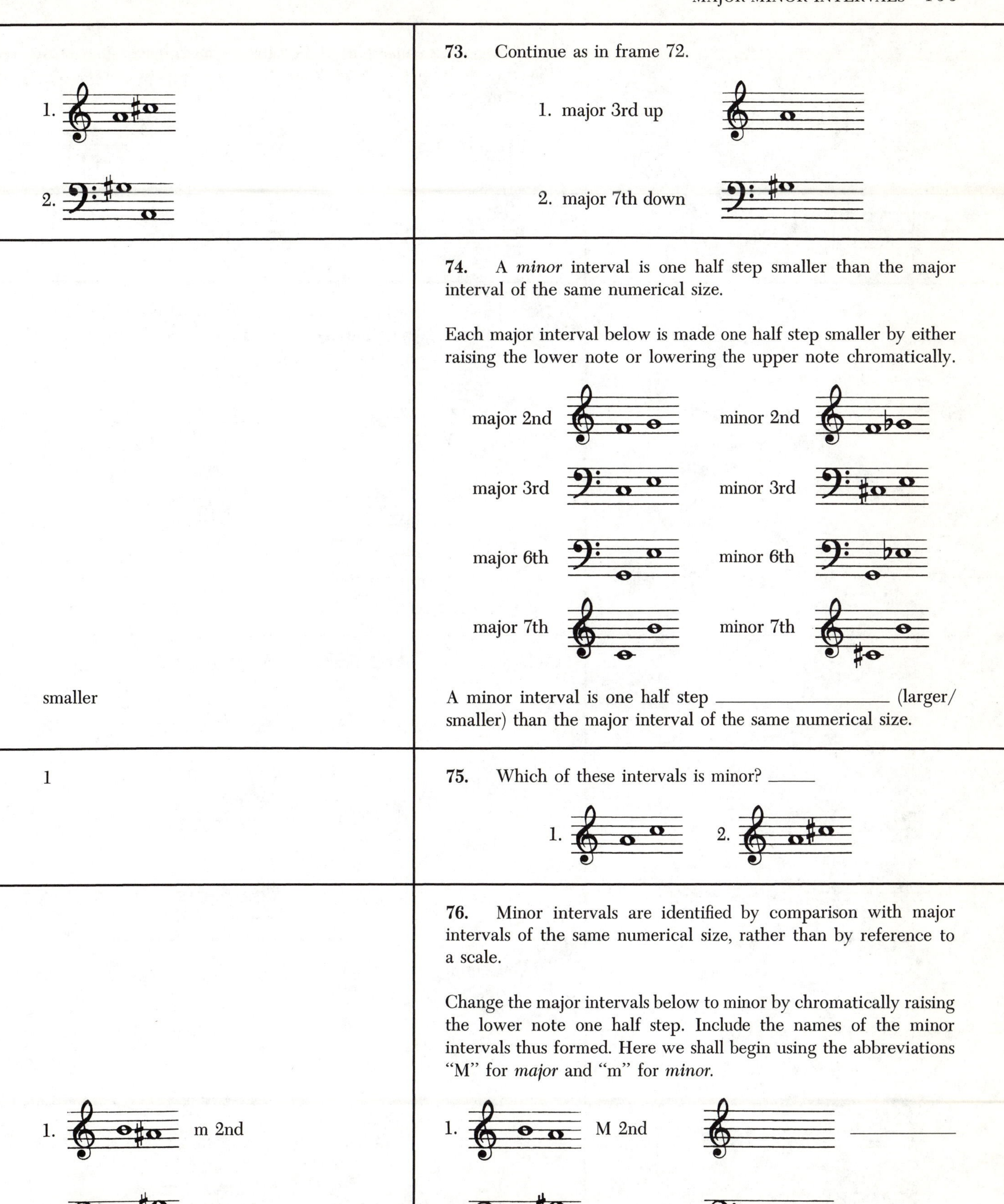

1.

2.

73. Continue as in frame 72.

1. major 3rd up

2. major 7th down

---

smaller

74. A *minor* interval is one half step smaller than the major interval of the same numerical size.

Each major interval below is made one half step smaller by either raising the lower note or lowering the upper note chromatically.

major 2nd — minor 2nd

major 3rd — minor 3rd

major 6th — minor 6th

major 7th — minor 7th

A minor interval is one half step ________________ (larger/smaller) than the major interval of the same numerical size.

1

75. Which of these intervals is minor? _____

1. 2.

---

1. m 2nd

2. m 7th

76. Minor intervals are identified by comparison with major intervals of the same numerical size, rather than by reference to a scale.

Change the major intervals below to minor by chromatically raising the lower note one half step. Include the names of the minor intervals thus formed. Here we shall begin using the abbreviations "M" for *major* and "m" for *minor.*

1. M 2nd ____________

2. M 7th ____________

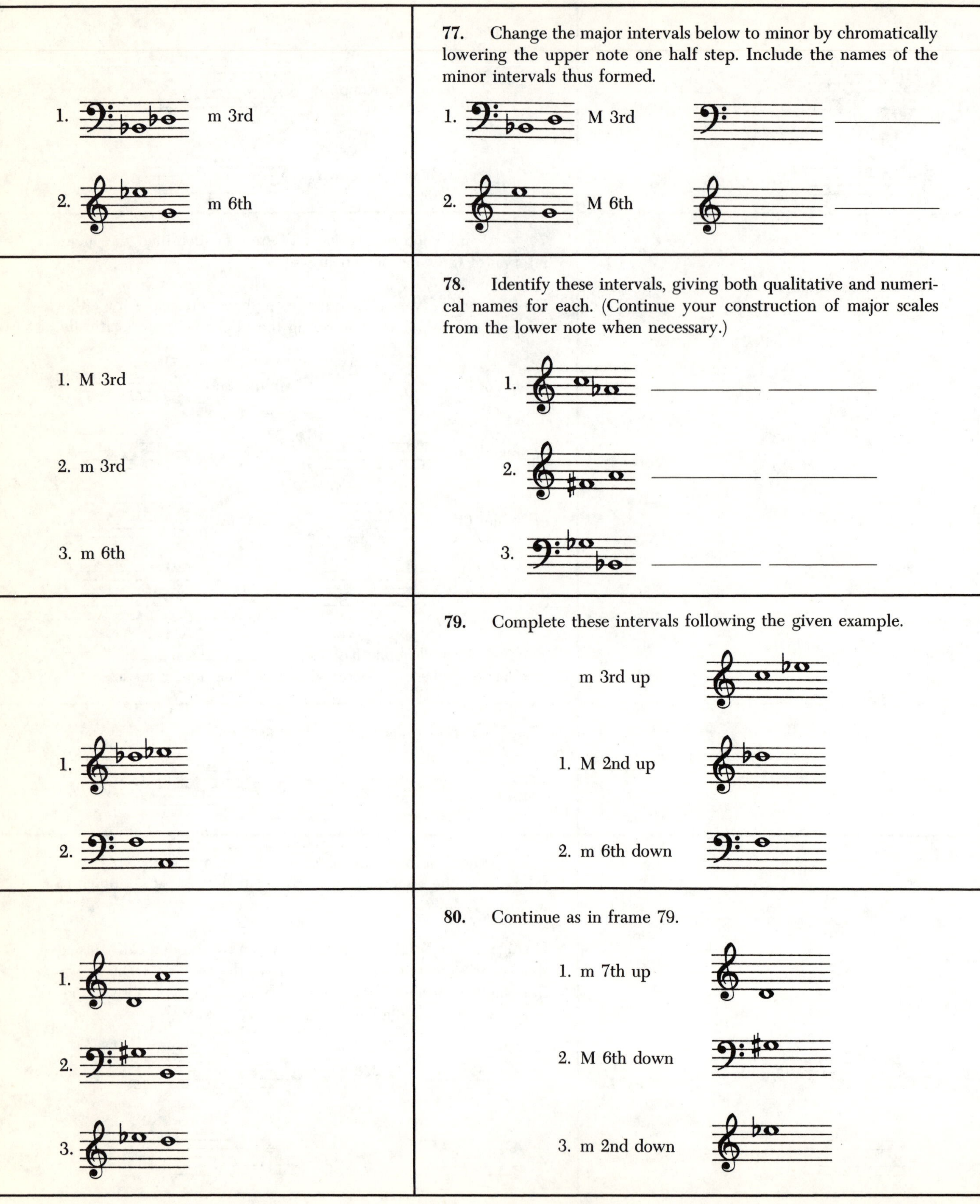

1. m 3rd
2. m 6th
77. Change the major intervals below to minor by chromatically lowering the upper note one half step. Include the names of the minor intervals thus formed.
1. M 3rd
2. M 6th
1. M 3rd
2. m 3rd
3. m 6th
78. Identify these intervals, giving both qualitative and numerical names for each. (Continue your construction of major scales from the lower note when necessary.)
1.
2.
3.
79. Complete these intervals following the given example.
m 3rd up
1. M 2nd up
2. m 6th down
1.
2.
80. Continue as in frame 79.
1. m 7th up
2. M 6th down
3. m 2nd down
1.
2.
3.

two 2nds 3rds 6ths 7ths (any order)	**81.** To arrive at qualitative interval names, into how many groups are numerical intervals divided? _____ The qualitative names major and minor refer to the interval group which consists of _____, _____, _____, and _____.
perfect diminished augmented (any order) prime	**82.** Primes, 4ths, 5ths, and octaves are either ____________, __________________, or __________________. The diminished ____________ does not exist.
major minor (either order) larger	**83.** 2nds, 3rds, 6ths, and 7ths are either ____________ or ____________. A major interval is one half step ____________ than a minor interval of the same numerical size.
5ths m (3rd) M (3rd)	**84.** An interval in the "perfect" interval group (primes, 4ths, _____, and octaves) goes from small to large in the following order: *diminished → perfect → augmented,* as illustrated below. d 4th P 4th A 4th Similarly, an interval in the "major-minor" interval group (2nds, 3rds, 6ths, and 7ths) goes from small to large in this order: *minor → major.* Complete the identification of the intervals below. _____ 3rd _____ 3rd (Play all of the intervals in this frame at the keyboard, listening for their progression from smaller to larger.)

(d 2nd) m 2nd M 2nd (A 2nd)

85. The range in size expressed by "m → M" may be extended in this interval group by the further use of the "diminished" and "augmented" principles.

d → m → M → A (illustrated below)

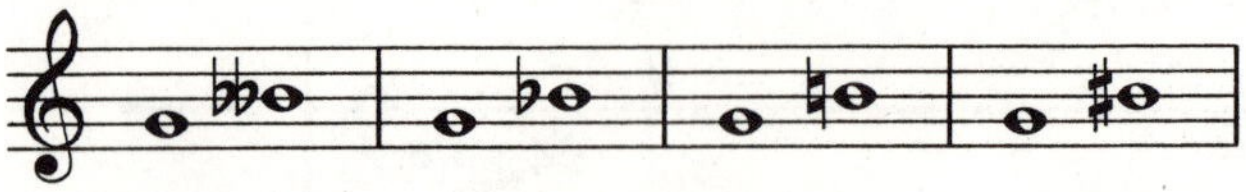

d 3rd m 3rd M 3rd A 3rd

Complete the identification of the intervals below.

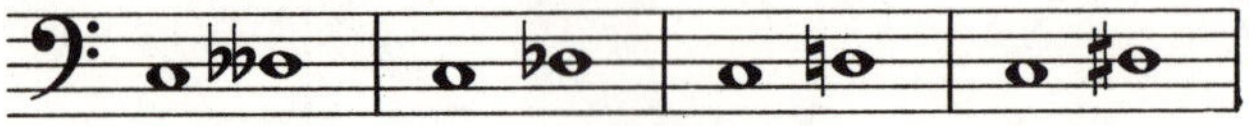

d 2nd ___ ___ ___ ___ A 2nd

diminished

augmented

86. From the information in frames 84 and 85, we may conclude the following:

1. An interval one half step *smaller* than minor is ________________ (diminished/augmented).

2. An interval one half step *larger* than major is ________________ (diminished/augmented).

1. A 2nd
2. A 3rd
3. A 6th

87. Change these major intervals to augmented by chromatically raising the upper note one half step. Identify each new interval.

1.  M 2nd ____ 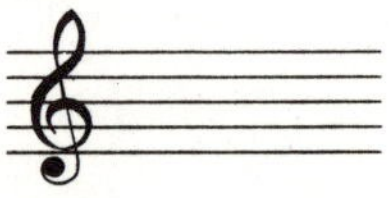
2.  M 3rd ____ 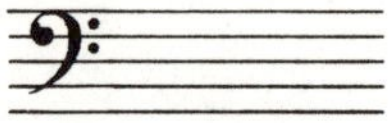
3.  M 6th ____

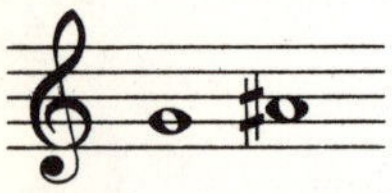

1. 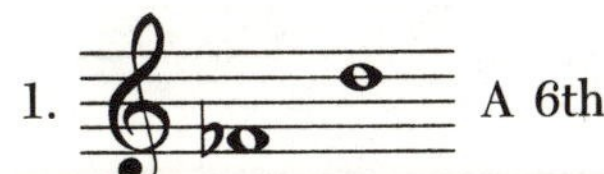 A 6th

2. 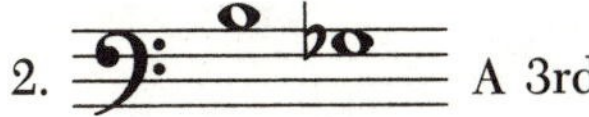 A 3rd

3. A 7th

88. Augment these major intervals by chromatically lowering the bottom note one half step, and identify each new interval.

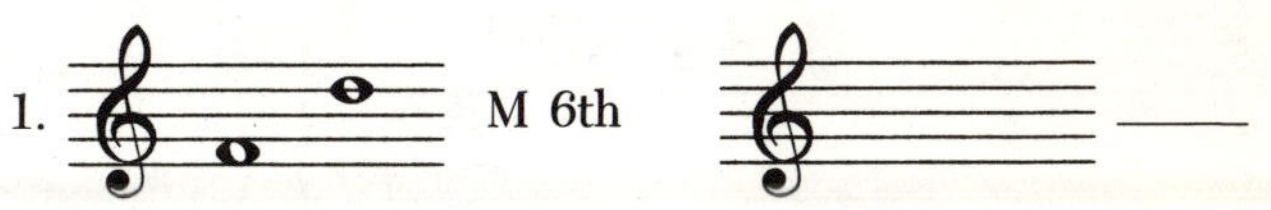

1. M 6th ____

2. M 3rd ____

3. M 7th ____

1. M 7th 3. A 6th

2. A 3rd 4. M 2nd

89. Identify these intervals.

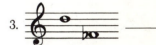

1. ____ 3. ____

2. ____ 4. ____

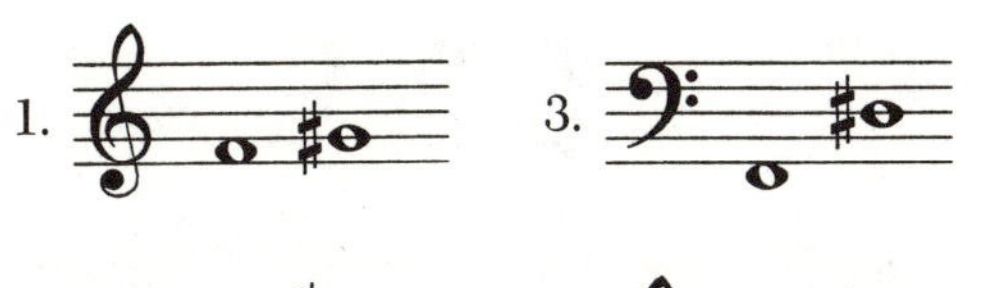

90. Construct these intervals above the given note. (You may find it helpful to construct the major interval first and then raise the upper note; see frame 87.)

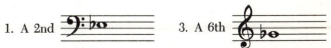

1. A 2nd 3. A 6th

2. A 3rd 4. A 7th

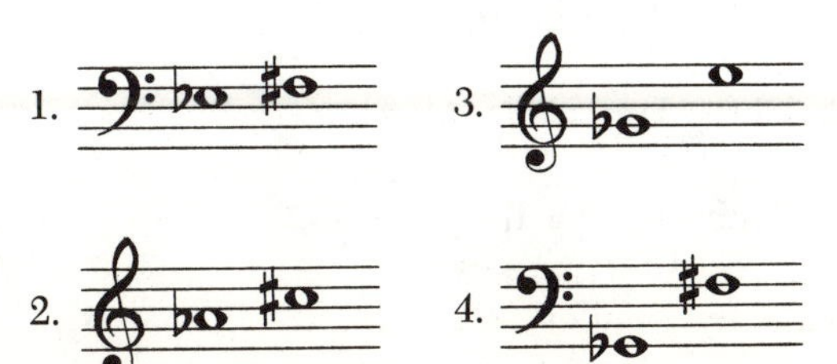

91. Continue as in frame 90.

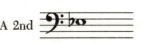

1. A 2nd 3. A 6th

2. A 3rd 4. A 7th

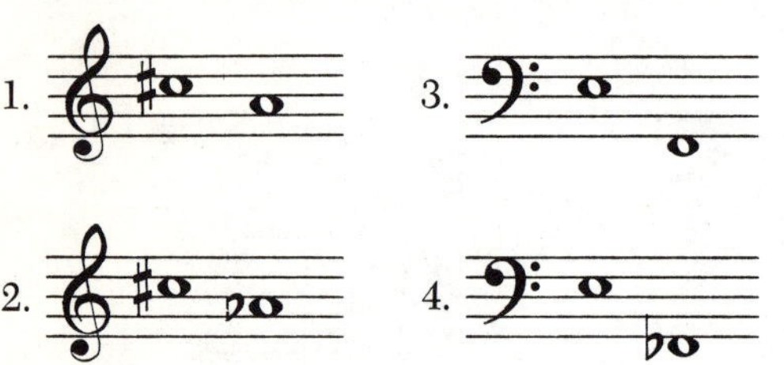
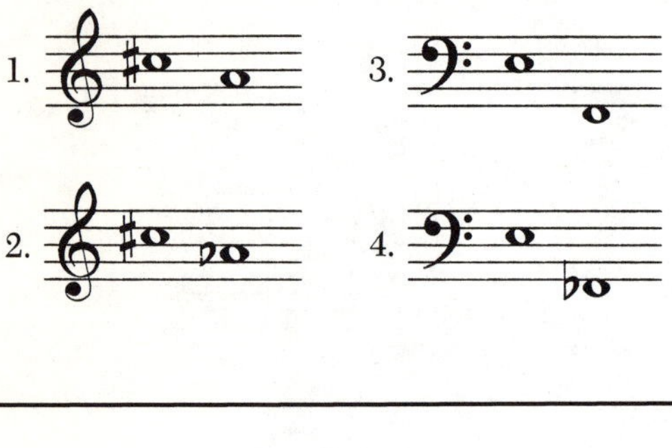

92. Construct these intervals *below* the given notes.

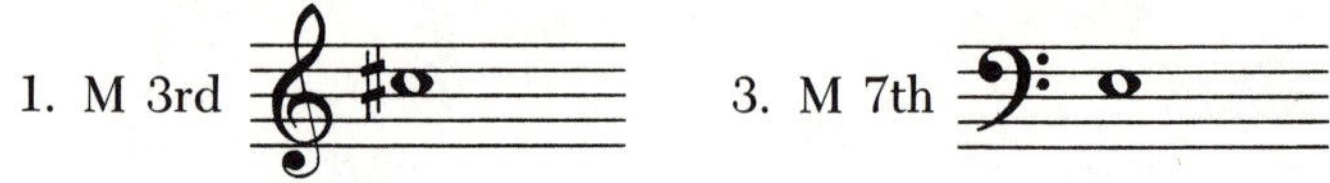

2. A 3rd 4. A 7th

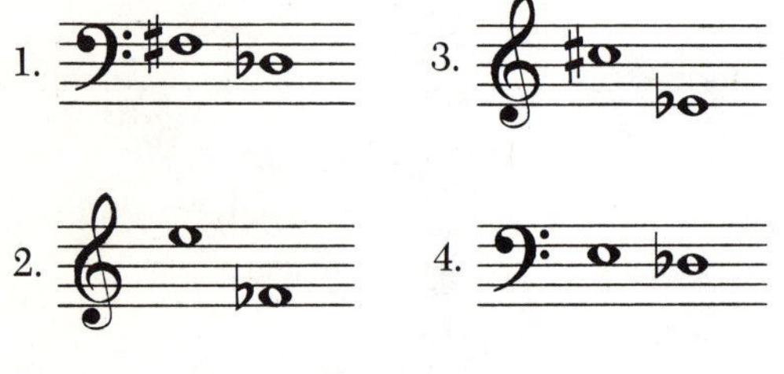

93. Continue as in frame 92.

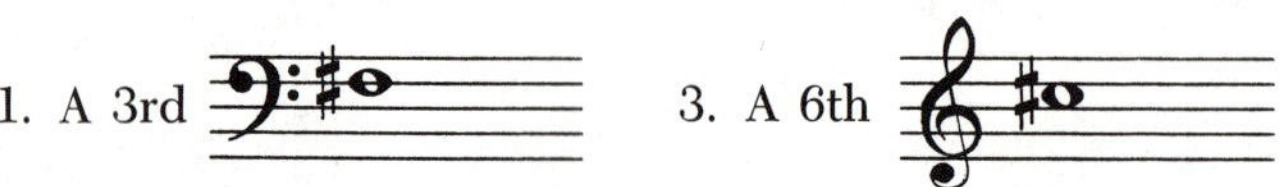

2. A 7th 4. A 2nd

1. M 3rd 4. m 7th

2. A 7th 5. A 6th

3. A 2nd 6. m 3rd

94. Identify these m, M, and A intervals.

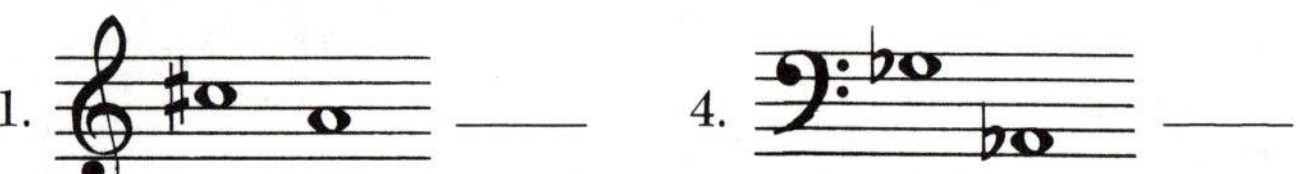

1. ____ 4. ____

2. ____ 5. ____

3. ____ 6. ____

1. A

2. m

3. d

95. d → m → M → A

1. An interval one half step larger than M is ____.

2. An interval one half step smaller than M is ____.

3. An interval one half step smaller than m is ____.

1. 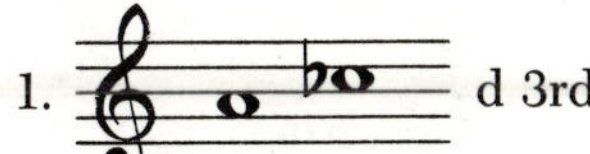 d 3rd

2.  d 6th

3.  d 7th

96. Change these minor intervals to diminished by chromatically *lowering* the *upper* note one half step, and identify each new interval.

1. m 3rd ____

2. m 6th ____

3. m 7th ____

1. d 3rd

2.  d 7th

3. d 2nd

97. Diminish these minor intervals by chromatically *raising* the *bottom* note one half step, and identify each new interval.

1. m 3rd ____

2. m 7th ____

3. m 2nd ____

1. d 7th

2. d 3rd

3. d 6th

98. Identify these intervals.

1.  ____

2. ____

3. 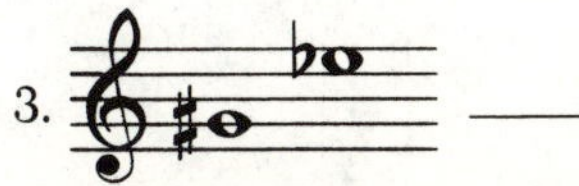 ____

1. d 2nd 2. P prime

99. Identify these intervals; then play them at the keyboard.

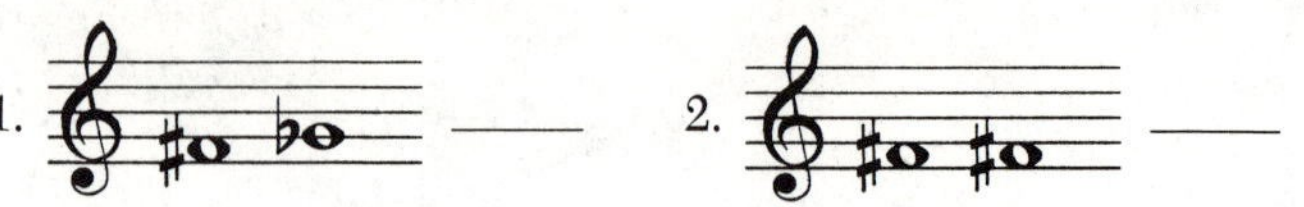

Observe that the two intervals *sound* the same. Many intervals sound the same but are spelled differently, such as m3 and A2, d5 and A4, A7 and P octave, and so forth. These intervals are spelled differently because of their characteristic functions in music. This will become clearer as your study of music advances.

---

1. M 3rd 4. m 3rd

2. d 3rd 5. d 7th

3. A 3rd 6. A 6th

100. Identify these d, m, M, and A intervals.

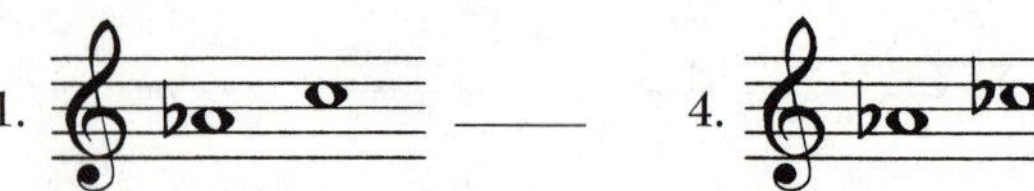

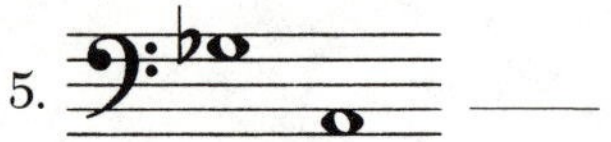

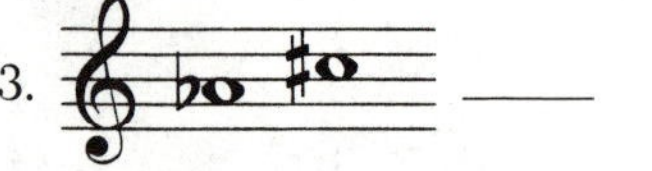

---

1. (D) E♭

2. (G) E♭

3. (D) B♯

101. The lower note is given in each interval below. Spell the upper note, following the example provided.

M 2nd up D ____ E ____

1. m 2nd up D ____ ____

2. m 6th up G ____ ____

3. A 6th up D ____ ____

---

1. (D♯) F♯ 4. (A) G♭

2. (D♯) B♯ 5. (A♭) B♭♭

3. (A♭) C♭ 6. (G♭) A

102. Spell these intervals either up or down, as indicated.

1. m 3rd up D♯ ____ ____
2. m 3rd down D♯ ____ ____
3. M 6th down A♭ ____ ____
4. d 7th up A ____ ____
5. M 7th down A♭ ____ ____
6. A 2nd up G♭ ____ ____

1. (G) F♭ 4. (A♯) B♭ 2. (E) C♭ 5. (A) B♭♭ 3. (D♭) F♯ 6. (F♯) E♯	**103.** Continue as in frame 102. 1. A 2nd down G ____ ____ 4. d 2nd up A♯ ____ ____ 2. d 6th up E ____ ____ 5. A 7th down A ____ ____ 3. d 6th down D♭ ____ ____ 6. M 7th up F♯ ____ ____
primes diminished perfect augmented (any order) diminished	**104.** The "perfect" interval group consists of ________, 4ths, 5ths, and octaves. The qualitative name of intervals in this group may be ________, ________, or ________. The ________ prime does not exist.
2nds 3rds 6ths 7ths diminished minor major augmented (any order)	**105.** The "major-minor" interval group consists of ____, ____, ____, and ____. Qualitative names of intervals in this group may be ________, ________, ________, or ________.

LISTENING FRAMES

2 d 4th	**106.** Listen again to Example 4-2, the beginning of Corelli's Trio Sonata, Op. 4, No. 8. Although the first five pitches are correct in each notation below, the sixth pitch varies. Which one notates the sixth pitch correctly? ____  The interval between pitches 5 and 6 is therefore a ____ ____.

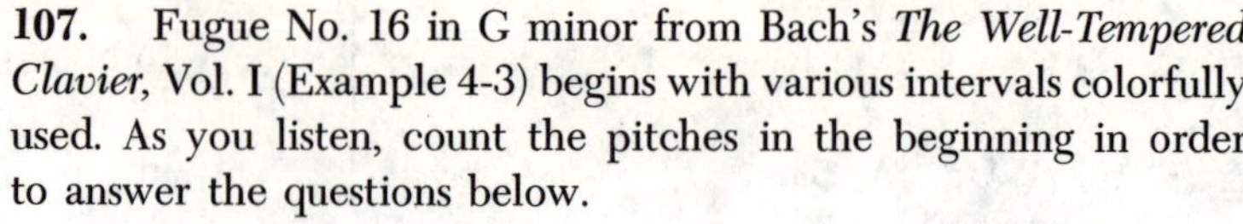

107. Fugue No. 16 in G minor from Bach's *The Well-Tempered Clavier,* Vol. I (Example 4-3) begins with various intervals colorfully used. As you listen, count the pitches in the beginning in order to answer the questions below.

1. The first two pitches form what ascending interval? _____ _____
2. The third and fourth pitches form what descending interval? _____ _____
3. The fifth pitch is the same as which previous pitch? ___________

1. m 2nd
2. m 2nd
3. third

108. Of the first five tones in Example 4-3, all but the third are notated below. Listen to the excerpt again and supply the third pitch, which is an eighth note. (Review the answers in the previous frame if necessary.)

The interval between pitches 2 and 3 is therefore a(n) _____ _____.

m 6th

109. Soon after the beginning of Example 4-3, a similar melody enters above the first. Listen carefully to this second melody when it appears, comparing it with the first.

1. The first two pitches of the second melody form what ascending interval? _____ _____ (P 5th / m 3rd / m 2nd).
2. The third and fourth pitches of the second melody form what descending interval? _____ _____ (M2nd / m 2nd).
3. Are the third and fifth pitches of this melody the same? _____

1. m 3rd
2. m 2nd
3. yes

MELODIC AND HARMONIC INTERVALS; INTERVAL INVERSIONS

110. Intervals occur in two forms: the two tones are sounded either consecutively or simultaneously.

When the two tones occur one after the other (consecutively), that interval is said to be a *melodic* interval.

When the two tones are sounded together (simultaneously), the interval is called a *harmonic* interval.

Is the following a melodic interval? ______

yes

---

111. In a ____________ interval, the two tones occur one after the other.

In a ______________ interval, the two tones sound together.

melodic

harmonic

---

112. Indicate whether each interval is melodic or harmonic.

1. ______________ 
2. ______________

1. melodic
2. harmonic

---

113. Continue as in frame 112.

1. ______________ 
2. ______________

1. harmonic
2. melodic

114. Identify these intervals and indicate whether each is melodic or harmonic, as shown in the given example.

harmonic d 4th

1. ______________ ___ __________

2. ______________ ___ __________

1. melodic A octave

2. melodic P 5th

115. Continue as in frame 114.

1. ______________ ___ __________

2. ______________ ___ __________

1. harmonic A 5th

2. harmonic A 4th

116. Complete these intervals as indicated.

1. M 6th up (harmonic)

2. A 2nd up (melodic)

1.

2.

117. Continue as in frame 116.

1. P 5th down (melodic)

2. A 5th down (harmonic)

1.

2.

118. Complete these *harmonic* intervals.

1. M 3rd up

2. P 4th up

1.

2.

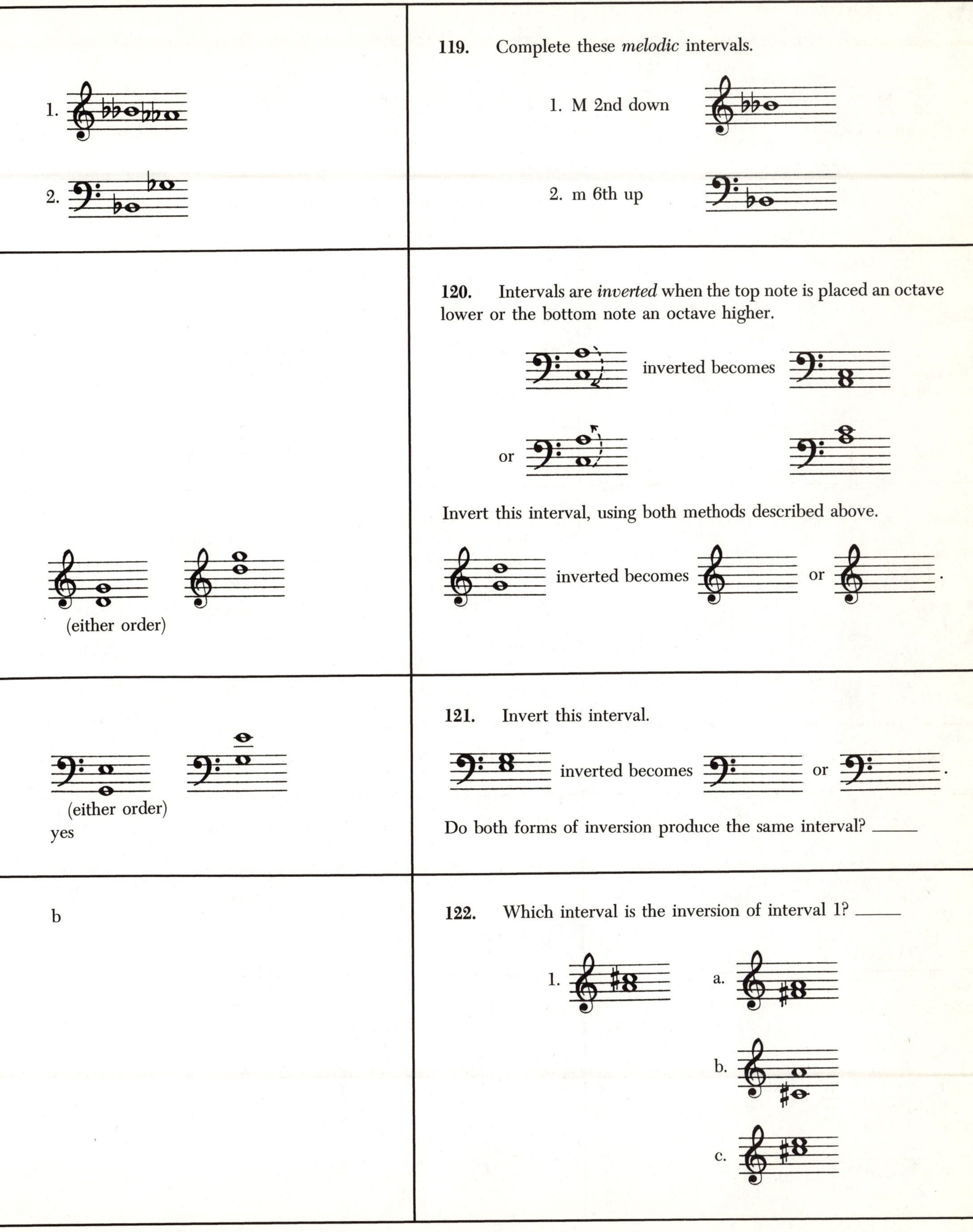

119. Complete these *melodic* intervals.

1. M 2nd down
2. m 6th up

Answers: 1. 2.

120. Intervals are *inverted* when the top note is placed an octave lower or the bottom note an octave higher.

inverted becomes

or

Invert this interval, using both methods described above.

inverted becomes or .

Answer: (either order)

121. Invert this interval.

inverted becomes or .

Do both forms of inversion produce the same interval? ______

Answer: (either order) yes

122. Which interval is the inversion of interval 1? ______

1. a. b. c.

Answer: b

(either order)

123. Invert this interval.

inverted becomes ______ or ______.

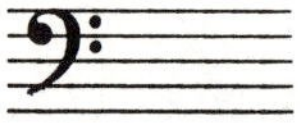

c

124. Which interval is the inversion of interval 1? _____

1.

a.

b.

c.

5th

125. Inverting an interval alters its numerical size. The inverted size can be found quickly by subtracting from nine the number representing the original interval.

A 2nd inverts to a 7th. (Two subtracted from nine equals seven.)

A 3rd inverts to a 6th. (Three subtracted from nine equals six.)

A 4th inverts to a ____________.

2nd 4th

126. A 7th inverts to a _____. A 5th inverts to a _____.

octave

127. Inverting an octave results in a prime.

inverted becomes ______ or ______.

Inverting a prime results in a(n) ____________.

1.  m 3rd

2.  P 4th

128. Invert these intervals by lowering the upper note an octave. Name the interval which is produced.

1. _____ ____________

2. _____ ____________

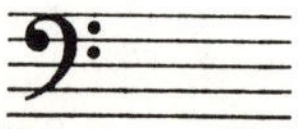

2nds 4ths primes	**129.** 7ths invert to ____. 5ths invert to ____. Octaves invert to ________.
perfect	**130.** The qualitative names of intervals also change with inversion except for one: perfect intervals remain perfect when inverted. Major intervals invert to minor. Minor intervals invert to major. Augmented intervals invert to diminished. Diminished intervals invert to augmented. When inverted, ________ intervals remain perfect.
a P 4th	**131.** Which interval is the inversion of interval 1? ____ It is a ____ ____. 1.  a.  b. 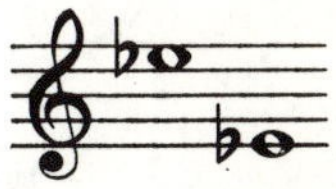 c. 
minor major	**132.** Major intervals inverted are ________. Minor intervals inverted are ________.
minor 2nd	**133.** An inverted major 3rd is a ________ 6th. An inverted minor 7th is a major ____.
minor 3rd perfect 4th	**134.** An inverted major 6th is a ________ ________. An inverted perfect 5th is a ________ ________.

1. m 6th

2. d 5th

135. Invert these intervals by raising the lower note an octave, and name the interval produced.

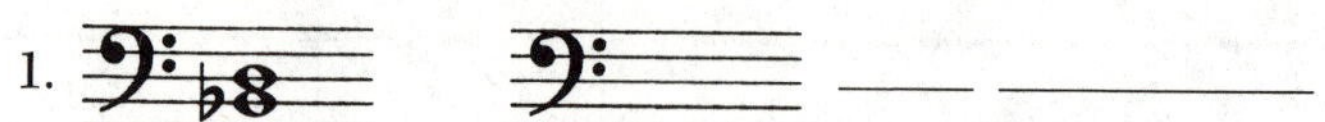

4th

augmented prime

136. An augmented 5th inverted is a diminished _____. An inverted diminished octave is a(n) _______________ _____________.

No. (The diminished prime does not exist. An inverted augmented octave is an augmented prime. This is the only exception to the principle that augmented intervals invert to diminished intervals.)

137. Study the inversion below.

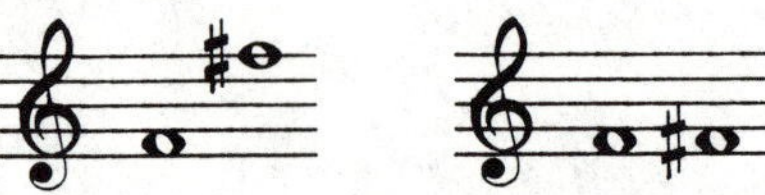

Is an inverted augmented octave a diminished prime? _____

d 7th

138. Some diminished and augmented intervals occur infrequently in music, while others are often found. The A 2nd, for instance, is part of the harmonic minor scale.

Circle the two notes which form the A 2nd in this D harmonic minor scale.

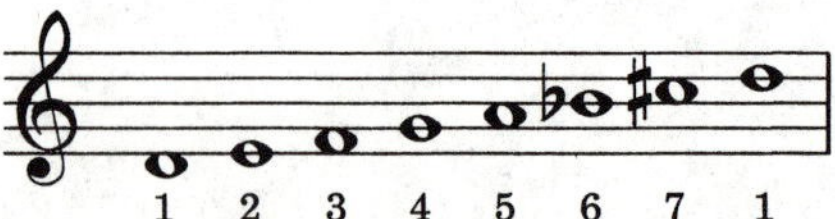

An inverted A 2nd is a _____ _____.

1. A 4th

2. d 5th

3. A 4th

139. The A 4th (or d 5th by inversion) occurs in several scales.

Name the intervals encompassed by the brackets in these scales.

1. 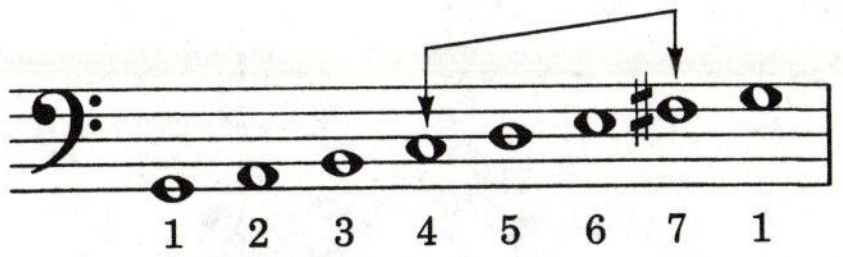 1 2 3 4 5 6 7 1 (G Major) ____ ____

2. 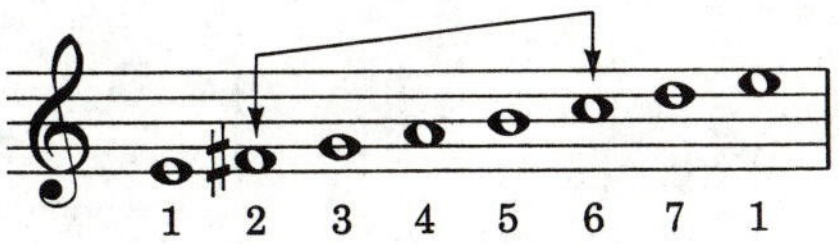 1 2 3 4 5 6 7 1 (E pure minor) ____ ____

3.  1 2 3 4 5 6 7 1 (B melodic minor ascending) ____ ____

---

1. d 7th

2. A 4th

3. d 3rd

140. Supply the inversions of these augmented and diminished intervals, which are frequently found in music.

(inversion)

1. A 2nd ____ ____

2. d 5th ____ ____

3. A 6th ____ ____

A

d

m

M

P

141. When inverted, d intervals become ____, and A intervals become ____.

Inverted M intervals are ____, and inverted m intervals become ____.

Inverted P intervals are always ____.

LISTENING FRAMES

1. (A) E♭

2. (A) D

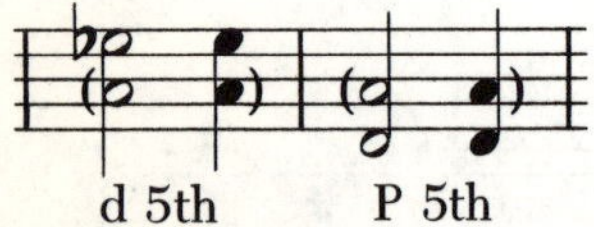

142. Spell these intervals:

1. d 5th up ___A___ ______

2. P 5th down ___A___ ______

These two intervals are used in their harmonic form in Camille Saint-Saëns' *Danse macabre,* Op. 40 (Example 4-4). In this passage the violin uses these intervals to evoke a dramatically sinister effect.

The first two measures are given below. After listening to Example 4-4, supply the missing notes in measures 3 and 4, and identify the intervals below the staff.

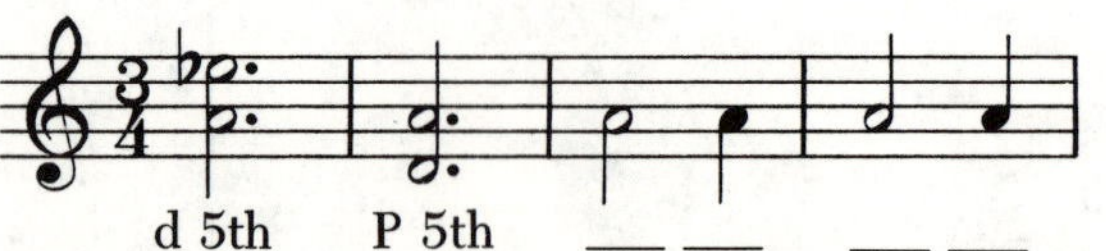

2

143. Immediately after the four measures given in frame 142, which of the following occurs? ______

1. The two intervals continue to alternate while the rhythmic motion becomes slower.

2. The two intervals continue to alternate in more rapid rhythmic motion.

3. Two other intervals are heard in the same rhythm as in the first four measures.

---

1. P

2. M

3. P

144. In Example 4-5, from Aaron Copland's Sonata for Violin and Piano, you will hear the violin play three harmonic intervals. The numerical names of these are given below. As you listen, determine the qualitative names of each. (The piano enters after the third harmonic interval begins.)

1. The first interval is a ______ 5th.

2. The second interval is a ______ 2nd.

3. The third interval is a ______ 4th.

M

145. Example 4-6, from Bartók's *Concerto for Orchestra* (second movement), uses harmonic intervals extensively. In this excerpt two muted trumpets play the same melody simultaneously a 2nd apart. Listen to Example 4-6 to determine the qualitative nature of the 2nds.

All of the 2nds are _____ (m / M).

SELF-QUIZ IV

1. The "perfect" intervals are __________, __________, __________, and __________.

2. The "major-minor" intervals are __________, __________, __________, and __________.

3. Spell these intervals either up or down as indicated.

   1. M 3rd down D _____
   2. d 3rd up G♯ _____
   3. A 6th down B♭ _____
   4. P 5th down D♭ _____
   5. A 2nd down A _____
   6. A octave up F♯ _____

4. Complete these melodic intervals.

   1. M 6th down 
   2. P octave down 
   3. M 3rd down

5. Complete these harmonic intervals.

   1. m 7th down 
   2. M 7th up 
   3. m 6th down

6. Identify these intervals.

   1.  _____ __________
   2.  _____ __________
   3. _____ __________

7. Invert this interval, and identify each inversion in the space provided.

   M3 inverted becomes _____ _____ or _____ _____

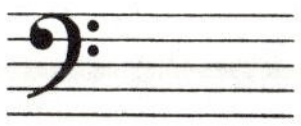

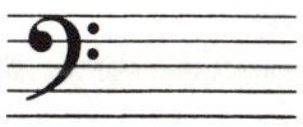

8. Augmented intervals invert to __________ intervals; diminished intervals invert to __________ intervals.

9. Major intervals invert to ________________ intervals; minor intervals invert to ____________ intervals.

10. Perfect intervals invert to ________________ intervals.

11. Supply the inversions of these intervals.

1. d 2nd _____ _____ (inversion) 2. A 5th _____ _____ (inversion) 3. d 7th _____ _____ (inversion)

CHAPTER ▪ V ▪ KEYS AND KEY SIGNATURES

Tonal organization in music frequently centers on a specific tone to which all other tones relate in various ways. This central tone is generally the first scale degree of the scale employed in the music and is often called the "tonic," "key center," or "key note." Key signatures serve to simplify notation by collecting the chromatic signs in the prevailing key and presenting them, following the clef, at the beginning of each line of music, thus eliminating the need to repeat them throughout the staff.

Major and minor keys are closely related to the major and minor scales they employ, usually identifiable by the key signature found in the music. Modes, however, involve different pitch relationships and usually are not associated with the idea of "key" as is found in music based on major and minor scales.

A thorough knowledge of scales and intervals is important in comprehending keys and key signatures and their relationships. Be certain that you understand the previous chapters before beginning the following material on keys and key signatures.

MAJOR KEY SIGNATURES; THE CIRCLE OF FIFTHS

1. This is an F major scale.

Complete the D major scale below by adding the necessary chromatic signs.

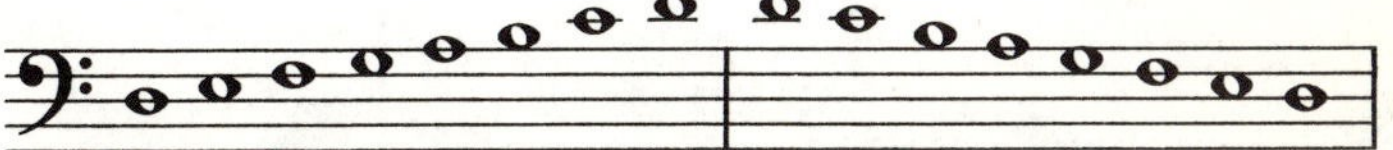

G major

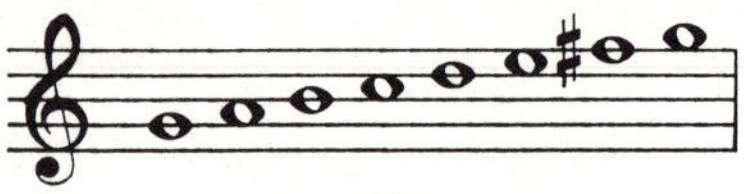

F major

2.

What is the name of the scale above? _____ ____________

Music employing primarily the notes of the G major scale is said to be in the *key* of G major.

The scale below is in the key of _____ ____________.

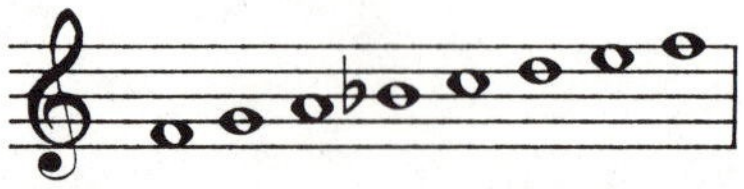

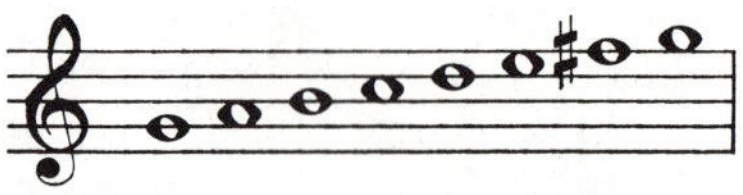

key G major

3.

This scale is in the _____ of G major. It is also the _____ ______ scale.

F major

4. Since music in the key of G major uses primarily the notes of the G major scale, all the F's in the music will be sharped, except when otherwise indicated.

Music in the key of F major employs the notes of the _____ ____________ scale.

B's

B's

5. Music in the key of F major requires all the _____ to be flatted, except when otherwise indicated in the music.

To eliminate the need for placing a flat before every B throughout an F major composition, a flat is placed at the beginning of each line of music at an appropriate pitch location on the staff. Note that it appears *after* the clef.

The flat at the beginning of the staff applies to all the _____ which follow.

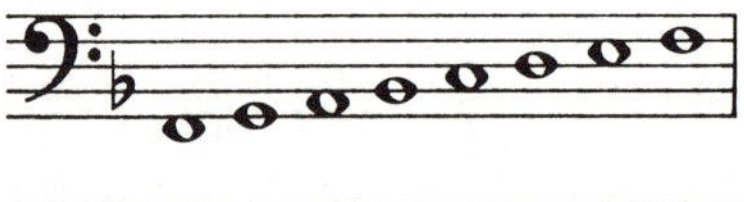

D major

6. Circle the notes affected by the sharps at the beginning of the staff. The notes affected may be in any octave.

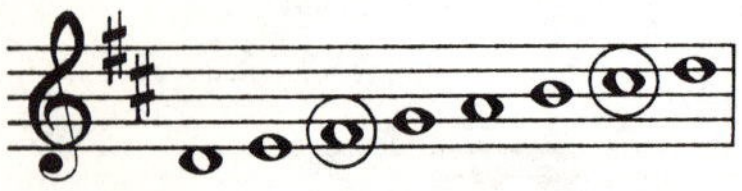

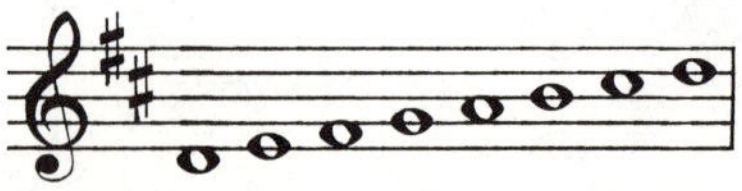

This example is in the key of _____ ____________.

B♭ major	**7.** Circle the notes affected by the flats at the beginning of the staff. This example is in the key of ____ ________.
signature	**8.** The chromatic signs placed at the beginning of a staff reflect those in the key of the music which follows. These chromatic signs are known as the *key signature.* The F major scale is shown below, followed by its key ____________.
key 1. after 2. before	**9.** The ____ signature of G major is shown below. It indicates that every F in the music is sharped, except when otherwise indicated. 1. The key signature appears ________ (before/after) the clef. 2. The key signature appears ________ (before/after) the meter signature.
1. G major 2. D pure minor	**10.** Write a key signature for each scale below. Indicate the name of each scale in the space provided, following the given example. B♭ major 1. ____________ 2. ____________

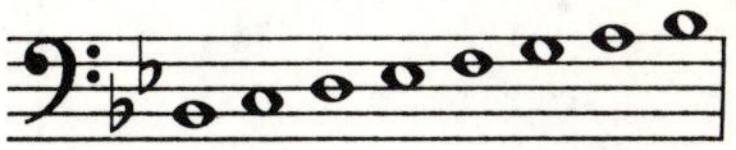

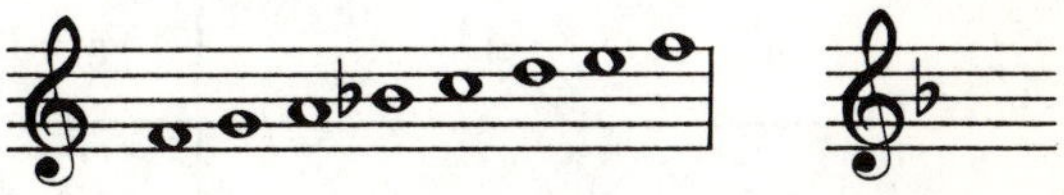

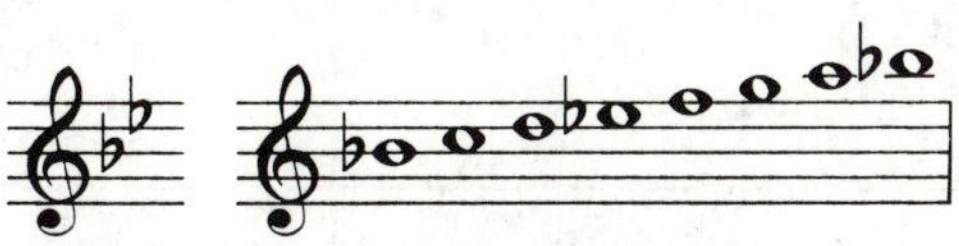

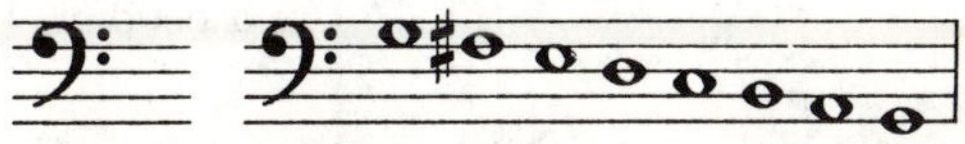

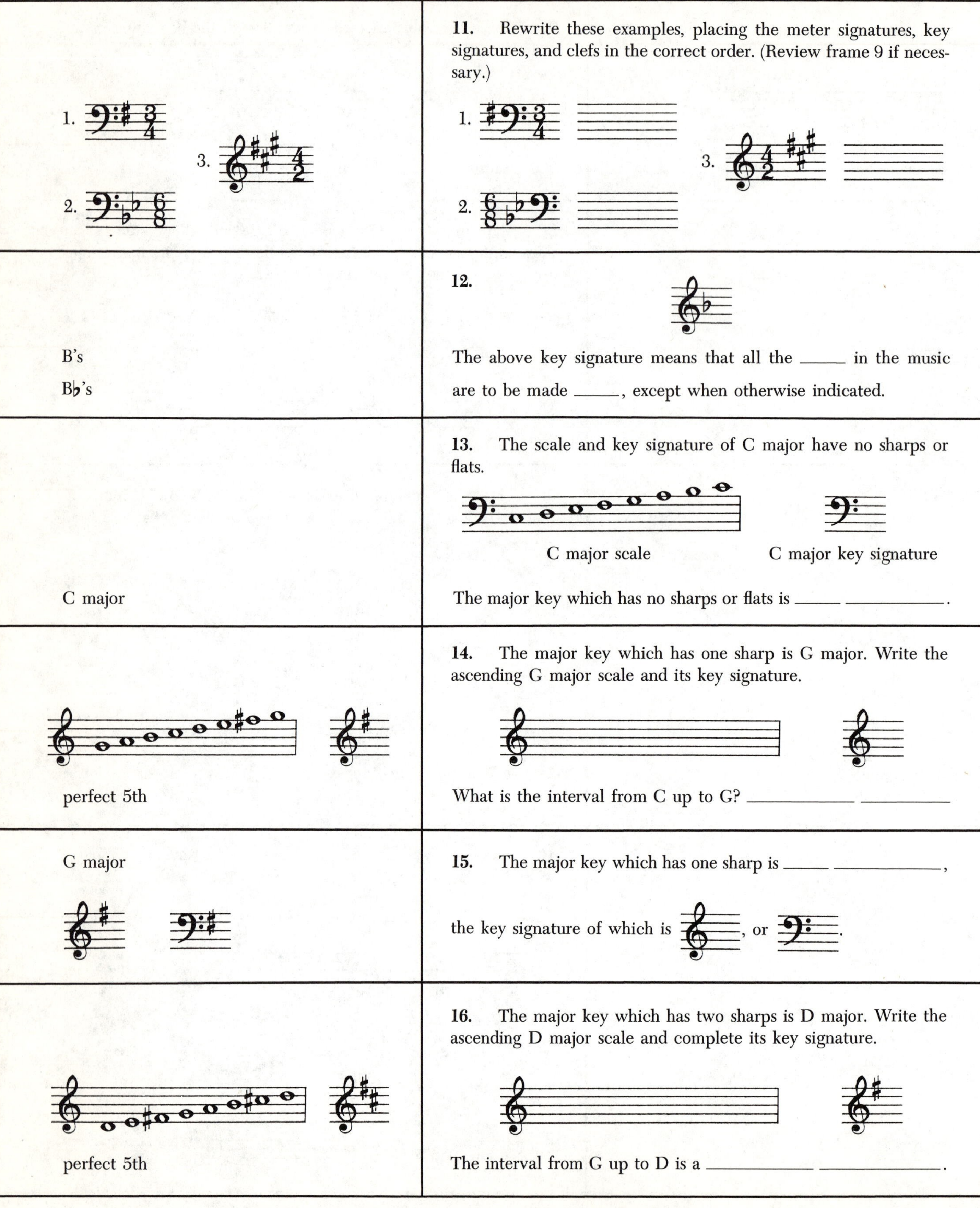

1. 2. 3.

11. Rewrite these examples, placing the meter signatures, key signatures, and clefs in the correct order. (Review frame 9 if necessary.)

1. 2. 3.

B's

B♭'s

12.

The above key signature means that all the ____ in the music are to be made ____, except when otherwise indicated.

C major

13. The scale and key signature of C major have no sharps or flats.

C major scale C major key signature

The major key which has no sharps or flats is ____ ________.

perfect 5th

14. The major key which has one sharp is G major. Write the ascending G major scale and its key signature.

What is the interval from C up to G? ________ ________

G major

15. The major key which has one sharp is ____ ________, the key signature of which is ____, or ____.

perfect 5th

16. The major key which has two sharps is D major. Write the ascending D major scale and complete its key signature.

The interval from G up to D is a ________ ________.

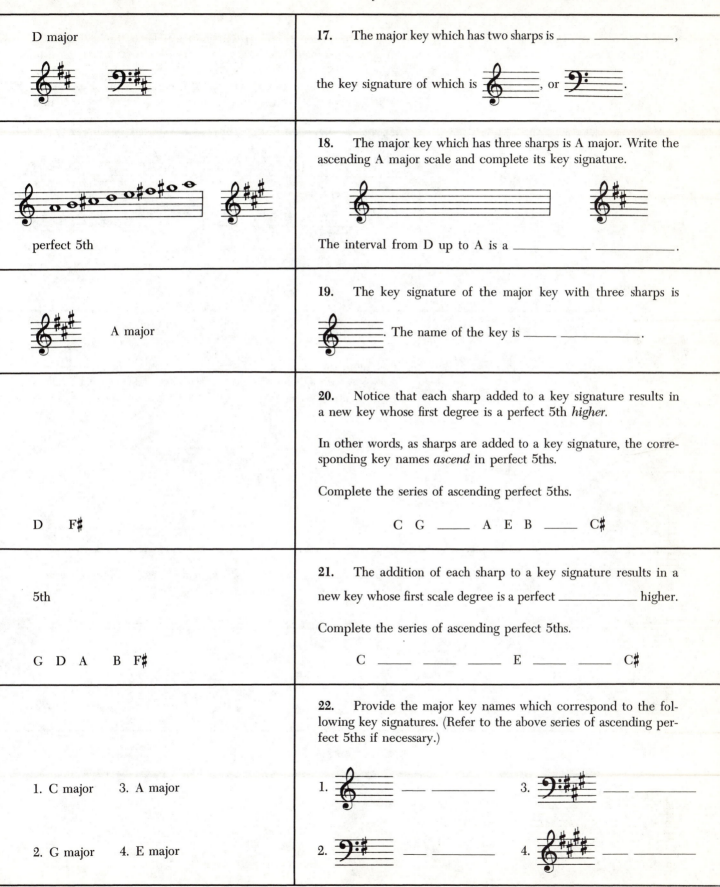

D major	**17.** The major key which has two sharps is ____ __________, the key signature of which is ________, or ________.
perfect 5th	**18.** The major key which has three sharps is A major. Write the ascending A major scale and complete its key signature. The interval from D up to A is a __________ __________.
A major	**19.** The key signature of the major key with three sharps is ________. The name of the key is ____ __________.
D F♯	**20.** Notice that each sharp added to a key signature results in a new key whose first degree is a perfect 5th *higher*. In other words, as sharps are added to a key signature, the corresponding key names *ascend* in perfect 5ths. Complete the series of ascending perfect 5ths. C G ____ A E B ____ C♯
5th G D A B F♯	**21.** The addition of each sharp to a key signature results in a new key whose first scale degree is a perfect __________ higher. Complete the series of ascending perfect 5ths. C ____ ____ ____ E ____ ____ C♯
1. C major 3. A major 2. G major 4. E major	**22.** Provide the major key names which correspond to the following key signatures. (Refer to the above series of ascending perfect 5ths if necessary.) 1. ____ ________ 3. ____ ________ 2. ____ ________ 4. ____ ________

23. The sequence of sharps as they are added to the key signature also follows a pattern of ascending perfect 5ths. The first sharp to appear is F♯; then C♯, then G♯, D♯, A♯, E♯, and B♯. Notice that the sharps occur in a fixed pattern of descending 4ths or ascending 5ths to maintain a consistent design while staying within the staff.

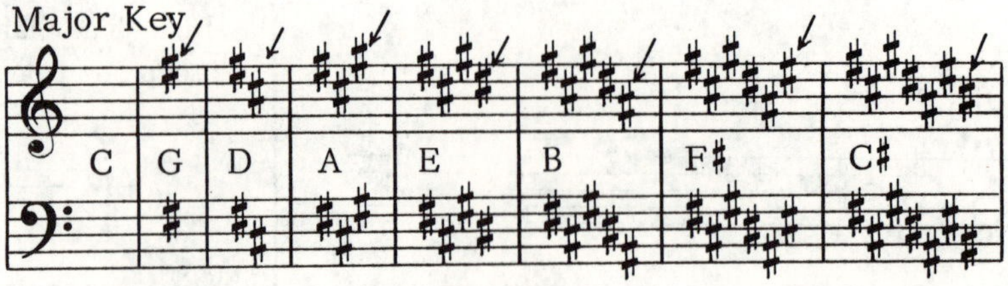

Major Key

C G D A E B F♯ C♯

The succession of keys above follows a pattern of ascending __________ __________.

perfect 5ths

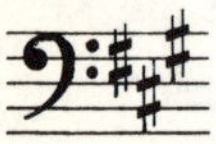

24. C __ __ A __ __ F♯ __ G♯ __ __ E♯ __

Complete the series of ascending perfect 5ths. Then provide the key signatures indicated below. (Begin memorizing the exact placement of sharps in key signatures but refer to the preceding frames if necessary.)

1. D major 
2. A major

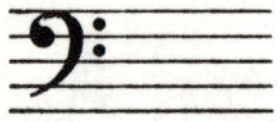

G D E B C♯ D♯ A♯ B♯

1. 
2.

25. Provide key signatures as indicated below. (Refer to preceding frames only if necessary.)

1. G major 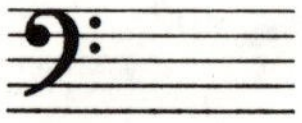
2. E major

1. 
2.

---

26. Continue as in frame 25.

1. B major 
2. C major

1.
2.

Bb Db Cb

27. Key signatures involving flats follow a pattern of *descending* perfect 5ths: each flat added to a key signature results in a new key a perfect 5th *lower.*

Complete the series of descending perfect 5ths.

C F ____ Eb Ab ____ Gb ____

F Bb Eb Db Gb

5ths

28. Complete the series of descending perfect 5ths.

C ____ ____ ____ Ab ____ ____ Cb

As flats are added to a key signature the corresponding key names descend in perfect __________.

1. F major 
2. Bb major

29. C F Bb Eb Ab Db Gb Cb

Following the above pattern of descending perfect 5ths, provide the major key name and corresponding major scale for each key signature. Observe the given example.

C major

1. ____ ________

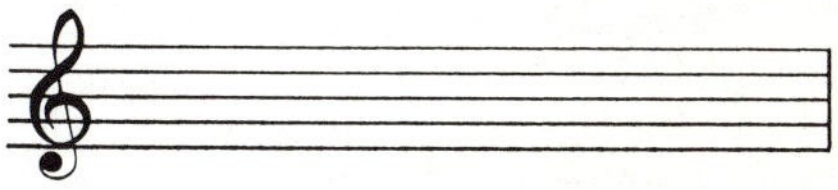

2. ____ ________

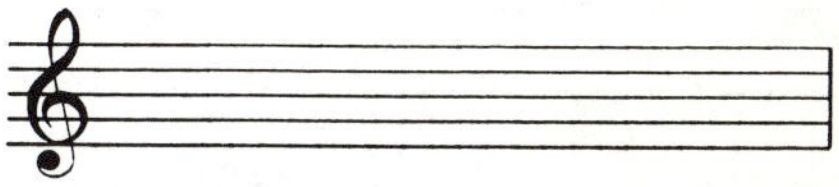

1. Eb major
2. Bb major

30. C F Bb Eb Ab Db Gb Cb

Referring to the above series of descending perfect 5ths, give the major key name of each key signature below. Observe the given example.

F major

1. ____ ________

2. ____ ________

1. A♭ major

2. G♭ major

3. D♭ major

31. Continue as in frame 30.

1. ____ __________

2. ____ __________

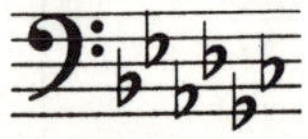

3. ____ __________

---

descending

32. The sequence of flats as they are added to the key signature also follows a pattern of descending perfect 5ths.

Major Key

C F B♭ E♭ A♭ D♭ G♭ C♭

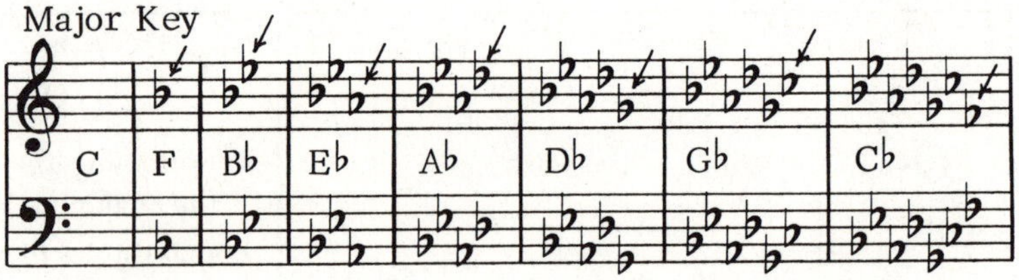

As with sharps, flats are placed in a fixed pattern. Here it is *ascending* 4ths and *descending* 5ths which maintain a consistent design while staying within the staff.

The succession of key names above follows a pattern of ______________ (ascending/descending) 5ths.

1.

2.

33. Write the key signatures of these keys. (Consult the descending perfect 5th series if necessary but begin memorizing the exact placement of flats.)

1. B♭ major

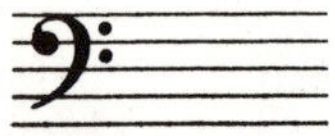

2. F major

1.

2.

34. Continue as in frame 33.

1. E♭ major

2. A♭ major

1. 2.	**35.** Continue as in frame 34. 1. G♭ major 2. D♭ major
ascending descending	**36.** Key signatures having sharps follow a series of ________ (ascending/descending) perfect 5ths. Key signatures having flats follow a series of ________ (ascending/descending) perfect 5ths.
D♭ A♭ E B enharmonic	**37.** Moving out from C, complete the perfect 5th series below. Pitch names moving to the right of C ascend; those moving to the left of C descend. G♭ ____ ____ E♭ B♭ F C G D A ____ ____ F♯ The pitches at each end of the series, G♭ and F♯, are *enharmonic,* which means that they are both played with the same key of the piano keyboard and therefore sound the same. G♭ and F♯ are ________.
alike yes	**38.** Enharmonic pitches have different pitch names but sound ________ (alike/different). Every pitch has either two or three possible enharmonic spellings (for example, C, B♯, D♭♭; E, D𝄪, F♭; A♭, G♯; etc.). Are these three pitches enharmonic? ____ F♯, G♭, E𝄪
1 2 5 6 9	**39.** Which groups of notes below are enharmonic? ____ ____ ____ ____ ____ 1. C♭, B 4. E, F♯ 7. E♭, C♯ 2. A, B♭♭ 5. E♯, F 8. A♯, B♭, C♭ 3. G, B♭ 6. A♭, G♯ 9. A♯, B♭, C♭♭

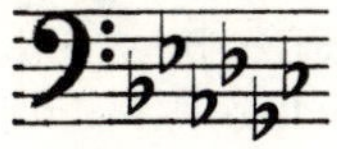

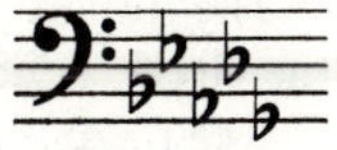

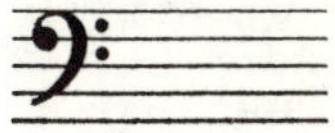

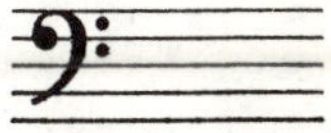

40. G♭ D♭ A♭ E♭ B♭ F C G D A E B F♯

Since G♭ and F♯ are enharmonic, the series of perfect 5ths (shown above) can be arranged in a circle which closes where G♭ and F♯ coincide. This is known as the *circle of 5ths.* The usual arrangement of the circle of 5ths, with C at the top of the circle, is shown at the left.

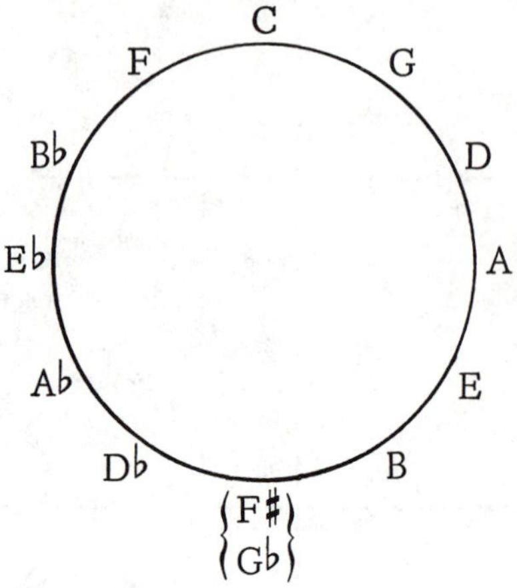

C G D A E B (F♯ / G♭) D♭ A♭ E♭ B♭ F

The diagram at the left is the circle of ____________.

5ths

41. Additional enharmonic pitches are added to the circle of 5ths below.

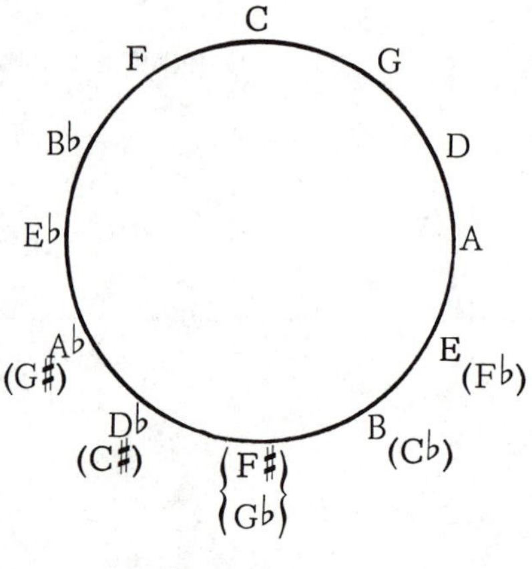

C G D A E (F♭) B (C♭) (F♯ / G♭) D♭ (C♯) A♭ (G♯) E♭ B♭ F

Starting at C, the clockwise direction shows the progression of sharp key names, and the counter-clockwise direction the progression of flat key names.

A♭ and G♯ are ____________________.

enharmonic

42. Provide signatures for these major keys. (Refer to the circle of 5ths in the preceding frame if necessary.)

1. G major 
2. D♭ major 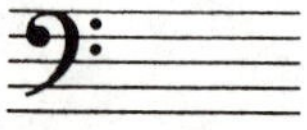
3. F major

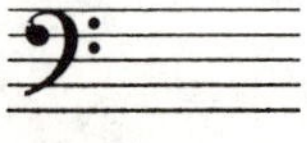

1. 
2. 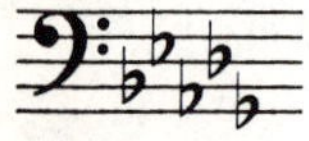
3.

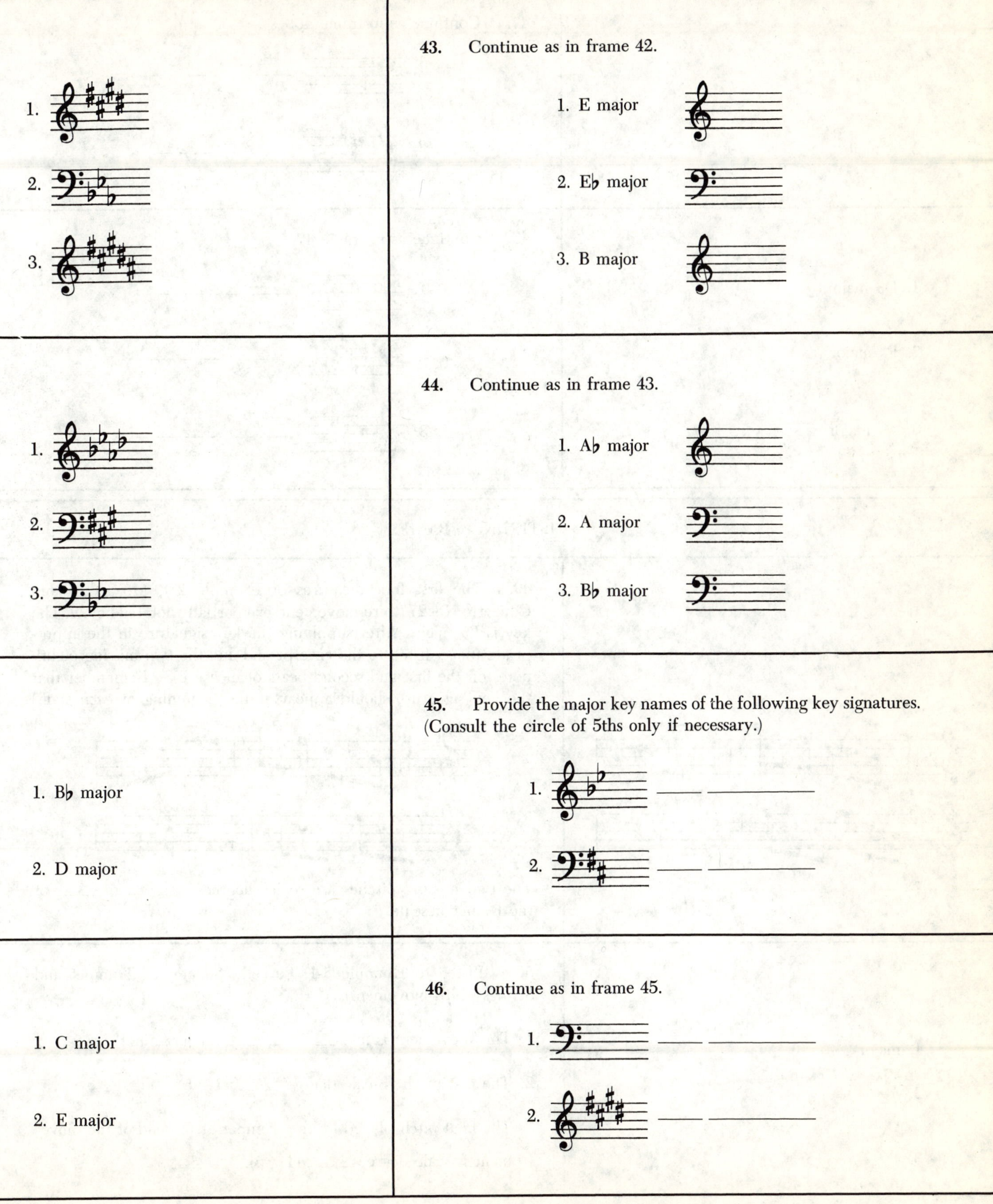

1.

2.

3.

43. Continue as in frame 42.

1. E major
2. E♭ major
3. B major

1.

2.

3.

44. Continue as in frame 43.

1. A♭ major
2. A major
3. B♭ major

---

1. B♭ major
2. D major

45. Provide the major key names of the following key signatures. (Consult the circle of 5ths only if necessary.)

1. ____ __________
2. ____ __________

---

1. C major
2. E major

46. Continue as in frame 45.

1. ____ __________
2. ____ __________

1. F major

2. A major

47. Continue as in frame 46.

1. ____ ________

2. ____ ________

1. D♭ major

2. F♯ major

3. A♭ major

48. Continue as in frame 47.

1. ____ ________

2. ____ ________

3. ____ ________

LISTENING FRAMES

7 1

49. The first four measures of Example 2-4, Mozart's Piano Concerto No. 27 (third movement) are partially notated below. The key is B♭ major. After supplying the key signature in the appropriate place, listen to the excerpt and add the two missing eighth notes on the first and second beats of measure 3. (Remember that the key signature should appear at the beginning of *each* staff.)

The two missing pitches are scales degrees _____ and _____ of the B♭ major scale.

1. major

2. 5

3. 1

50. Listen to Example 5-1, Purcell's Sonata for Trumpet and Strings (third movement).

1. This movement is in a ____________ (major/minor) key.

2. The first pitch is scale degree _____ (1 / 5).

3. The final pitch played by the trumpet at the end of the movement is scale degree _____ (1 / 5).

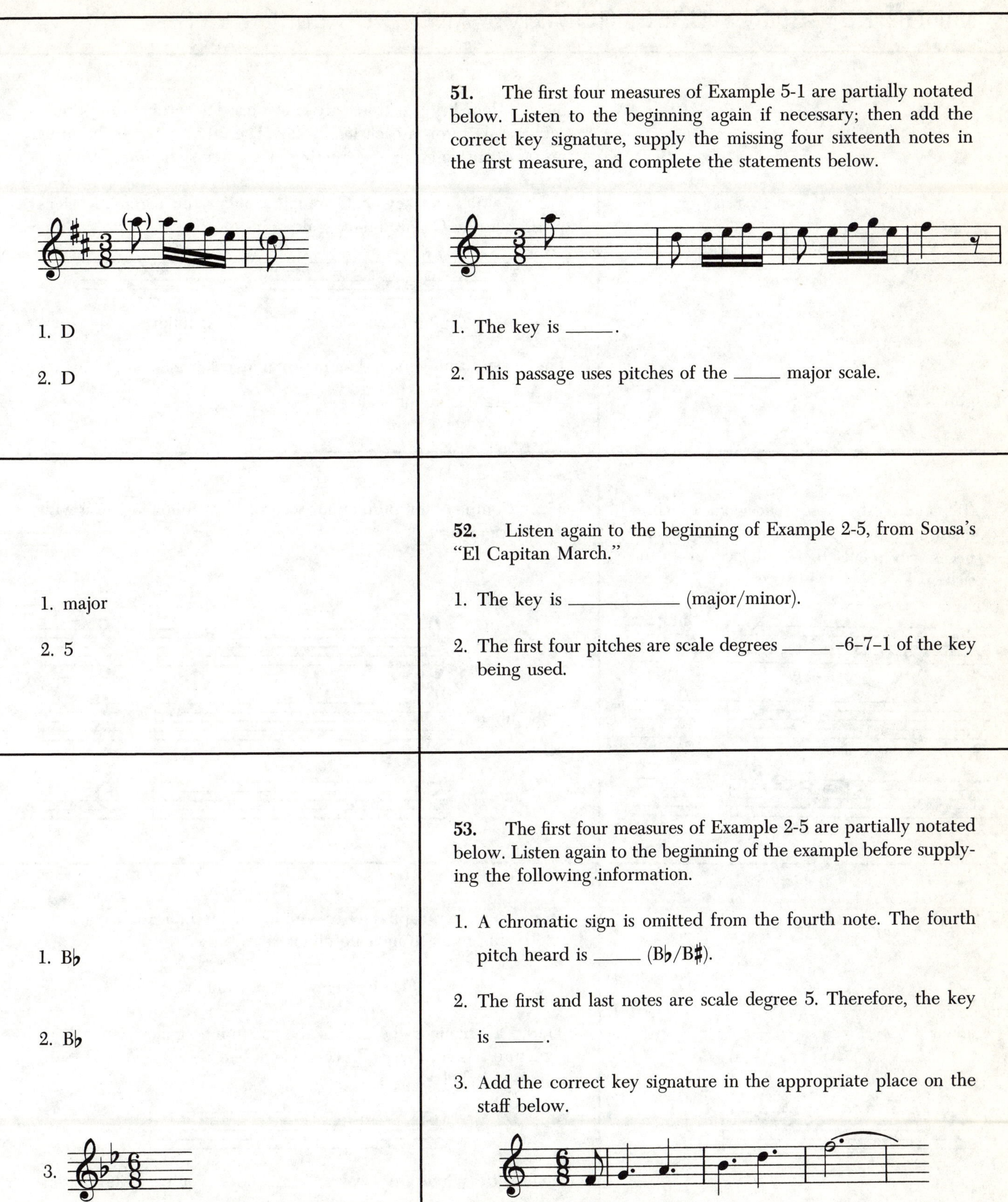

1. D

2. D

51. The first four measures of Example 5-1 are partially notated below. Listen to the beginning again if necessary; then add the correct key signature, supply the missing four sixteenth notes in the first measure, and complete the statements below.

1. The key is ____.

2. This passage uses pitches of the ____ major scale.

1. major

2. 5

52. Listen again to the beginning of Example 2-5, from Sousa's "El Capitan March."

1. The key is __________ (major/minor).

2. The first four pitches are scale degrees ____ -6-7-1 of the key being used.

1. B♭

2. B♭

3.

53. The first four measures of Example 2-5 are partially notated below. Listen again to the beginning of the example before supplying the following information.

1. A chromatic sign is omitted from the fourth note. The fourth pitch heard is ____ (B♭/B♮).

2. The first and last notes are scale degree 5. Therefore, the key is ____.

3. Add the correct key signature in the appropriate place on the staff below.

MINOR KEY SIGNATURES; RELATIVE AND PARALLEL KEYS

54. Minor key signatures are constructed according to the *pure minor* scale form in each minor key. The other minor scale forms are not considered in constructing minor key signatures.

For example, the key of G minor contains the chromatic signs present in the G *pure minor* scale only.

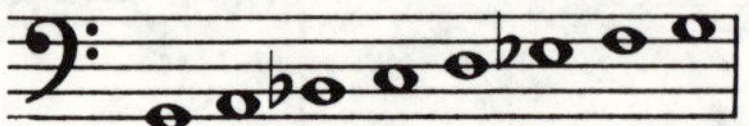

G pure minor scale

G minor key signature

The scale form which determines minor key signatures is the __________ minor scale.

pure

---

55. Complete the pure minor scales below, following each with its key signature.

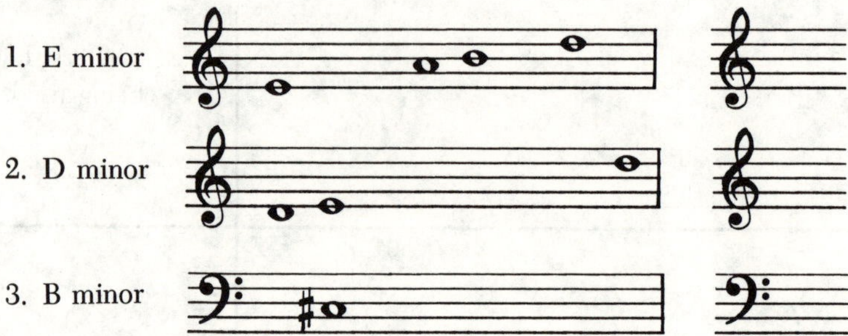

(Remember the fixed placement of chromatic signs in the key signature; they do not necessarily reflect the exact location in the scale.)

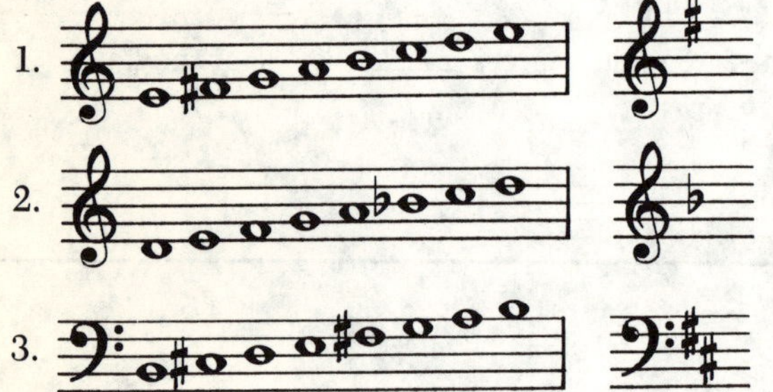

---

56. Hereafter, capital letters will be used to indicate major keys, and small letters to indicate minor keys.

F = F major f = f minor

Thus, "a" signifies the __________ (minor/major) key whose signature has no sharps or flats. Complete the ascending a pure minor scale below.

Small letters indicate __________ keys, while capital letters indicate __________ keys.

minor

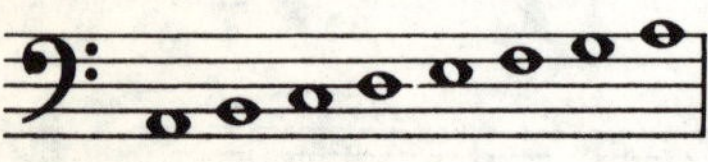

minor

major

a C signature	**57.** The minor key whose signature has no sharps or flats is _____. The major key whose signature has no sharps or flats is _____. Therefore, C and a share the same key __________________.
(treble staff with one flat) (treble staff with one flat) d	**58.** The key signature of F (major) is (treble staff). The key signature of d (minor) is (treble staff). F and _____ share the same key signature.
(bass staff with one sharp) (bass staff with one sharp) G same	**59.** The key signature of G is (bass staff). The key signature of e is (bass staff). _____ and e share the __________ key signature.
relative minor major	**60.** Major and minor keys which share the same signature are said to be *relative.* Thus, the *relative minor* of C is a; the *relative major* of a is C. F and d are ________________. e is the relative __________ of G. G is the relative __________ of e.

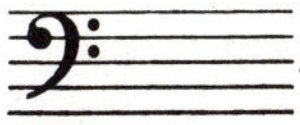

61. Some other relative major and minor keys are shown below.

MAJOR	MINOR	KEY SIGNATURE
B♭	g	 (treble clef, two flats)
E♭	c	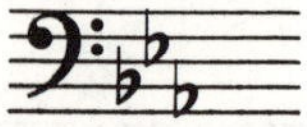 (bass clef, three flats)
A	f♯	 (treble clef, three sharps)

Relative keys share the same _____ _______________.

key signature

62. Notice that in each instance the minor key can be located a minor 3rd below its relative major key.

MAJOR	MINOR	KEY SIGNATURE
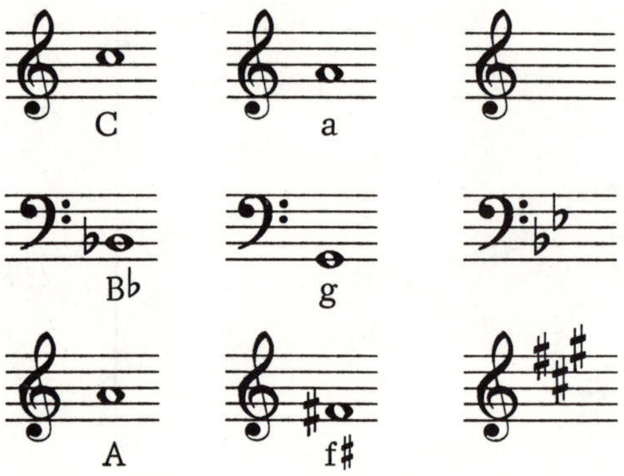 C	a	(treble clef, no sharps or flats)
B♭	g	(bass clef, two flats)
A	f♯	(treble clef, three sharps)

Relative major and minor keys lie a __________ 3rd apart and share the same _____ _______________.

minor

key signature

63. A minor key is located a __________ _____ below its relative major key.

minor 3rd

Conversely, a major key is located a __________ _____ above its relative minor key.

minor 3rd

1. (G) e

2. F (d)

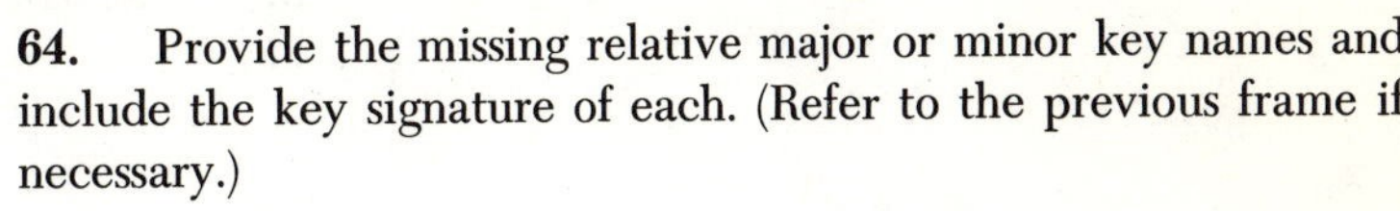

64. Provide the missing relative major or minor key names and include the key signature of each. (Refer to the previous frame if necessary.)

	MAJOR	MINOR	KEY SIGNATURE
1.	G	____	
2.	____	d	

---

1. (A) f♯

2. A♭ (f)

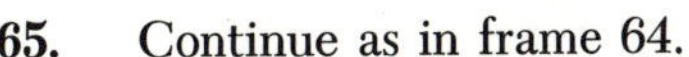

65. Continue as in frame 64.

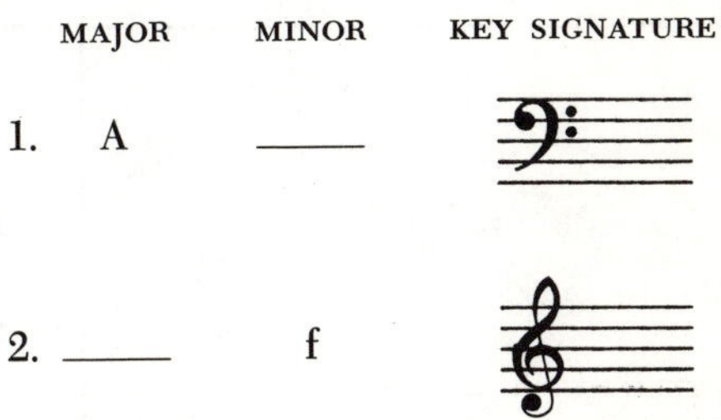

	MAJOR	MINOR	KEY SIGNATURE
1.	A	____	
2.	____	f	

---

e♭ d♯
(either order)

66. The circle of 5ths applies to minor keys and signatures as well as major ones. It is made clearer, however, by locating the minor key with no sharps or flats (a minor) at the top of the circle. Again, a sharp is added for each ascending perfect 5th, and a flat is added for each descending perfect 5th.

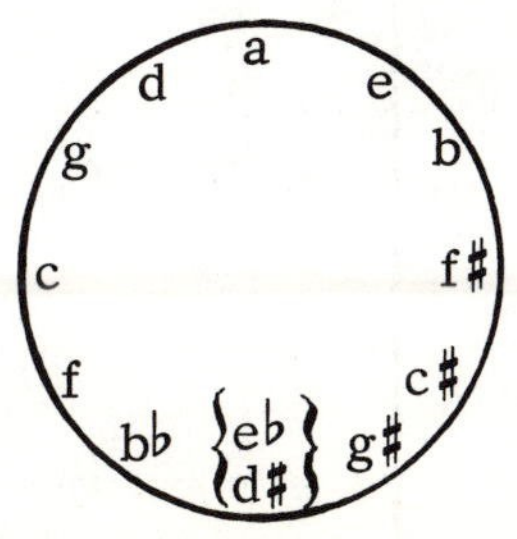

The enharmonic pitches in the circle of 5ths at the left are ____ and ____.

1. e

2. b

3. g

4. f

67. Referring to the circle of 5ths, identify the following minor key signatures. Observe the given example.

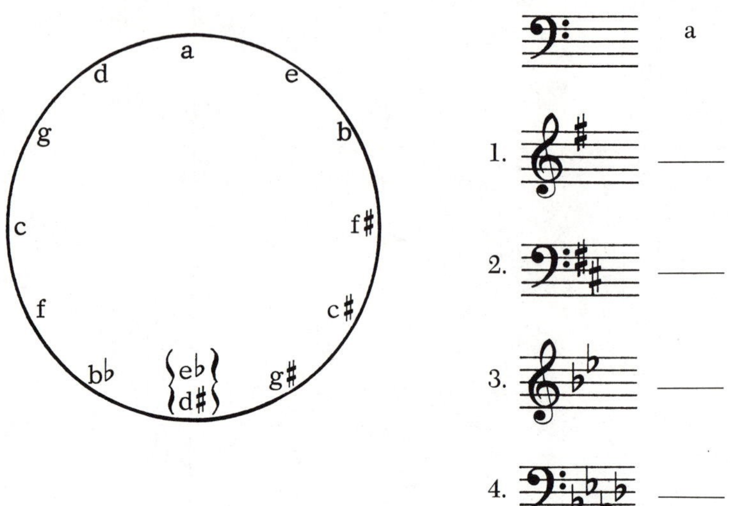

below

68. The complete circle of 5ths including both major and minor keys is shown below. Major keys lie outside the circle; the relative minor keys are inside. In this circle, relative major and minor keys are adjacent, and the clockwise addition of sharps and counterclockwise addition of flats is maintained for all major and minor keys.

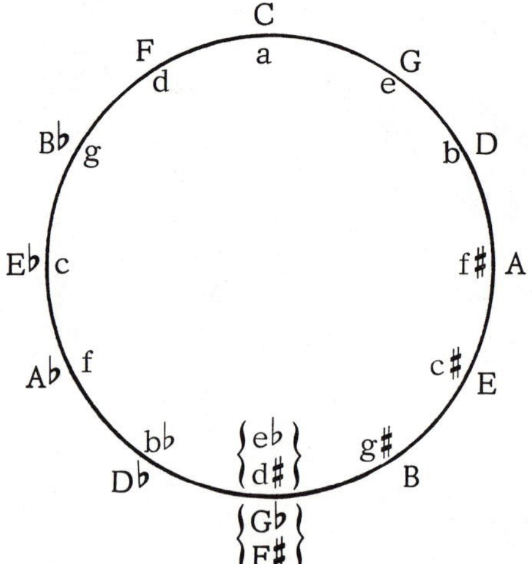

A minor key is located an m 3rd ______ (above/below) its relative major key.

1. (B♭) (g)  [treble staff with 2 flats]
2. (A) f♯ [bass staff with 3 sharps]
3. A♭ (f)  [bass staff with 4 flats]
4. (E) c♯ [treble staff with 4 sharps]

69. Supply the missing signatures or relative key names. (Refer to the circle of 5ths in the preceding frame if necessary.)

	MAJOR	MINOR	KEY SIGNATURE
1.	B♭	g	
2.	A	____	
3.	____	f	
4.	E	____	

---

1. E♭ c
2. D b
3. A♭ f

70. Identify these key signatures.

KEY SIGNATURE	MAJOR	MINOR
1. 	____	____
2. 	____	____
3. 	____	____

---

relative 3rd
relative

71. Major and minor keys sharing the same key signature are said to be ________________ and lie a minor _____ apart.

The ________________ minor of A♭ is f.

---

major
minor b♭

72. The relative __________ of g is B♭.

The relative __________ of D♭ is _____.

---

relative major
[bass staff with 5 sharps]

73. B is the ______________ ______________ of g♯.

The key signature of both B and g♯ is [empty bass staff].

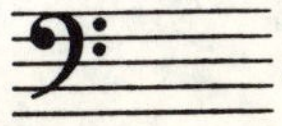

1 7 no	**74.** Which two of the following keys have the same first scale degree? _____ _____ 1. F 5. d♯ 2. g 6. C♯ 3. A♭ 7. f 4. B 8. E Do they share the same key signature? _____
parallel	**75.** Major and minor keys which share the same first scale degree are *parallel.* For example, D is the *parallel major* of d, and d is the _______________ minor of D. D d
parallel scale degree signature	**76.** E and e are _______________. They share the same first __________ __________ but not the same key _______________.
parallel relative	**77.** Major and minor keys which share the same first scale degree are _______________. Major and minor keys which share the same key signature are _______________.
parallel relative parallel	**78.** The __________ major of b♭ is B♭. The __________ major of b♭ is D♭. The _______________ minor of C♯ is c♯.
c♯ E♭ f♯	**79.** The relative minor of E is _____. The parallel major of e♭ is _____. The relative major of _____ is A. (Be careful to make clear the distinction between upper and lower case letters.)

Answers	Frames
1. g♯ 2. F♯ 3. D 4. D♭	**80.** Complete the following statements, and provide the key signature shared by the relative keys. 1. The relative minor of B is ____. 2. The parallel minor of ____ is f♯. 3. The relative major of b is ____. 4. The parallel major of d♭ is ____.
pure enharmonic	**81.** Minor key signatures are constructed according to the ____________ minor scale. Two notes with different pitch names which are played with the same key of the piano keyboard are called ____________________.
B♭ g	**82.** The major key with two flats in its signature is ____. The minor key with two flats in its signature is ____.
1. two flats 2. four flats 3. three sharps	**83.** Complete these sentences following the given example. The signature of D contains two sharps. 1. The signature of B♭ contains ____________ ____________. 2. The signature of A♭ contains ____________ ____________. 3. The signature of f♯ contains ____________ ____________.
1. five sharps 2. five flats 3. three sharps 4. four flats	**84.** Continue as in frame 83. 1. The signature of B contains ____________ ____________. 2. The signature of b♭ contains ____________ ____________. 3. The signature of A contains ____________ ____________. 4. The signature of f contains ____________ ____________.

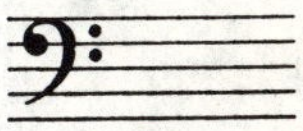

1. G e

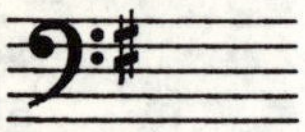

2. E♭ c

85. Identify the keys to which each group of chromatic signs belongs, and provide the corresponding key signature.

	MAJOR	MINOR	KEY SIGNATURE
1. ♯	____	____	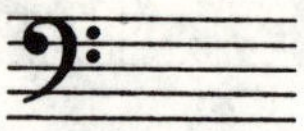
2. ♭♭♭	____	____	

1. E c♯

2. C a

3. F♯ d♯

86. Continue as in frame 85.

	MAJOR	MINOR	KEY SIGNATURE
1. ♯♯♯♯	____	____	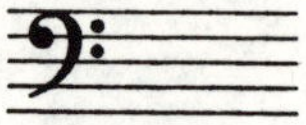
2.	____	____	
3. ♯♯♯♯♯♯	____	____	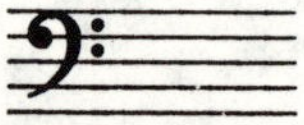

1.  (G) g

2. 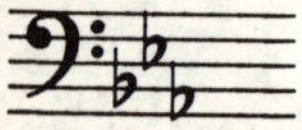 (E♭) e♭

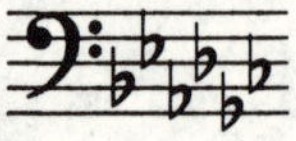

87. Supply the missing signatures and key names of these parallel major and minor keys.

	KEY SIGNATURE	MAJOR	PARALLEL MINOR	KEY SIGNATURE
1.		G	____	
2.	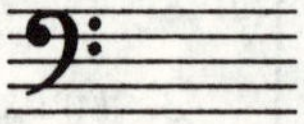	E♭	____	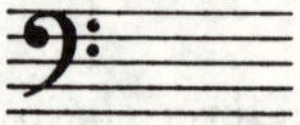

1.  B (b)

2.  F♯ f♯

88. Continue as in frame 87.

	KEY SIGNATURE	MAJOR	PARALLEL MINOR	KEY SIGNATURE
1.	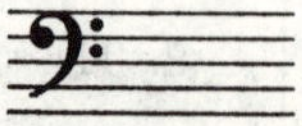	____	b	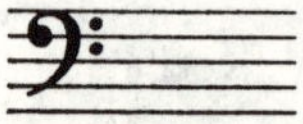
2.		____	____	

1. 

2. 

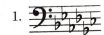

3. 

89. Provide the signature for each key.

1. A♭

2. g♯

3. f♯

1.

2.

3. 

90. Continue as in frame 89.

1. F

2. b

3. c

1.

2. 

91. Continue as in frame 90.

1. G♭

2. c♯

Answers	Frame
1. D 2. D♭ 3. A 4. F	**92.** Identify these major key signatures. 1. ____ 2. ____ 3. ____ 4. ____
1. B 2. E♭ 3. G♭ 4. F♯	**93.** Continue as in frame 92. 1. ____ 2. ____ 3. ____ 4. ____
1. d 2. f 3. b 4. c♯	**94.** Identify these minor key signatures. 1. ____ 2. ____ 3. ____ 4. ____

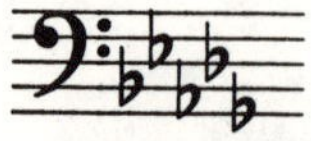

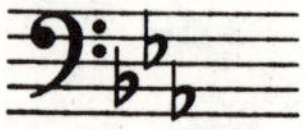

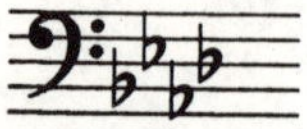

	95. Continue as in frame 94.
1. f♯	1. ____
2. a♭	2. ____
3. e	3. ____
4. g	4. ____

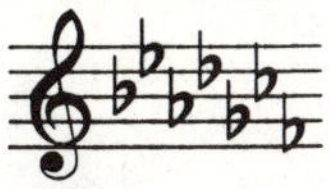

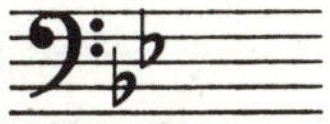

LISTENING FRAMES

	96. Listen to Example 5-2, from Haydn's Symphony No. 94 (second movement), which presents a melodic fragment in two ways. A short pause on the recording separates the two. As you listen to the example, carefully observe both their similarities and differences.
1. major	1. The key of the first passage is ____________ (major/minor).
2. minor	2. The key of the second passage is ____________ (major/minor).
3. louder	3. The second passage is ____________ (louder/less loud) than the first.
	97. Listen to Example 5-2 again if necessary in answering the following.
1. the same	1. The first pitch in each passage is ____________________ (the same/different).
2. parallel	2. The first pitch in both the two passages is also the first scale degree. Since the two passages share the same first scale degree, they are in ____________________ (relative/parallel) major and minor keys.
3. c (c minor, the parallel minor of C major)	3. The first excerpt is in C. Therefore, the second is in _____.

lower	**98.** The notation of the first passage in Example 5-2 is shown below. The circled pitches are one HS ______ (higher/lower) in the second passage.
	99. From the information in the three previous frames you should be able to complete the notation of the *second* passage in Example 5-2 below. Supply the correct key signature, and include any other necessary chromatic signs.
	100. Example 5-3 is from Bach's *Brandenburg Concerto* No. 2 (third movement). Two excerpts are heard, separated on the recording by a brief pause. Each begins on the first scale degree of the melody that follows. Listen to and compare both passages before answering the following.
1. M	1. The first melody, played by the trumpet, is in an ____ (M / m) key.
2. m	2. The second melody, played by the oboe, is in an ____ (M / m) key.
3. different	3. The pitch of the first scale degree heard at the beginning of the two melodies is ______ (the same/different).
	101.
1. m 3rd	1. In Example 5-3, the interval between the first scale degrees of each melody is an ____ ____ (m 3rd / M 7th).
2. relative	2. Therefore, the key of the second passage is the ______ (relative/parallel) minor of the key of the first.
3. d	3. The key of the first passage is F. Since the key of the second is the relative minor, it must be in ____.

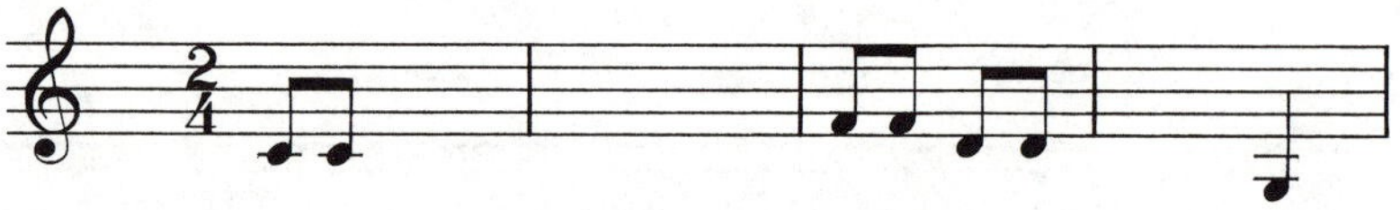

SELF-QUIZ V

1. Rewrite these examples, placing the meter signatures, key signatures, and clefs in the correct order.

2. Sharp key names ________________ (ascend/descend) in P 5ths.

3. Flat key names ________________ (ascend/descend) in P 5ths.

4. Every pitch has either two or three possible enharmonic spellings. Give the enharmonic spellings for each pitch below.

   1. A _____ _____ 2. D♯ _____ _____ 3. C♭ _____ _____ 4. G♯ _____

5. Provide key signatures for these *major* keys.

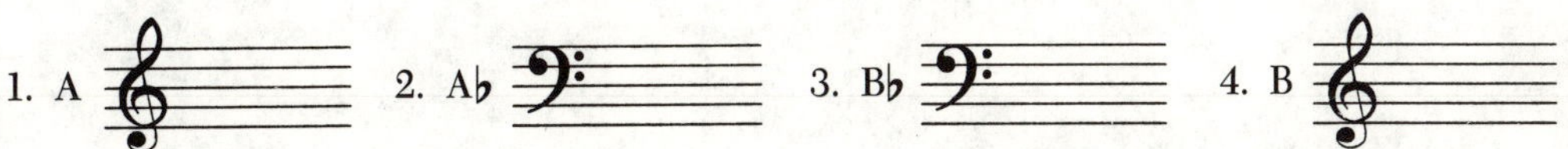

6. The minor scale form which determines minor key signatures is the ________________ minor scale.

7. Which keys below are relative? _____ _____ _____

   1. E, g♯ 2. D, b 3. A, f 4. A♭, f 5. B, g♯ 6. B, d

8. The interval separating relative major and minor keys is a(n) _____ _____.

9. Provide the missing relative major and minor key names and key signatures in the following.

	MAJOR	MINOR	KEY SIGNATURE
1.	B♭	_____	
2.	_____	c♯	
3.	_____	_____	

10. Parallel major and minor keys share the same __________ __________ __________.

11. Relative major and minor keys share the same _____ __________.

12. Provide the signature for each key below.

1. f♯ 2. F♯ 3. D♭ 4. e♭

13. Identify these key signatures.

MAJOR: ______ ______ ______ ______

MINOR: ______ ______ ______ ______

CHAPTER ▪ VI ▪ TRIADS

Harmony in music occurs when two or more tones sound simultaneously and all the tones relate to each other according to recognizable patterns of harmonic perception. One of the basic elements in harmony is the *chord,* which results when several tones sound concurrently. Chords can be produced by combining any number of harmonic intervals. By the seventeenth century, Western music had developed a harmonic system in which chords are constructed in thirds, usually called "tertian" harmony. The basis of this system is the *triad,* which is a three-tone chord constructed in harmonic thirds, as explained in the following frames. The four triad types discussed in this chapter form the basic harmonic units underlying traditional harmonic practices, all of which relate to the concepts of key and scale as presented in previous chapters.

It is important to be able to recognize the four triad types, aurally as well as notationally, in order to perceive their relationships in harmonic music. Therefore, frequent use of the piano will prove of great benefit in this chapter and is strongly recommended.

MAJOR AND MINOR TRIADS

	1. A *chord* consists of three or more tones of different pitch written or sounded together.
3 (1 has only two notes. 2 has three notes, but they do not sound together.)	**2.** In musical notation, the notes of a chord are placed in vertical alignment on the staff, indicating that the tones are sounded simultaneously. Which example below is a chord? _____ 1.  2. 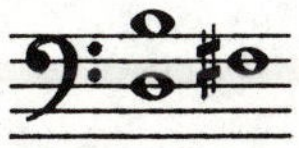 3. 
three	**3.** A chord consists of _____ or more tones of different pitch sounded or written together.

3rds	**4.** Chords in traditional harmony are constructed in 3rds, as shown below. , , and all sounded together are written . The above chord is constructed in _____.
	5. Construct a chord of *three* notes built upward in 3rds. The bottom note is given.
	6. Continue as in frame 5.
2 (1 has too many notes. 3 is not built in 3rds.)	**7.** A chord of *three* notes built in 3rds is a *triad.* Which chord below is a triad? _____ 1. 2. 3.
triad	8. A ____________ is a chord of three notes built in 3rds.
no	**9.** A triad is a chord which is limited to three different pitches built in thirds. Is every chord a triad? _____
2 4 (2 is not built in 3rds. 4 has too many notes.)	**10.** Which chords below are not triads? _____ _____ 1. 3. 2. 4.

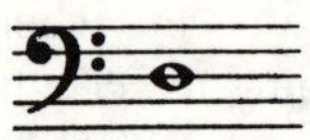

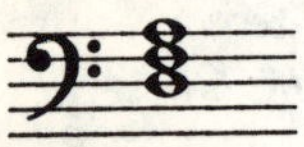

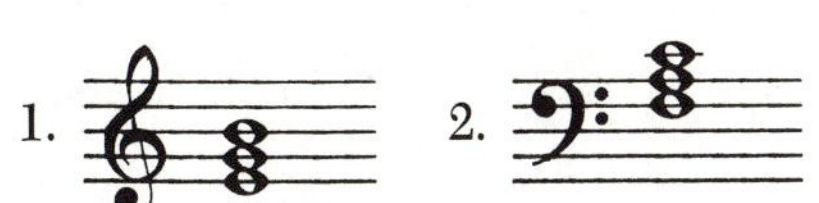

11. Construct triads upward from the given notes. (Do not use chromatic signs.)

F

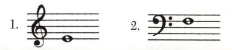

12. A triad is built upward from its basic tone, rather than downward. The tone on which a triad is built is the *root.*

In this triad, C is the root.

In this triad 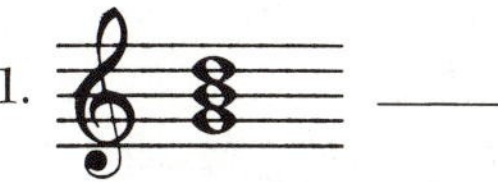, the root is _____.

---

1. G

2. B♭

13. Name the root in each of these triads.

1. _____

2. _____

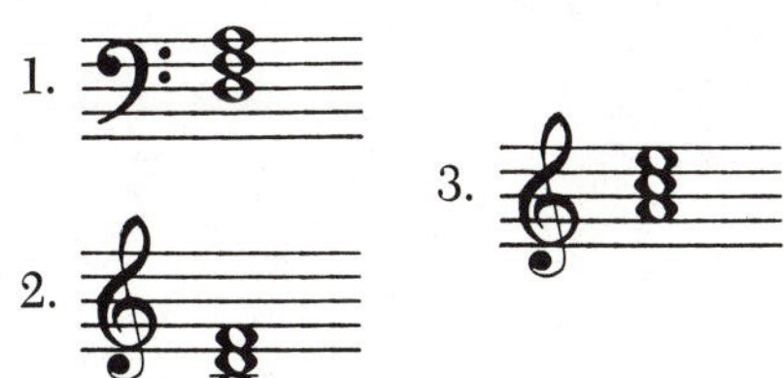

14. Construct triads upward from the given roots. (Do not use chromatic signs.)

---

root

E

15. Triads are spelled in upward order from the root.

This triad is spelled C E G. C is the ____________.

In the triad E G B, the root is _____.

1. (G) B D

2. (D) F A

3. (A) C E

16. Spell triads upward from the given roots. (Do not use chromatic signs.)

1. G _____ _____

2. D _____ _____

3. A _____ _____

---

1. C (E G)

2. D (F A)

17. Supply roots for these triads, using no chromatic signs.

1. _____ E G

2. _____ F A

F

D

18. The note which lies a 3rd above the root of a triad is called the *third* of the triad.

In this triad , the third is _____.

Which note is the root? _____

---

1.  2. 

19. Without using chromatic signs, supply the third in each triad.

1.  2. 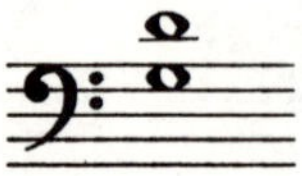

---

1. (A) C (E)

2. (B) D (F)

3. (G) B (D)

20. Without using chromatic signs, supply thirds in these triad spellings.

1. A _____ E

2. B _____ F

3. G _____ D

---

fifth

F

21. The note a 5th above the root is called the *fifth* of the triad.

In this triad , C is the __________.

Which note is the root? _____

fifth

A

22. Every triad has a root, a third, and a ____________.

In this triad , _____ is the fifth.

---

1.  2. 

23. Supply the fifth in each triad. The root and third are given. (Do not use chromatic signs.)

1.  2. 

5th

3rd

24. 

The numerical interval between the root and the third of a triad is a 3rd.

What is the numerical interval between the root and the fifth? _____

What is the numerical interval between the third and the fifth? _____

---

minor

25. In this triad the interval between the root and the third is a major 3rd.

 = M 3rd

What interval separates the third and the fifth? ____________ (major/minor) 3rd

---

minor 3rd

major 3rd

26. In this triad the interval between the root and the third is a ____________ _____.

The interval between the third and the fifth is a ____________ _____.

---

major 3rd

27. In traditional harmony all basic triads consist of major and minor 3rds, combined in various ways.

Write the name of the interval between the root and third of this triad.

 ____________ _____

major 3rd	**28.** There are four possible arrangements of major and minor 3rds in forming triads. major 3rd + minor 3rd minor 3rd + major 3rd minor 3rd + minor 3rd major 3rd + __________ ____
triad	**29.** These four arrangements of major and minor 3rds create four types of triads, each of which sounds distinctly different from the others. Major 3rd + minor 3rd is one type of __________.
major 3rd minor 3rd	**30.** The triad consisting of a major 3rd + a minor 3rd (going from the root upward) is known as *major.* This triad is a major triad. What interval separates the root and the third? __________ ____ What interval separates the third and the fifth? __________ ____
major minor 5th	**31.** A major triad consists of a __________ 3rd + a __________ 3rd (going from the root upward). The interval between the root and fifth of a major triad is a perfect ____.
	**32.** The major triad may be constructed from scale degrees 1, 3, and 5 of the major scale. 1 2 3 4 5 6 7 1 major triad Construct a major triad from scale degrees 1, 3, and 5 of this scale. 1 2 3 4 5 6 7 1

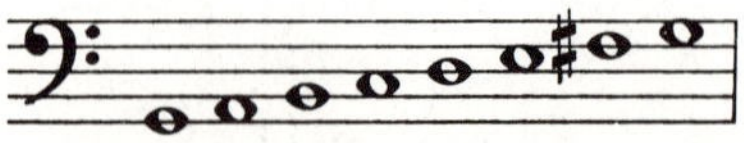

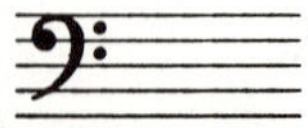

major 3rd

2

33. In a major triad the interval between the root and the third is a ________ ____.

Which triad below is major? ____

1.  2. 

---

1. major 3. major

34. Write "major" beneath the triads which are major.

1.  2.  3. 

---

major

minor 3rd

35. A major triad may be produced by combining scale degrres 1, 3, and 5 of a ________ scale.

The interval between the third and the fifth of a major triad is a ________ ____.

---

1.  2. 

36. Supply thirds to form major triads, using chromatic signs when necessary. Do not change the given root and fifth.

1.  2. 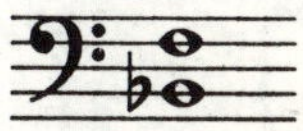

---

1. 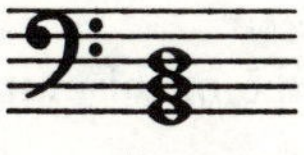 2. 

37. Supply thirds and fifths to form major triads. Do not alter the given roots.

1.  2. 

---

1. (B♭) D F

2. G (B) D

3. E♭ G (B♭)

38. Complete the spelling of major triads below.

1. B♭ ____ ____

2. ____ B ____

3. ____ ____ B♭

---

major minor

perfect 5th

39. A major triad consists of a ____ 3rd + a ____ 3rd.

The interval from root to fifth is a ________ ____.

3	**40.** Which triad below is not major? _____ 1. 2. 3.
minor major	**41.** Another of the four triad types is shown below. Its structure consists of a __________ 3rd + a __________ 3rd (going from the root upward). A triad consisting of a minor 3rd + a major 3rd is known as *minor.*
minor 1	**42.** A __________ triad consists of a minor 3rd + a major 3rd. Which triad is minor? _____ 1. 2.
	43. Minor triads may be constructed from scale degrees 1, 3, and 5 of any minor scale. 1 2 3 4 5 6 7 1 minor triad Construct a minor triad from scale degrees 1, 3, and 5 of this minor scale. 1 2 3 4 5 6 7 1
minor perfect	**44.** Both major and minor triads consist of major and minor 3rds. The interval between the root and third of a major triad is a major 3rd; the interval between the root and third of a minor triad is a __________ 3rd. A __________ 5th separates the root and fifth of both triads.

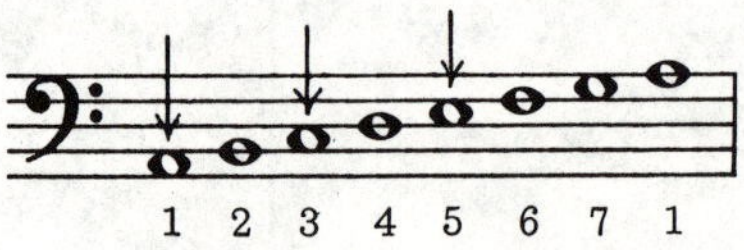

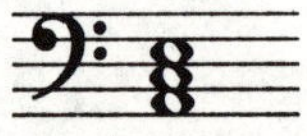

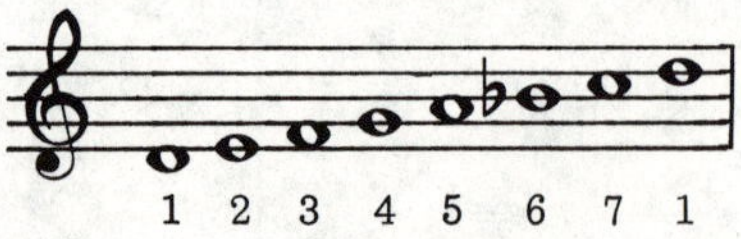

major 3rd 2	**45.** In a minor triad the interval between the third and fifth is a __________ ____. Which triad is minor? ____ 1. 2.
minor	**46.** A minor triad may be produced by combining scale degrees 1, 3, and 5 of a __________ scale. Supply the third to form a minor triad below.
1. 2.	**47.** Complete these minor triads. The roots and fifths are given. 1. 2.
1. 2.	**48.** Supply the thirds and fifths of these minor triads. 1. 2.
1. (B) D F♯ 2. F A♭ (C) 3. C♯ (E G♯)	**49.** Complete the spelling of these minor triads. 1. B ____ ____ 2. ____ ____ C 3. ____ E G♯
major major perfect 5th	**50.** Major triads consist of a __________ 3rd + a minor 3rd. Minor triads consist of a minor 3rd + a __________ 3rd. The interval separating the root and fifth of both major and minor triads is a __________ ____.

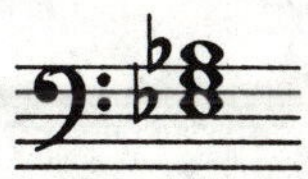

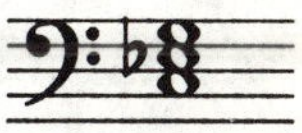

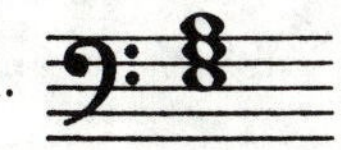

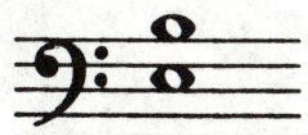

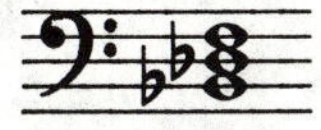

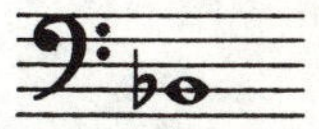

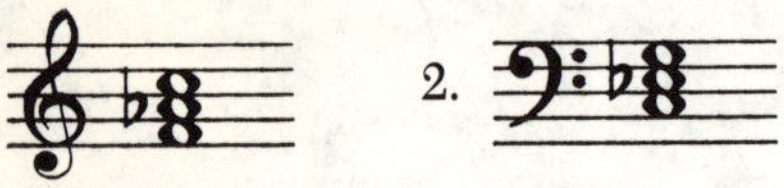

51. Change these major triads to minor by applying one chromatic sign to each third.

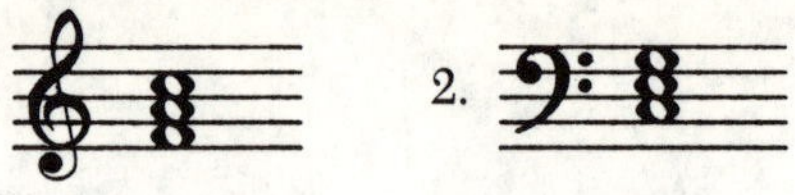

1. 2.

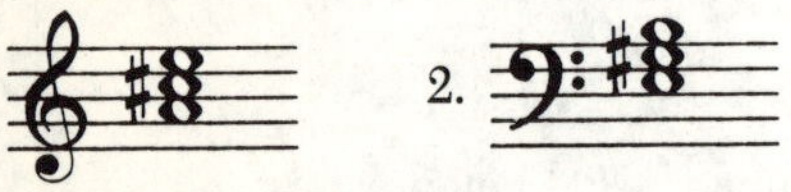

52. Change these minor triads to major by applying one chromatic sign to each third.

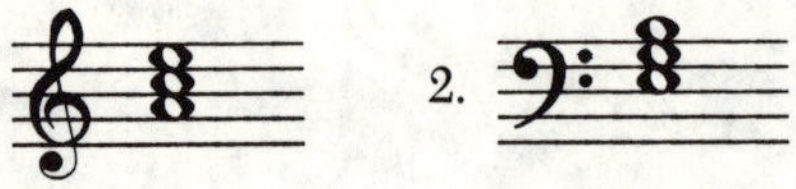

1. 2.

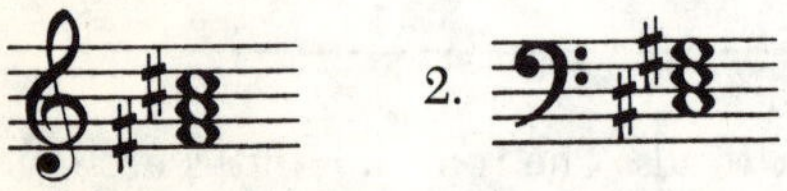

53. Without altering the third, change these major triads to minor. Two chromatic alterations are necessary in each.

1. 2.

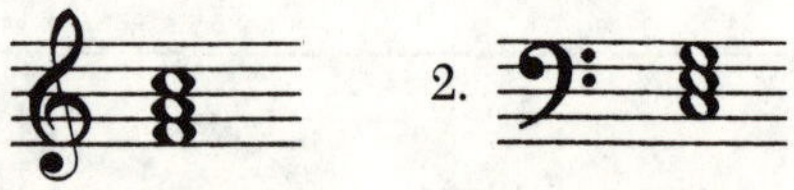

1. m 3. M

2. M 4. m

54. Using the abbreviations "M" for major and "m" for minor, identify these triads.

1. ___ 3. ___

2. ___ 4. ___

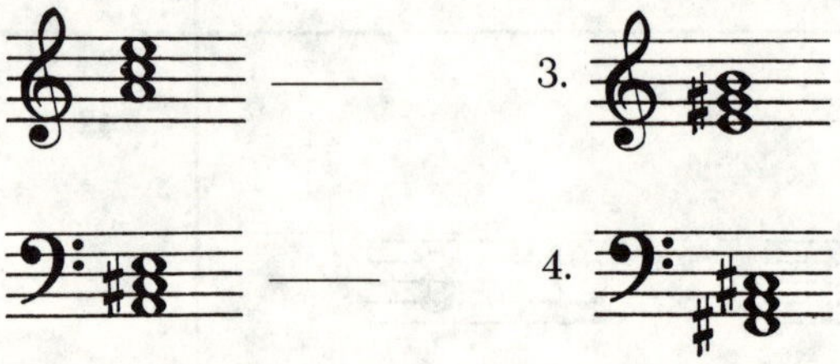

1. M 3. m

2. m 4. m

55. Continue as in frame 54.

1. ___ 3. ___

2. ___ 4. ___

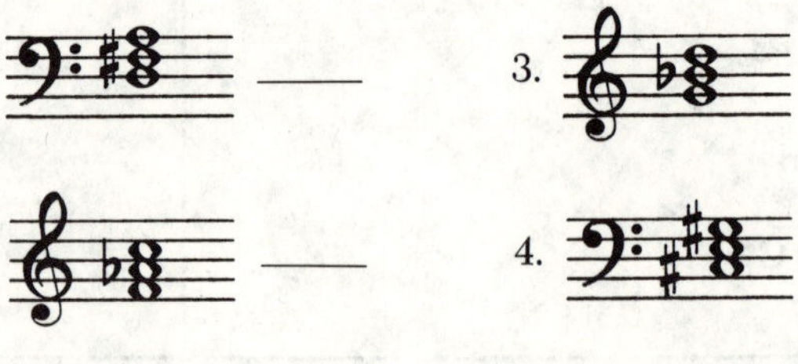

1. 2. 3.

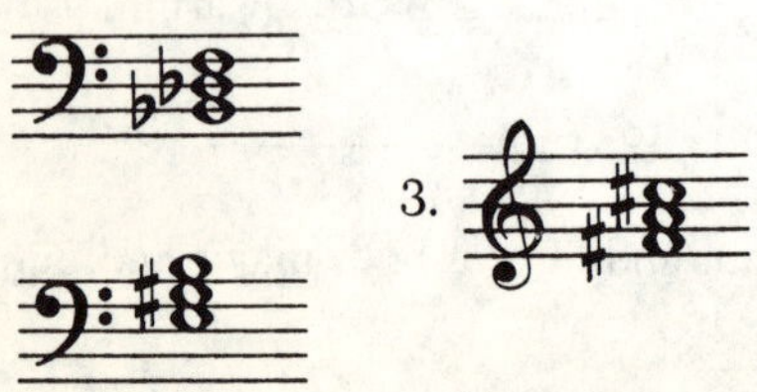

56. Construct on each root a triad as indicated.

1. m 2. M 3. m

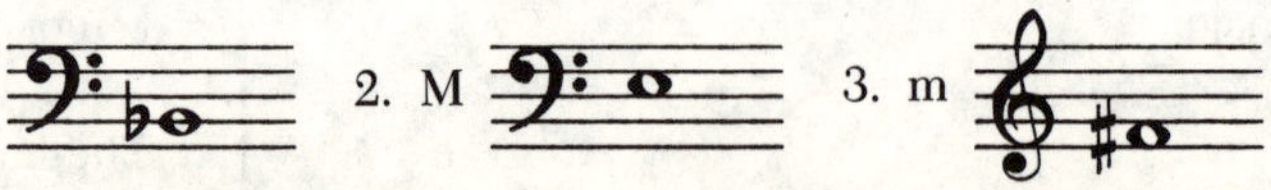

LISTENING FRAMES

57. Listen to Example 6-1, the beginning of Brahms' Symphony No. 3 (first movement). Listen carefully to the first and third chords.

1. The first chord is a _____ (M / m) triad.
2. The third chord is a _____ (M / m) triad.

Answers: 1. M 2. M

58. In Example 6-1, the third chord adds melodic and rhythmic activity. Listen again to the excerpt, comparing the pitches used in both the first and third chords. Which statement below most accurately describes the comparison? _____

1. The roots of the two triads are different.
2. Although the third chord has added melodic and rhythmic activity, both triads are the same.

Answer: 2

59. Example 6-2 is the beginning of Frédéric Chopin's Prelude No. 20 for piano. The rhythm of the upper line in the first measure is notated below. After listening to the example, write "m" under the two notes where minor triads are heard.

Answer:

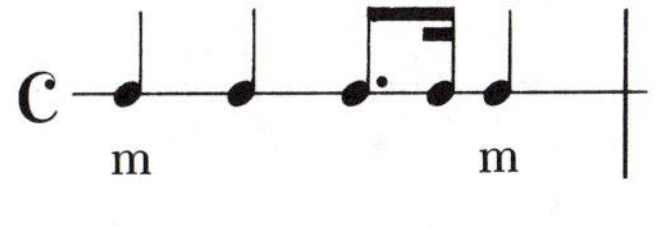

60. Listen to all of Example 6-2. The final chord is _____ (M / m).

Is the final triad the same as the first? _____ (The same triad may be sounded in different octaves.)

Answers: m; yes

DIMINISHED AND AUGMENTED TRIADS

61. Which triad below is neither major nor minor? _____

1.  2.  3. 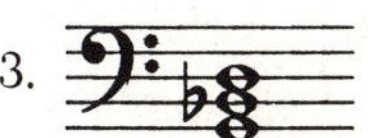

Answer: 2

diminished	**62.** Another of the four triad types consists of two minor 3rds. It is called *diminished.* The name "diminished" reflects the interval separating the root and fifth, which is a ______________ 5th.
minor 2	**63.** A diminished triad consists of two __________ 3rds. Which triad below is diminished? ____ 1. 2.
diminished diminished 5th	**64.** The triad consisting of a minor 3rd + a minor 3rd is known as ______________. The interval from root to fifth in a diminished triad is a ______________ ____.
1. 2.	**65.** Supply the fifths to form diminished triads. The roots and thirds are provided. 1. 2.
1. 2.	**66.** Build diminished triads on the given roots. 1. 2.
1. 2.	**67.** Complete the diminished triads whose *fifths* are given below. 1. 2.
(G) B♭ D♭ D (F) A♭	**68.** The diminished triad whose root is G is spelled G ____ ____. The diminished triad whose third is F is spelled ____ F ____.

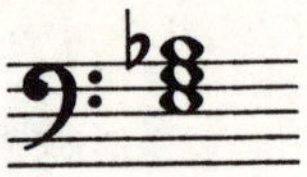

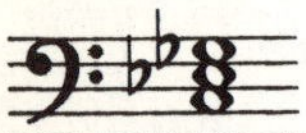

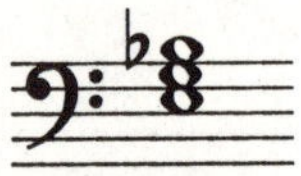

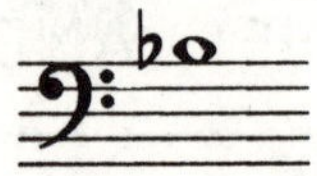

1. (C♯) E G 2. A♯ (C♯) E 3. D♯ F♯ (A)	**69.** Complete these diminished triad spellings. 1. C♯ ____ ____ 2. ____ C♯ ____ 3. ____ ____ A
1. 2.	**70.** Change each minor triad to diminished by chromatically altering the fifth. 1. 2.
1. 2.	**71.** Change each diminished triad to minor by chromatically altering the fifth. 1. 2.
1. m 3. d 2. M	**72.** Identify these triads, using the abbreviations "M" for major, "m" for minor, and "d" for diminished. 1. ____ 3. ____ 2. ____
1. d 3. m 2. M 4. d	**73.** Identify these triads, using the abbreviations established. 1. ____ 3. ____ 2. ____ 4. ____
major minor diminished (any order)	**74.** The three types of triads covered thus far are ________, __________, and ______________.

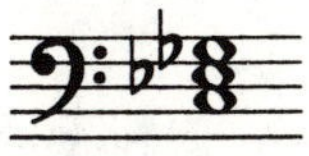

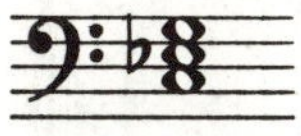

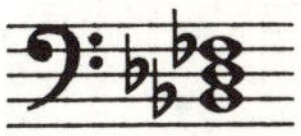

75. The last triad consists of two major 3rds. It is called *augmented.*

The name "augmented" reflects the interval between the root and fifth, which is a(n) ________________ 5th.

augmented

---

76. The triad consisting of a __________ 3rd + a __________ 3rd is known as augmented.

The triad consisting of a minor 3rd + a minor 3rd is known as ________________.

major major

diminished

---

77. The ________________ triad consists of two major 3rds.

Which triad is augmented? _____

1.  2.

augmented

2

---

78. The interval between root and fifth in an augmented triad is a(n) ________________ _____.

Which triad is augmented? _____

1.  2.

augmented 5th

1

79. Supply fifths to form augmented triads. The roots and thirds are provided.

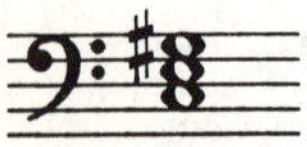

1.  2.

1.  2.

---

80. Build augmented triads on the given roots.

1.  2.

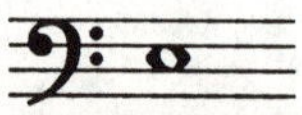

1. 2.

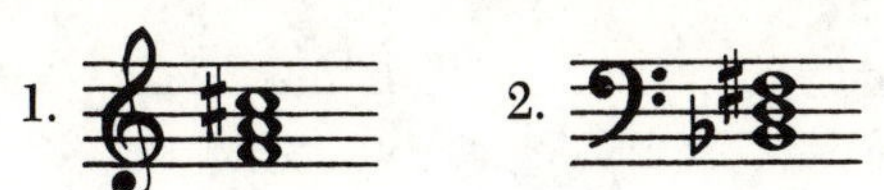

81. Complete the augmented triads whose fifths are given below.

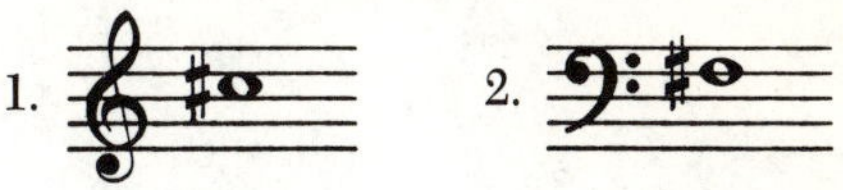

82. Complete the augmented triads whose thirds are given below.

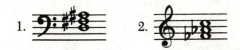

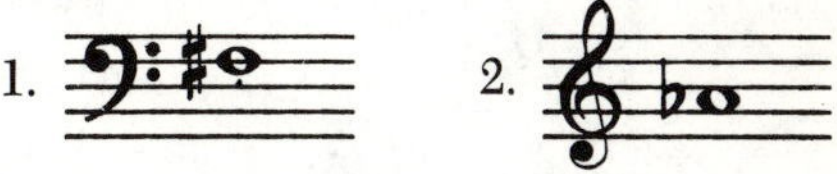

83. Complete these augmented triad spellings.

1. G♭ (B♭) D
2. C♭ (E♭) G

1. _____ B♭ _____
2. _____ E♭ _____

84. Complete these augmented triad spellings.

1. G B (D♯)
2. A (C♯) E♯
3. (B) D♯ F𝄪

1. _____ _____ D♯
2. _____ C♯ _____
3. B _____ _____

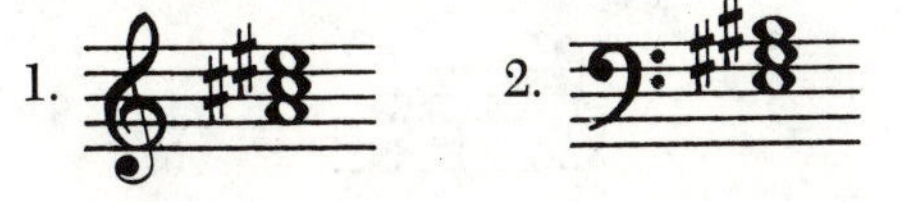

85. Change each major triad to augmented by chromatically altering the fifth.

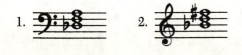

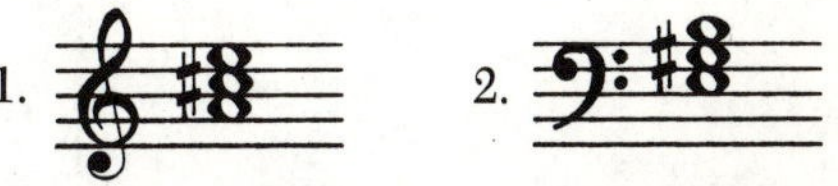

86. Change each minor triad to augmented by applying one chromatic sign to each.

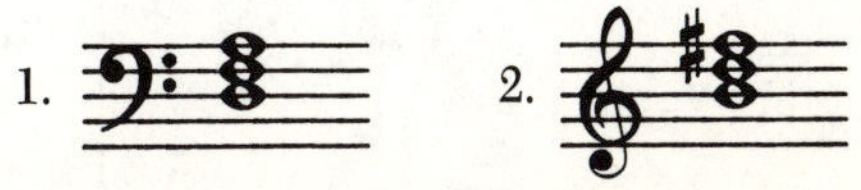

87. Write the type of triad which corresponds to each structure described below.

1. major 3rd + minor 3rd ______major______
2. minor 3rd + minor 3rd ____________
3. minor 3rd + major 3rd ____________
4. major 3rd + major 3rd ____________

1. (major)
2. diminished
3. minor
4. augmented

88. Give the interval between the root and fifth of each triad.

1. major ____________ 5th
2. minor ____________ 5th
3. diminished ____________ 5th
4. augmented ____________ 5th

1. perfect
2. perfect
3. diminished
4. augmented

89. Identify the following triads, using the abbreviations previously established with the addition of "A" for augmented.

1.  ____ 2.  ____ 3. ____

1. M 2. A 3. m

90. Continue as in frame 89.

1. 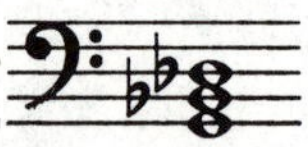 ____ 3. ____

2. 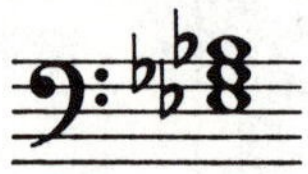 ____ 4. ____

1. d 3. d

2. m 4. A

91. Naming of triads becomes more explicit when the root is also identified. For example, the major triad whose root is F is called the F major triad. When naming triads in this way, the name of the root always comes first.

The minor triad whose root is G is the ____ ________ triad.

G minor

1. (D M)
2. B♭ M
3. F♯ m

92. Name these triads, using the abbreviations previously established.

		ROOT	TRIAD TYPE
1.		D	M
2.		____	____
3.		____	____

1. F m
2. A d
3. B A

93. Continue as in frame 92.

1.	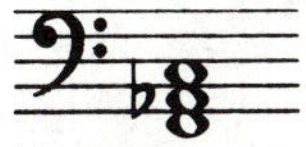	____	____
2.		____	____
3.		____	____

1. 
2. 

94. Build the triads indicated.

1. A♭ M 
2. C♯ m 

1. 
2. 
3. 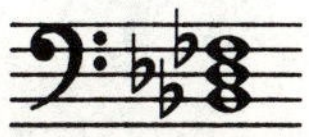

95. Continue as in frame 94.

1. A A 
2. G♯ m 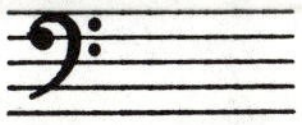
3. B♭ d 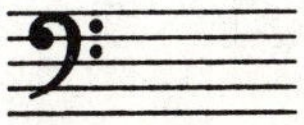

minor major	**96.** The diminished triad consists of two ____________ 3rds. The augmented triad consists of two ____________ 3rds.
root	**97.** The note upon which a triad is built is called the ______.

LISTENING FRAMES

C ♩ ♩ ♩. ♬ ♩ | ♩ ♩ ♩. ♬ ♩ | (m) A (m) | M M M	**98.** Listen again to Example 6-2, Chopin's Prelude No. 20. The rhythm of the upper melodic line in the first two measures is notated below. The first and fourth triads in the first measure were previously identified as minor. The first two measures contain one augmented triad and three major triads. Write "A" or "M" under the notes where these triad types are heard. C ♩ ♩ ♩. ♬ ♩ | ♩ ♩ ♩. ♬ ♩ | (m) (m)
1. second 2. m	**99.** Listen to Example 1-4, the opening of Brahms' Symphony No. 4 (last movement), consisting of eight chords that become the harmonic basis for the entire movement. 1. Of the first three chords, which one is diminished? ____________ 2. The first chord is _____ (M / m / d / A).
1. m 2. M	**100.** Listen to Example 1-4 again. 1. Chords three and four are both _____ (M / m / d / A). 2. The final chord in the excerpt, triad No. 8, is _____ (M / m / d / A).

DIATONIC TRIADS; TRIAD INVERSIONS

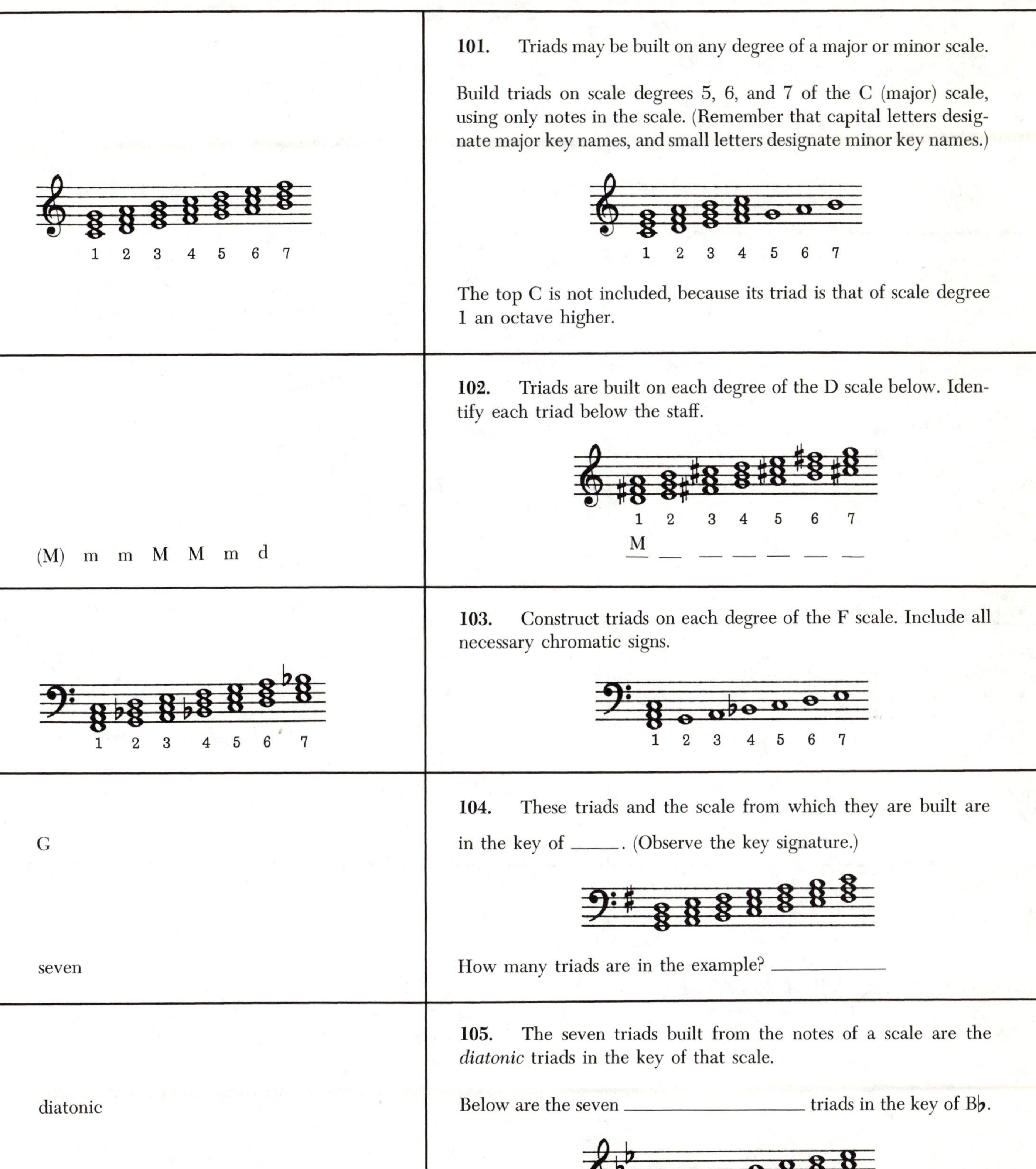

101. Triads may be built on any degree of a major or minor scale.

Build triads on scale degrees 5, 6, and 7 of the C (major) scale, using only notes in the scale. (Remember that capital letters designate major key names, and small letters designate minor key names.)

The top C is not included, because its triad is that of scale degree 1 an octave higher.

(M) m m M M m d

102. Triads are built on each degree of the D scale below. Identify each triad below the staff.

---

103. Construct triads on each degree of the F scale. Include all necessary chromatic signs.

G

104. These triads and the scale from which they are built are in the key of _____. (Observe the key signature.)

seven

How many triads are in the example? __________

---

diatonic

105. The seven triads built from the notes of a scale are the *diatonic* triads in the key of that scale.

Below are the seven ________________ triads in the key of B♭.

106. Write the seven diatonic triads in the key of A♭. (It is usually easier to write the scale first.)

seven

diatonic

107. How many diatonic triads exist in each key? ____________

The triad E♭ G B♭ is ________________ in the key of E♭.

harmonic

108. Diatonic triads in minor keys may be built from the notes of any form of minor scale. This book, however, will concentrate upon diatonic triads corresponding to the *harmonic* minor scale, since their usage is more frequent.

The seven diatonic triads in g (minor) are shown below. They are built from the notes of the g ______________ minor scale.

1 2 3 4 5 6 7

(The harmonic minor scale contains half steps at 2 to 3, 5 to 6, and 7 to 1.)

harmonic minor

(m) d A m M M d

109. Name the e diatonic triads below. The triads are built from the notes of the e ______________ ____________ scale.

1 2 3 4 5 6 7

m __ __ __ __ __ __

1 2 3 4 5 6 7

110. Write the diatonic triads in d. The harmonic minor scale is provided. Include all the necessary chromatic signs.

1 2 3 4 5 6 7

diatonic

111. A triad may be diatonic in several different keys. The major triad C E G corresponds to scale degrees 1, 3, and 5 in C; 4, 6, and 1 in G; 5, 7, and 2 in F; 5, 7, and 2 in f; and 6, 1, and 3 in e.

Therefore, C E G is ______________ in those keys.

F

F♯

112. The triad G B♭ D corresponds to scale degrees 2, 4, and 6 in the key of ____.

B D♯ F♯ corresponds to scale degrees 4, 6, and 1 in the key of ____.

A

3 5 7

113. C♯ E G♯ is diatonic in ____ (A / a).

It is built from scale degrees ____, ____, and ____ in that key.

1 2 3 4 5 6 7

114. Apply the necessary chromatic signs to form the diatonic triads in f♯. Complete the harmonic minor scale first, supplementing the key signature.

1 2 3 4 5 6 7

---

f

m d A m M M d

115. Identify these triads. The key is ____ (F / f).

____ ____ ____ ____ ____ ____ ____

---

seven

116. How many diatonic triads exist in each key? ________

G B D

2 4 6

117. Spell the triad which corresponds to scale degrees 6, 1, and 3 in b. ____ ____ ____

F♯ A C corresponds to scale degrees ____, ____, and ____ in e.

---

3 5

7

augmented

118. A♭ C E corresponds to scale degrees ____, ____, and ____ in f.

It is a(n) ________ triad.

Answers	Frames
2 3	**119.** A triad is *inverted* when its third or fifth is on the bottom rather than the root. Which triads below are inverted? _____ _____ 1. ←root 2. ←root 3. ←root
1 3	**120.** A triad is in *root position* when its root is the bottom note. Which triads below are in root position? _____ _____ 1. ←root 2. ←root 3. ←root
A (D) F A	**121.** The triad members (root, third, and fifth) do not alter their identity, nor does the sequence of spelling change, when a triad is inverted. In all three triads below, the root is D, the third is F, and the fifth is _____. In root position, all three triads are spelled D _____ _____. 1. 2. 3.
B♭ D	**122.** A triad is in *first inversion* when the third is the bottom note. Triad 2 is the first inversion of triad 1. 1. ←third 2. ←third The root of both triads above is _____. The third is _____.
third 3	**123.** In first inversion triads, the __________ is the bottom note. Which triad below is the first inversion of triad 1? _____ 1. 2. 3.

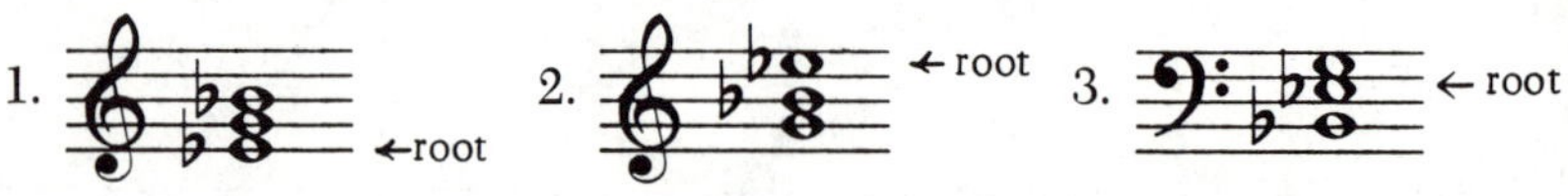

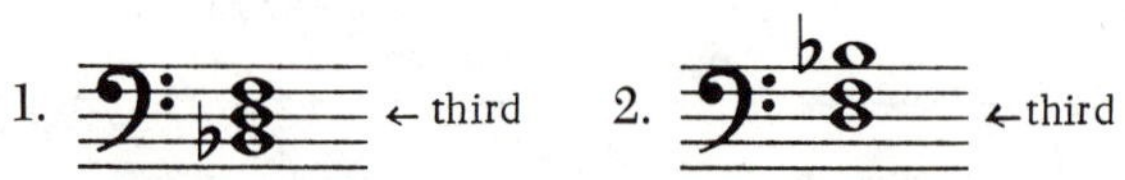

first inversion	**124.** When the third is the bottom note, a triad is in ________ ________________. Write the first inversion of the triad below.
2 A C E♭	**125.** Which triad is the first inversion of triad 1? _____ (Inversions may occur in any octave.) 1. 2. 3. In root position, all three triads are spelled _____ _____ _____.
D D F♯ A	**126.** A triad is in *second inversion* when the fifth is the bottom note. Triad 2 is triad 1 in second inversion. 1. ←fifth 2. ←fifth The root of both triads is _____. In root position, both triads are spelled _____ _____ _____.
second inversion 2 3	**127.** When the fifth is the bottom note, a triad is in ________ ________________. Which triad below is triad 1 in second inversion? _____ Which is triad 1 in first inversion? _____ 1. 2. 3.
fifth third	**128.** In second inversion triads, the ____________ is the bottom note. In first inversion triads, the ____________ is the bottom note.

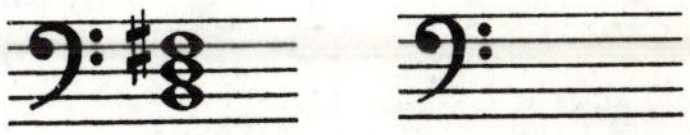

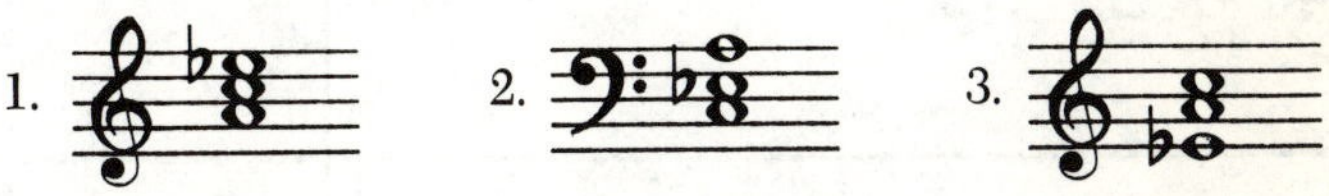

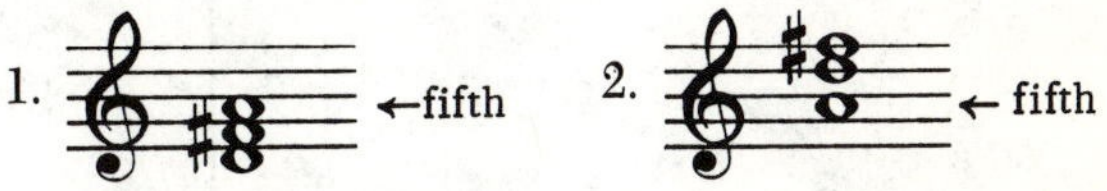

129. Write the second inversion of this triad.

root

130. In root position triads, the __________ is the bottom note.

Construct the E major triad in root position.

3

diminished

131. Although all triads are constructed in 3rds, inversion rearranges the 3rds so that the original structure may no longer be obvious. When arranged so that the structure of 3rds appears, a triad is in root position.

Which triad below is in root position? _____

It is a(n) ______________ triad.

1.  2.  3.

root

position

no

132. When structured in 3rds, a triad is in ______________ ______________.

Is this triad in root position? _____

133. To identify the root, third, and fifth of an inverted triad, rearrange the notes until the structure of 3rds (root position) appears, as in this example.

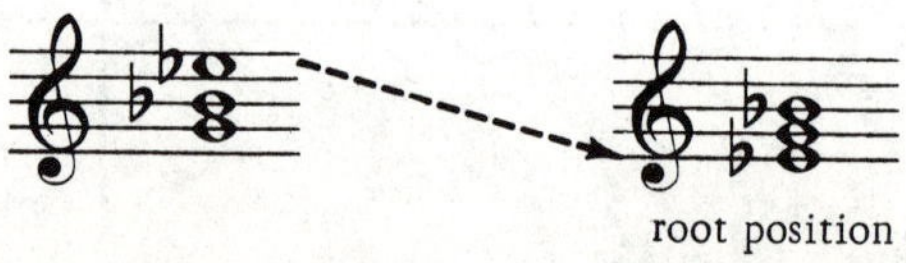

root position

first

The first triad above is in __________ inversion.

second	**134.** Reconstruct this triad so that the structure of 3rds appears. root position The first triad above is in ____________ inversion.
1. 2.	**135.** Reconstruct these inverted triads in root position. 1. 2.
F♯ A C♯ first	**136.** Mentally (or on a separate piece of paper) reconstruct this triad in root position. In root position, this triad is spelled _____ _____ _____. It is in ____________ inversion.
D♭ F A♭ second	**137.** Mentally reconstruct this triad in root position. This triad is spelled _____ _____ _____. It is in ____________ inversion.
G B♭ D♭ first inversion	**138.** This triad is spelled _____ _____ _____. It is in ____________ ________________.

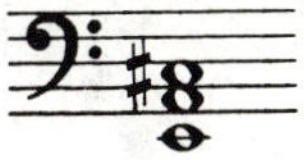

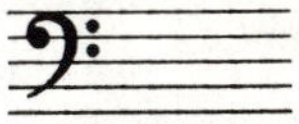

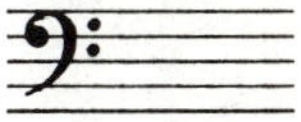

A C♯ E♯ root position augmented	**139.** This triad is spelled ___ ___ ___. It is in __________ ______________. It is a(n) ______________ triad.
F	**140.** The notes of a triad may be transferred to other octaves without altering the spelling or identity of triad members. Each triad below is spelled F A C and is in first inversion. The root of each triad above is _____.
	141. Each of the three triads below is spelled D F A and is in root position. Reconstruct the root position triad below so that the structure of thirds appears.
second	**142.** Reconstruct this triad so that the structure of 3rds appears. The first triad above is in __________ inversion.
second major	**143.** Reconstruct this triad in 3rds. The first triad above is in __________ inversion. It is a(n) __________ triad.

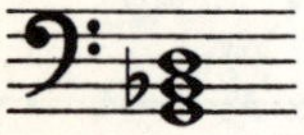

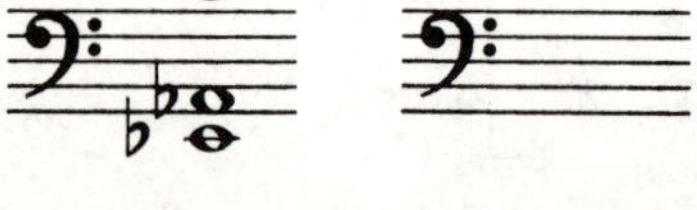

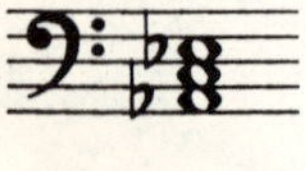

1. (m first inversion)

2. d first inversion

3. m second inversion

144. Name each triad, using the established abbreviations, and indicate its inversion.

1.  m first inversion

2. ____ ____ ____

3. ____ ____ ____

G

145. The notes of a triad may also encompass octave repetitions without altering the spelling or identity of triad members.

Each triad below is spelled G B♭ D and is in root position.

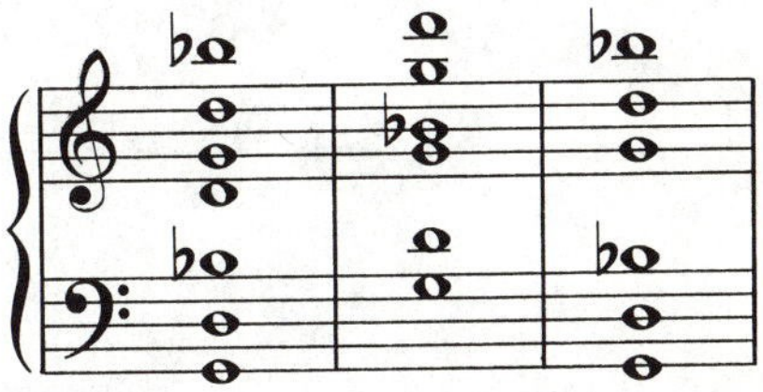

The root of each triad above is ____.

or

146. Reconstruct this triad in 3rds.

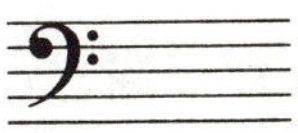

E minor

or

2

147. Reconstruct both triads in 3rds. They are both ____ ____ triads.

1.

2.

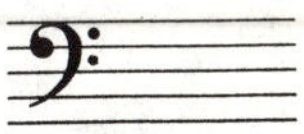

Which triad above is in second inversion? ____

diatonic	**148.** There are seven __________ triads in each key.
F♯ A C♯ 7 2 4	**149.** Spell the triad which corresponds to scale degrees 4, 6, and 1 in c♯. ____ ____ ____ G♯ B D corresponds to scale degrees ____, ____, and ____ in A.
f major	**150.** D♭ F A♭ corresponds to scale degrees 6, 1, and 3 in what key? ____ It is a(n) ________ triad.
A C♯ E major	**151.** Spell the triad built from scale degrees 5, 7, and 2 in d. ____ ____ ____ It is a(n) ________ triad.
e♭ minor	**152.** A♭ C♭ E♭ corresponds to scale degrees 4, 6, and 1 in the key of ____. It is a(n) ________ triad.
1. augmented 2. minor 3. diminished 4. major	**153.** Name the four kinds of triads whose structures are given below. 1. major 3rd + major 3rd ________ 2. minor 3rd + major 3rd ________ 3. minor 3rd + minor 3rd ________ 4. major 3rd + minor 3rd ________
perfect 5th augmented 5th diminished 5th	**154.** The interval between the root and fifth of major and minor triads is a(n) ________ ____. From root to fifth of an augmented triad is a(n) ________ ____. From root to fifth of a diminished triad is a(n) ________ ____.

1. (M first inversion)
2. M second inversion
3. m root position

155. Name each triad and indicate whether it is in root position, first inversion, or second inversion.

1.  M first inversion
2. 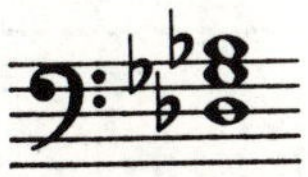
3.

---

1. M root position
2. d first inversion
3. A first inversion

156. Continue as in frame 155.

1. 
2. 
3.

---

1. 
2.

157. Write root position triads as indicated. (Build triads in 3rds.)

1. G♭ M 
2. A♯ d

---

1. 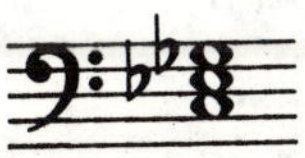
2.

158. Continue as in frame 157.

1. C d 
2. B A

1.  2. 

159. Write the augmented triads whose thirds are given.

1.  2. 

1. A (C♯) E
2. A (C♯) E♯
3. A♯ (C♯) E

160. Complete these triad spellings.

1. major _____ C♯ _____
2. augmented _____ C♯ _____
3. diminished _____ C♯ _____

1. E♭ G♭ (B♭)
2. B♭ D♭ (F♭)
3. B♭ D (F♯)

161. Continue as in frame 160.

1. minor _____ _____ B♭
2. diminished _____ _____ F♭
3. augmented _____ _____ F♯

LISTENING FRAMES

m

162. The tones of a triad are often presented consecutively, or "outlined," rather than all at once. Listen again to Example 4-2, from Corelli's Trio Sonata, Op. 4, No. 8.

At the beginning the violin sounds successive tones of a triad as the triad climbs upward. This triad is _____ (M / m / d / A).

M

163. Another triad outline is heard in the first two measures of Example 2-4, the beginning of Mozart's Piano Concerto No. 27 (third movement), the rhythm of which is notated below.

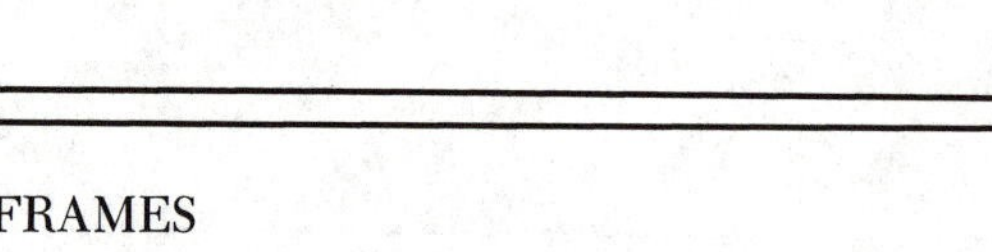

The triad outlined here is _____ (M / m / d / A).

164. Triad outlines, repeated triads, and associated repeated pitches are heard several times in Example 5-1, Purcell's Sonata for Trumpet and Strings (last movement). Near the end they are particularly noticeable, forming triads built from the first scale degree.

Since the key is D, the repeated triads on the first scale degree are spelled _____ _____ _____.

D F♯ A

Is the final triad in the movement spelled D F♯ A? _____

yes

165. Listen to Example 6-3, the "Crucifixus" from Bach's Mass in B minor. The first four measures are notated below. (The bracketed chords are discussed in frame 167.)

Listen first to the bass line, which is repeated continuously throughout the movement. Does it ever change? _____

yes (in the last three measures)

166. An expressive feature that occurs throughout the movement in Example 6-3 is the melodic minor second downward, as in measures 5 and 6 (notated below).

Listen to the movement again, concentrating this time on the chorus, and identify as many such intervals as you can.

	167. Study the notation of the first four measures in frame 165 and answer the following questions, which are numbered to correspond to the brackets over the notation.
1. yes	1. The key is e. Are the first two chords in measure 1 built from the first scale degree? _____
2. C major first	2. The root of this chord is _____. Its triad type is ___________. This chord is in ___________ inversion.
3. B minor first	3. The root is _____. The triad type is _____. It is in ___________ inversion.
4. A minor first	4. The root is _____. The triad type is ___________. It is in ___________ inversion.
5. yes second	5. Is the root of this chord the first scale degree (E)? _____ It is in ___________ inversion.
6. B major fifth	6. The root is _____. The triad type is ___________. This triad, in root position, is built from which scale degree? ___________
M	**168.** The final chord in Example 6-3 is _____ (M / m / d / A).
relative	The key center changes at the very end to G (major). G and e are _______________ (relative/parallel) keys.
(G) B D	The final chord is therefore spelled G _____ _____.
	Listen to Examples 6-3 and 1-2, comparing the bass lines. Both examples employ similar bass lines, but the musical effect of each is quite distinct.

SELF-QUIZ VI

1. The four types of triads are _____, _____, _____, and _____.

2. The interval between the root and the fifth of a triad may be a P 5th, _____ 5th, or _____ 5th.

3. Name each triad below, using abbreviations established in the chapter.

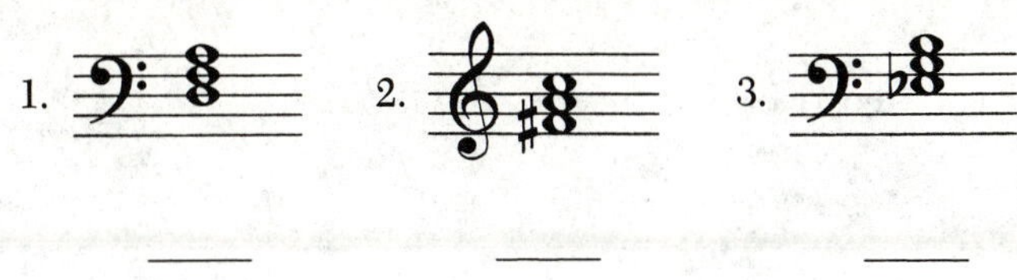

	1.	2.	3.
ROOT	_____	_____	_____
TRIAD TYPE	_____	_____	_____

4. Construct the indicated triads.

1. F m   2. D A   3. A d

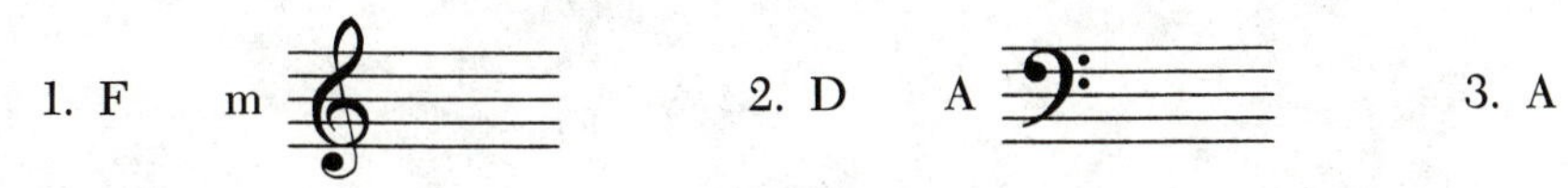

5. _________________ triads are built on degrees of the major and minor scale.

6. How many diatonic triads exist in any key? ___________

7. In minor keys, diatonic triads are usually constructed according to which form of minor scale?

____

8. F♯–A–C♯ corresponds to scale degrees 3–5–7 in the key of _____.

9. E–G♯–B is diatonic in _____ (E / g♯ / both).

10. Which triad below is the first inversion of triad 1? _____

1.   2.   3.

11. Complete these triad spellings.

	ROOT	3rd	5th		ROOT	3rd	5th
1. M	_____	F♯	_____	5. m	_____	_____	F
2. d	A♯	_____	_____	6. A	_____	C♯	_____
3. A	_____	_____	F♯	7. d	A♭	_____	_____
4. m	_____	_____	B♭	8. M	_____	_____	G𝄪

12. Name each triad type below, and indicate whether it is in root position, first inversion, or second inversion.

	TRIAD TYPE	ROOT	ROOT POSITION OR INVERSION
1.	____	____	__________
2.	____	____	__________
3.	____	____	__________
4.	____	____	__________
5.	____	____	__________
6.	____	____	__________

ANSWERS TO SELF-QUIZZES

Italicized numbers in parentheses designate frames in the chapter in which the material is first presented.

Self-Quiz I

1. notation (*1–3*)

2. Pitch (*2–3*)

3. 1. F or bass (either order) (*25–31*) 2. G or treble (either order) (*14–24*)

4. chromatic (signs) accidentals (*49–89*)

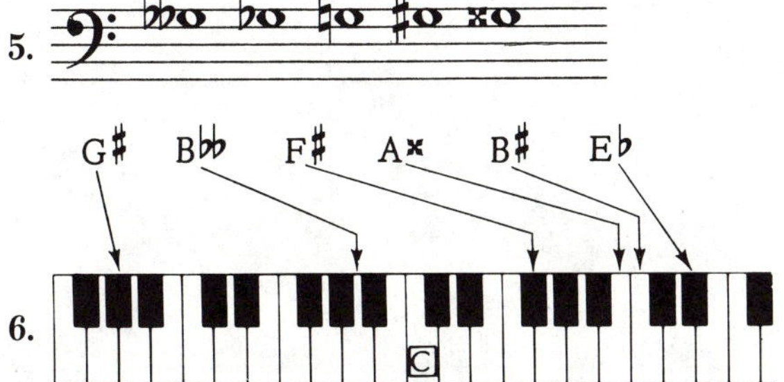

7. octave (*108–110*)

8. ottava (*120*)

9. 1, 4, 5

10. leger (*32*) ottava (*120*)

Self-Quiz II

1. meter (*6*)

2. Quintuple (*21*)

3. (*75–78*)

4. 1. 2. 3. 4. (*58–60*)

5. 1. = = (*100–107*)
2. = = (*104*)

6. 1. 2. (*108–109*)

7. meter, beat unit, and beat type (any order) (*134*)

8. 1. triple simple 3. quintuple simple
2. triple compound
(*181*)

9. three (*162*)

10.

11. duple compound

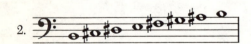

compound

Self-Quiz III

1. 3 to 4 7 to 1 (either order) (*35*)

2. 1.

2.

3. pure, melodic, and harmonic (any order) (*56, 65, 86*)

4. 1 5 (*51*)

5. melodic (*65*)

6. harmonic (*89*)

7. Aeolian (*131*)

8. 1.  (*35–43*)

2. (*56–64*)

3. (*65–77*)

4. (*86–100*)

9. 1. G harmonic minor
2. A major
3. E pure minor (or descending melodic minor)
4. C♯ ascending melodic minor

10. 1. D E F♯ G A B C♯ D
2. F♯ E♯ D C♯ B A G♯ F♯
3. E♭ D♭ C♭ B♭ A♭ G♭ F E♭
4. A♭ B♭ C♭ D♭ E♭ F♭ G A♭
5. E♭ D♭ C♭ B♭ A♭ G♭ F E♭

(Compare No. 3 with No. 5. If your answer was incorrect in either, review frame 74.)

11. 1. Aeolian
2. Locrian
3. Ionian
4. Dorian
5. Phrygian
6. Lydian
7. Mixolydian (*129*)

12. Phrygian Locrian (either order) (*137*)

13. Ionian (*128*, *129*, *144*)

14. 1. D E F♯ G♯ A B C♯ D 2. B C♯ D E F♯ G♯ A B

15. 1. G♯ F♯ E D♯ C♯ B A G♯ 2. G♯ F♯ E D C♯ B A G♯

16. 1. E Mixolydian
2. C Phrygian
3. C♯ Locrian

17. 1.
2.

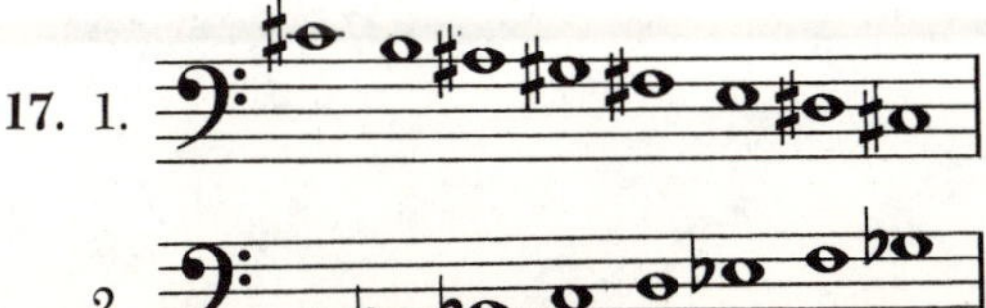

Self-Quiz IV

1. primes 4ths 5ths octaves (any order) (*17–19*)

2. 2nds 3rds 6ths 7ths (any order) (*63–65*)

3. 1. (D) B♭ 2. (G♯) B♭ 3. (B♭) D♭♭ 4. (D♭) G♭ 5. (A) G♭ 6. (F♯) F𝄪

4. 1. 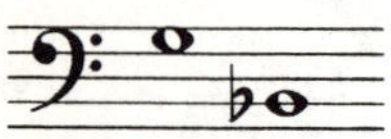 2.  3.  (*110*)

5. 1.  2. 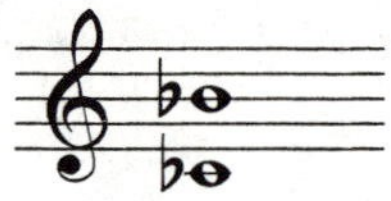 3. 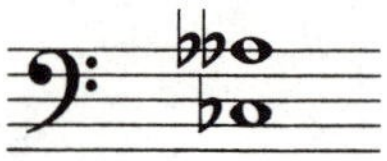 (*110*)

6. 1. M 7th 2. M 7th 3. m 7th

7. 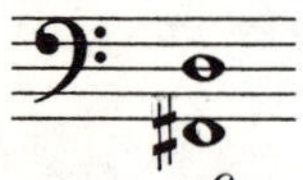  (*120*)

m6 m6

(either order)

8. diminished augmented (*130*)

9. minor major (*130*)

10. perfect (*130*)

11. 1. A 7th 2. d 4th 3. A 2nd

Self-Quiz V

1. 1.  2.  3.  (*9*)

2. ascend (*20*)

3. descend (*27*)

4. 1. (A) B♭♭ G𝄪 2. (D♯) E♭ F♭♭ 3. (C♭) B A𝄪 4. (G♯) A♭ (*37–39*)

5. 1.  2.  3.  4.

6. pure (*54*)

7. 2 4 5 (*60–63*)

8. m 3rd (*62, 63*)

9. 1. (B♭) g

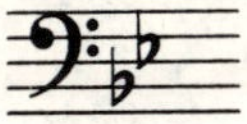

2. E (c♯)

3. G♭ e♭

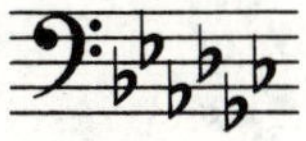

10. first scale degree (*75*)

11. key signature (*60*)

12. 1.  2.  3.  4.

13.

	1.	2.	3.	4.
MAJOR:	E	D♭	E♭	B
MINOR:	c♯	b♭	c	g♯

Self-Quiz VI

1. M, m, d, A (any order)

2. d 5th A 5th (either order)

3.

ROOT	1. D	2. F♯	3. E♭
TRIAD TYPE	m	d	A

4. 1.  2.  3.

5. Diatonic (*105*)

6. seven

7. harmonic (*108*)

8. D

9. both

10. 3 (*119–129*)

11.

1. D	(F♯)	A	5. B♭	D♭	(F)
2. (A♯)	C♯	E	6. A	(C♯)	E♯
3. B♭	D	(F♯)	7. (A♭)	C♭	E♭♭
4. E♭	G♭	(B♭)	8. C𝄪	E𝄪	(G𝄪)

12.

	TRIAD TYPE	ROOT	ROOT POSITION OR INVERSION
1.	m	C	root position
2.	M	E	root position
3.	M	A	first inversion
4.	d	F	first inversion
5.	A	D	first inversion
6.	m	G	second inversion

INDEX

Only frames in which concepts are defined or described are listed. Roman numerals indicate chapter numbers; Arabic numerals indicate frame numbers. Numbers in *italics* refer to the *page numbers* of material in the introductions to sections within chapters. Where an entry lists more than one frame, the principal frame is printed in **boldface** type (with the exception of Listening Frame entries).

A 5
B 6
C 7
D 8
E 9
F 0
G 1
H 2
I 3
J 4